Projections of Power

STUDIES IN

COMMUNICATION,

MEDIA, AND

PUBLIC OPINION

A series edited by

Susan Herbst and

Benjamin I. Page

ROBERT M. ENTMAN

Projections of Power

Framing News, Public Opinion, and U.S. Foreign Policy

The University of Chicago Press

Chicago & London

Robert M. Entman is professor of communication and political science at North Carolina State University. He is the author of *Democracy without Citizens: Media and the Decay of American Politics* (1989), coauthor of *The Black Image in the White Mind: Media and Race in America* (2000, with Andrew Rojecki), and coeditor of *Mediated Politics: Communication in the Future of Democracy* (2001, with W. Lance Bennett).

The University of Chicago Press, Chicago 60637
The University of Chicago Press, Ltd., London
© 2004 by The University of Chicago
All rights reserved. Published 2004
Printed in the United States of America
13 12 11 10 09 08 07 06 05 04   1 2 3 4 5

ISBN: 0-226-21071-5 (cloth)
ISBN: 0-226-21072-3 (paper)

Library of Congress Cataloging-in-Publication Data

Entman, Robert M.
    Projections of power : framing news, public
opinion, and U.S. foreign policy / Robert M. Entman.
        p.   cm.—(Studies in communication, media, and
public opinion)
    Includes bibliographical references and index.
    ISBN 0-226-21071-5 (cloth : alk. paper)—
ISBN 0-226-21072-3 (pbk. : alk. paper)
        1. United States—Foreign relations—1989–
    2. United States—Foreign relations—1981–1989.
    3. United States—Foreign relations—Public
opinion. 4. Mass media—Political aspects—United
States. 5. Press and politics—United States. 6. Public
opinion—United States. I. Title. II. Series.

E840 .E57 2004
327.73′009′045—dc21

                                        2003009777

For Clay and Wib, who were there at the beginning

CONTENTS

● ●

ACKNOWLEDGMENTS

I would first like to thank my former colleagues and graduate students at Northwestern University, who created the environment that nurtured the early work on this study. On the faculty side, Jim Ettema, Susan Herbst, Mike Janeway, Ben Page, Jim Webster, Steve Wildman, and David Zarefsky in particular made my time at Northwestern as intellectually stimulating as I could have hoped. The truly extraordinary cohort of graduate students I was privileged to work with and learn from includes Scott Althaus, Bea Chestnut, Jill Edy, Limor Peer, Pat Phalen, and Andy Rojecki, all of whom have labored on one or another facet of the research reported here and have gone on to become respected scholars themselves. Professor Rojecki provided essential critiques of the manuscript and it is a measurably better book for his skilled attention. John Tryneski, senior editor at the University of Chicago Press, has nurtured this project with skill and tact; I thank him and the readers of the manuscript for their sage advice. In addition I would like to thank Lance Bennett for his pioneering work on media and foreign policy, and for his cheerful and creative collaboration on the book series we coedit for the Cambridge University Press.

At North Carolina State University, colleagues provided support and understanding, and I am grateful to them all. I would especially like to thank Dean Linda Brady for helping me through a stint as head of the department of communication, and Jane Mabe, Debbie Pell, and Bev McTaggart for their crucial assistance.

The Markle Foundation supported the earliest work on this study, undertaken while I was a guest scholar at the Woodrow Wilson Center in 1988–89, and some later research as well. That assistance was indispensable and my gratitude to the foundation is profound.

Finally, my long-suffering family put up with me as I slogged away on this and two other books. May my lovely and amazing Emily, my wonderful son Max, already a mensch at seventeen, and my dear wife Francie—may all of us—live in peace and understanding, an end toward which I hope this book might in some small way contribute.

1. PROJECTING POWER IN THE NEWS

• •

On the morning after the terrorist assaults of September 11, 2001, President George W. Bush spoke. "The deliberate and deadly attacks which were carried out yesterday against our country were more than acts of terror, they were acts of war," he said. "This will require our country to unite in steadfast determination and resolve. . . . This will be a monumental struggle of good versus evil, but good will prevail."[1] In these remarks and many others, Bush defined a problem in simple and emotional terms as an act of war[2] and identified its clear cause as an enemy that was evil. Bush and other officials used these same words many times after 9/11; he invoked *evil* five times and *war* twelve times in his 2002 State of the Union speech.

Repeating these terms helped frame September 11th to "unite" the country behind the Bush administration's interpretation and response to the attacks and to exclude other understandings. By conveying an unambiguous and emotionally compelling frame,[3] Bush promoted assent from Congress and the media—and overwhelming public approval.[4] Calling the post-9/11 policy a "war" on terrorism was a contestable but effective political choice. Among other things, President Bush did *not* do what presidents normally do when the country goes to war: for instance, call for sacrifices from the civilian population, propose tax increases to cover new expenditures, or bolster the Veterans Administration. Indeed he did the very opposite, urging Americans to consume more, asking Congress to cut taxes and VA services. In essence Bush's framing strategy, if successful, would yield the best of both political worlds: the advantage of the heightened deference that accrues to presidents in wartime without the drawback of forcing alteration in the administration's domestic agendas or imposing unpopular costs on the average American.

The success of the White House approach is evident in the comments of CBS news anchor Dan Rather, a week after the attacks: "George Bush is the president, he makes the decisions, and, you know, as just one American, he wants me to line up, just tell me where." The seventy-year-old Rather even said he would willingly don a uniform—and presumably engage in combat himself.[5] His remarks embody the patriotic fervor that swept through the media in the wake of the terrorist attacks as framed by Bush's fiery rhetoric. Whatever his feelings, Rather would have been unlikely to align himself so unabashedly with a president's policy in normal times.[6]

The media are not always as cooperative with the White House as Dan Rather and others were in the immediate aftermath of September 11th. Scholars have devoted a significant amount of attention to the connection between what the media report and what government *wants* them to report. Ideally, a free press balances official views with a more impartial perspective that allows the public to deliberate independently on the government's decisions. But in practice, the relationship between governing elites and news organizations is less distant and more cooperative than the ideal envisions, especially in foreign affairs. The question is really one of degree: just how close is the association? Does it become cozier in some conditions than in others? How exactly is this connection reflected in the news? And what are the effects on foreign policy and democratic accountability? These are the subjects of this book.

The attacks of September 11, 2001, may have "changed everything," as a cliché of the time had it, but at least on first impression, one thing it did not change was the news media's traditional promotion of patriotic rallies around presidents when America appears under attack. Reflecting the surge of outrage and nationalistic fervor, the news made little room for any but official, government-sanctioned interpretations. Even the mildest dissent was immediately condemned. It would be unrealistic to expect much else in light of the stunning, unprecedented, and heinous nature of the violence. But other aspects of the coverage are noteworthy for those interested in how the media's role may have changed since the Soviet Union crumbled and collapsed and the Cold War ended. For within just a few weeks of September 11, once the emotional reaction had receded a bit and discussion of exactly what to *do* became the order of the day, journalistic deference to the White House began ever so slightly to recede. Not that dissent achieved anything like the visibility and memorability of the patriotic rhetoric and symbols pervading both news and popular culture. Still, even the overwhelmingly popular war on the Taliban government of Afghanistan did not escape critical appraisal in the media, and, more tellingly, after the Taliban fell, the president's attempt to shift the focus of American military power to Iraq met significant resistance.

Had the "war on terrorism" provided as unifying a framework as the Cold War mindset once did, particularly in its earliest years—had news organizations lapped up the White House line as fervently as their predecessors during the Red Scare of the 1940s and 1950s—America might well have been waging unilateral war against Saddam Hussein by autumn 2002, and with massive public support. Instead, by that time, President Bush's attempt to weave a seamless connection between Osama bin Laden, the new demon, and the familiar villainy of Saddam Hussein had run into objections and questions from leaders across the political spectrum; dissenters included prominent Republicans, Democrats, reporters, and editorial writers. The resistance in the summer of 2002 forced Bush to change course. He rejected calls from administration hawks to wage war unilaterally and quickly, and instead sought approval from the Congress and the United Nations. The point is not that the media alone compelled the president to adjust his stance—media choices are rarely if ever sufficient in themselves to alter public policy. Top public officials inside and outside the administration exert more decisive influence over the president. But that influence is conditioned in part by how fully the media cooperate with the administration, as against its opponents. Arguably, had the major news organizations ignored or trivialized the opposition to immediate war against Iraq, the political environment might have remained sufficiently acquiescent for Bush to pursue the original plans. Republican hawks lent credence to this analysis: they charged that leading media had deliberately played up the internal GOP dissent to advance their own liberal, dovish agenda.[7] Whatever the merit of that specific charge, this book seeks to demonstrate that the media are now indeed forces presidents must reckon with, even in foreign policy, even when proposing military operations that, like Afghanistan and Iraq, turn out to yield predictable and popular early success.

The public naturally desired protection against a terrifying global conspiracy whose shadowy agents, having established a strong presence in the United States, posed a direct, palpable threat to security on American soil far outweighing any domestic danger ever posed by the "international communist conspiracy." If Edelman was right to argue that the public turns to presidents for symbolic reassurance in the face of catastrophic threat,[8] then the media's failure to provide unalloyed support for the leader in this time suggests something new. Whatever else the events of September 11th may have transformed, however, it was not the catalyst for this particular development on the part of the media, which had been in transition for some time, arguably ever since the disastrous U.S. involvement in Vietnam. That national tragedy undermined Americans' sense of their nation as invincible and righteous, and spawned a degree of uncertainty and conflict among leaders that has persisted since the fading of the Cold War. What September 11th did accomplish was to highlight the uncertainties, and to reveal that despite America's status as the sole superpower, it is not invulnerable. Understanding the nature, evolution, and extent of the new, less dependably deferential role for media in the context of this new, still-evolving international system is the central purpose of this book.

Hegemony and Indexing

Political communication scholars have developed two major approaches to understanding the government–media nexus in foreign policy: *hegemony* and *indexing*. Both perceive the media as too subservient to government, and both endorse more democracy in foreign policy. Hegemony theorists believe that government officials keep the information available to the public within such narrow ideological boundaries that democratic deliberation and influence are all but impossible.[9] Although these scholars acknowledge that leaders sometimes conflict with each other, they stress elites' agreement on first principles, a harmony that impedes the flow of independent information and consistently (although not inevitably) produces progovernment propaganda—and public consent or acquiescence to White House decisions.

In contrast, the indexing approach makes elite disagreement its centerpiece. It argues that the media "index" or reflect elite debate rather closely. If sufficiently vigorous disputes over the White House line erupt inside the foreign policy establishment, critical views appear in the news.[10] In perhaps the most thorough exposition of indexing, Mermin summarizes its basic conclusion: "[T]he press . . . does not offer critical analysis of White House policy decisions unless actors inside the government (most often in Congress) have done so first. This means the media act, for the most part, as a vehicle for government officials to criticize each other."[11] Thus, the media make "no independent contribution (except at the margins) to foreign policy debate."[12] Contrary to the hegemony view, indexing theorists believe that when elites disagree about foreign policy, media reflect the discord in ways that may affect foreign policy, and that means their role, though still limited, transcends mere transmission of propaganda.

Although offering many insights, the hegemony and indexing models—based largely on events during the Cold War—do not fit with some of the findings discussed in this book. Not surprisingly, the models cannot fully account for changes in international politics and media behavior since the Soviet Union began withering away. It seems time, then, for a new model.

Framing and the Cascade Model

The White House, its supporters, and its critics peddle their messages to the press in hopes of gaining political leverage. The media's political influence arises from how they respond—from their ability to frame the news in ways that favor one side over another. In fact, I argue, that influence has been growing since before the certitudes of the Cold War began to fade. Under the pressure of the civil rights and anti–Vietnam War movements and the Watergate scandals, government and governing processes opened up.[13] Openness lent urgency to contests over the public framing of issues, clashes in which the president, though always the one to beat, is no sure winner. This book advances a model of cascading activation as a way to explain who wins. The model highlights what the hegemony model neglects: that the collapse of the Cold War consensus has meant differences among elites are no longer the exception but the rule. Patriotic deference to the president does not come automatically or last indefinitely, and hegemonic control is a tenuous feature of some but not all foreign policy news. And although indexing convincingly emphasizes elite opposition as a vital determinant of whether the news will deviate from the White House line, it does not explain fully why leaders sometimes contest the president's frame and other times keep quiet, or just how *much* elite dissent will arise, or what it will focus on. Nor do previous models delineate comprehensively the public's role in the larger system of communication linking presidents, elites outside the administration (including foreign leaders), journalists, news texts, and citizens. Building particularly on the work of Hallin, Bennett, and Mermin, this book offers some initial answers in the form of the *cascading activation* model.

UNDERSTANDING FRAMES

The first step in building the cascade model is to develop a clearer conceptual grasp of framing. Although this concept has become more of a unifying thread in political communication research,[14] it has been vulnerable to criticism as an imprecise catchall that means slightly different things to each researcher employing it. A review and synthesis of the research literature yields the following stab at a standard definition of framing: *selecting and highlighting some facets of events or issues, and making connections among them so as to promote a particular interpretation, evaluation, and/ or solution.*

This study explores two classes of framing, substantive and procedural. Substantive frames perform at least two of the following basic functions in covering political events, issues, and actors:

- Defining effects or conditions as problematic
- Identifying causes
- Conveying a moral judgment
- Endorsing remedies or improvements

For September 11th, the problematic effect was of course thousands of civilian deaths from an act of war against America; the cause, the Taliban government of Afghanistan, its de facto leaders, Mullah Mohammed Omar and Osama bin Laden, and the latter's al-Qaeda terrorist network; the moral judgment, condemnation of these agents as evil; and the initial remedy, war against Afghanistan. All four of these framing functions hold together in a kind of cultural logic, each helping to sustain the others with the connections among them cemented more by custom and convention than by the principles of syllogistic logic. In this book I emphasize the two most important framing functions: problem definition, which often virtually predetermines the rest of the frame, and remedy, because it directly promotes support (or opposition) to public policy.[15]

Procedural frames have a narrower focus and function. Procedural framing suggests evaluations of *political actors' legitimacy,* based on their *technique, success,* and *representativeness.* Scholars of domestic politics[16] have frequently observed that procedural—or "game" or "horserace"—framing occupies much of the news. The same holds for foreign news. As we will see in later chapters, procedural framing does little to motivate or equip the public to engage in political deliberation, although it can have other important political effects. The remainder of this chapter focuses on substantive framing.

The words and images that make up the frame can be distinguished from the rest of the news by their capacity to stimulate support or opposition to the sides in a political conflict. We can measure this capacity by *cultural resonance* and *magnitude.*[17] Those frames that employ more culturally resonant terms have the greatest potential for influence. They use words and images highly salient in the culture, which is to say *noticeable, understandable, memorable,* and *emotionally charged.*[18] Magnitude taps the *prominence* and *repetition* of the framing words and images. The more resonance and magnitude, the more likely the framing is to evoke similar thoughts and feelings in large portions of the audience. However, some highly resonant words or images may not need much repetition—say, airliners flying into the World Trade Center on September 11th.[19] Their meaning was almost certainly understood and indelibly engraved into memory with one or two viewings.[20]

KNOWLEDGE NETWORKS AND SPREADING ACTIVIATION

Scholars have used the term "frame" interchangeably with such closely related concepts as schemas,[21] heuristics,[22] and scripts.[23] To clarify matters, this study applies the term "schemas" to interpretive processes that occur in the human mind, and applies "frames" to texts.[24] Schemas are clusters or nodes of connected ideas and feelings stored in memory.[25] These clusters neighbor each other psychologically and perhaps even physiologically, so are likely to be thought of together.[26]

Kintsch[27] suggests that schemas are connected in *knowledge networks.* A schema for September 11th might include the World Trade Center, airplane hijackers, Osama bin Laden, the New York fire department, and New York mayor Rudolph Guiliani (among others). A partial diagram of this event schema, occupying a small portion of a person's knowledge net, might look like figure 1.1. Each idea would have or quickly develop an emotional association—presumably, for Americans, positive feelings about the World Trade Center, the fire department, and Guiliani, but negative feelings toward the hijackers and Osama bin Laden. The new September 11th schema draws on the news coverage of the events of that day and on the existing knowledge network (for example, ideas about the Republican Party and foreigners) as well. Once the new schema is stored in long-term memory, all succeeding information about any one of these ideas has the potential to bring to mind (online, into working memory) associated feelings and concepts from the knowledge network.

Lodge and Stroh[28] observe that this process of bringing thoughts and feelings to mind works "through the mechanism of *spreading activation.*" The idea of spreading activation plays a central part in the cascade model.[29] Thus a new report showing a picture of Osama bin Laden will likely reactivate the audience's negative feelings and bring to mind conscious or unconscious memories of the burning World Trade Center, the heroes of the fire department, and so forth. The theory of spreading activation underlines the importance of the order in which information is presented. Early stimuli arising from new events and issues generally have primacy, since activation spreads out from the initial idea.[30] There is thus a very practical reason for political leaders to worry, as did President Bush after September 11th, about imposing their own frames on an event from the start. A dominant frame in the earliest news coverage of an event can activate and spread congruent thoughts and feelings in individuals' knowledge networks, building a new event schema that guides responses to all future reports. First impressions may be difficult to dislodge.[31]

This discussion does not pretend to capture the eternal and fixed essence of political framing but is instead itself a heuristic, a shortcut guide to dealing with what might otherwise be the unmanageable complexity of news texts. The concepts and terminology proposed here constitute one attempt to reduce confusion and imprecision in the scholarly literature about the

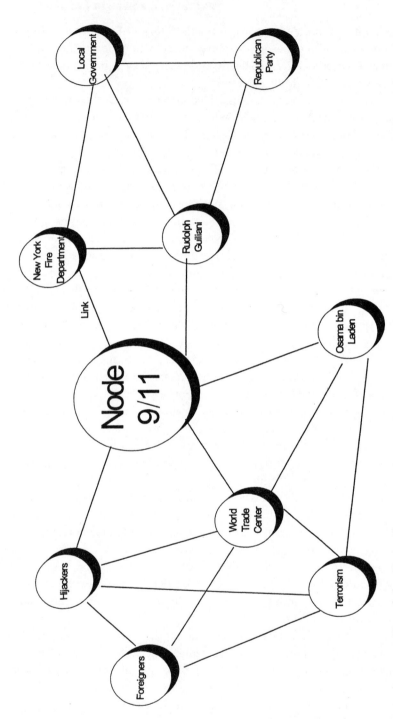

FIGURE 1.1 *Knowledge Network*

nature and functions of framing. It is not the only way to, as it were, frame framing.[32] The appendix to this chapter provides further conceptual discussion of framing and schemas, with examples from the events of September 11, 2001.

Cascading Activation

The cascading activation model is designed to help explain how thoroughly the thoughts and feelings that support a frame extend down from the White House through the rest of the system—and who thus wins the framing contest and gains the upper hand politically.[33] Figure 1.2 illustrates the cascading flow of influence linking each level of the system: the administration, other elites, news organizations, the texts they produce, and the public. The cascade model assumes that the concept of spreading network activation applies at each level of the system. The spreading activation of thoughts or nodes on a knowledge network within an individual's mind (whether a Congress member, a reporter, or citizen) has parallels in the way ideas travel along interpersonal networks and in the spread of framing words and images across the different media.[34]

Figure 1.2 suggests how ideas cascade downward from the administration's first public expressions about an event. Activation of thoughts and feelings in the minds of journalists and leaders almost immediately spawns conversations that spread ideas between participants. Journalists canvass their networks of legitimate and customary sources (for example, the White House and Pentagon press secretaries, key members of Congress) to learn how they are connecting ideas and feelings: are sources saying the same things in unison, are they arguing with each other, are they quiet on particular matters? During this time, too, reporters and editors talk to each other, compare impressions, and monitor competitors' coverage. The more often journalists hear similar thoughts expressed by their sources and by other news outlets, the more likely their own thoughts will run along those lines, with the result that the news they produce will feature words and visuals that confirm the same framing. If ideas expressed are more varied, framing may be less one-sided.

The metaphor of the cascade was chosen in part to emphasize that the ability to promote the spread of frames is stratified; some actors have more power than others to push ideas along to the news and then to the public. The president and top advisors enjoy the most independent ability to decide which mental associations to activate and the highest probability of having their thoughts become part of the general circulation of ideas,[35] and congressional leaders enjoy more autonomy and influence than backbenchers.

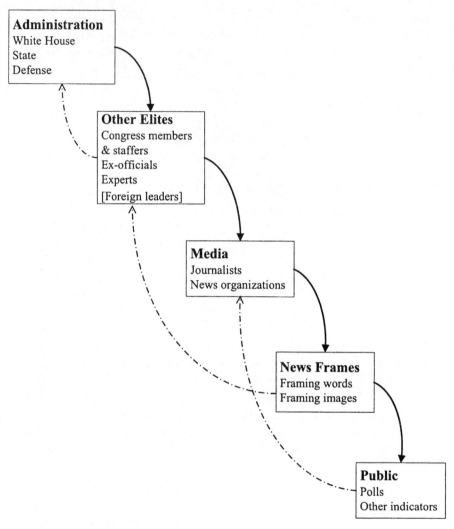

FIGURE 1.2 *Cascading Network Activation*

Analogously, informal networks of association among news organizations also set up a pecking order, with the pinnacle occupied by the *New York Times* and a few other top news organizations whose cues are followed by the rest of the media.

As with real-world cascading waterfalls, each level in the metaphorical cascade also makes its own contribution to the mix and flow (of ideas).

Each can be thought of as a network of individuals and organizations, jostling to influence the political environment, and being affected by it in turn. The top level, the *administration,* is distinguished from the *elite network* that connects Washington insiders who do not work in the executive branch: members of Congress and their staffs, and sources from the community of Washington policy experts and lobbyists (former government officials, think tank denizens, university sages, interest groups, and public relations firms).[36] I generally refer to this group as "other elites" or "nonadministration elites," though I also use "leaders" and "officials" to relieve stylistic monotony. When the officials under discussion work for the executive branch, although they too are elites, the distinction is signaled by such terms as "administration" or "White House."

The network of *journalists* consists of reporters, columnists, producers, editors, and publishers who work for the important national media. They communicate regularly with colleagues inside and beyond their own organizations. Administration figures and other elites maintain social and professional contact with upper-tier journalists, exchanging information off the record and on, at receptions, conferences, and elsewhere. This interface between journalists and elites is a key transmission point for spreading activation of frames, and it is not always easy to determine where the line between "elite" and "journalist" should be drawn, or who influences whom. Arguably, a few top editors, correspondents, and editorialists exercise more sway over the spread of ideas than all but the most powerful public officials. A counterargument is that journalists simply reflect rather than influence the play of power because they so rigidly follow standard operating procedures. Yet even if organizational norms and standard procedures largely determine the media's decisions, these determinations help indirectly and directly to shape and limit the talk, actions, and options of those who govern.[37] That makes them important objects of inquiry.[38]

The news media of particular interest are the broadcast television network news operations of ABC, CBS, and NBC; the two elite newsmagazines, *Time* and *Newsweek;* and the two leading newspapers, the *New York Times* and the *Washington Post.* The role of the all-news cable channels is also noted where significant. Although these outlets sometimes differ in their reporting and commentary on foreign events and issues, more striking is their broad similarity.[39] In order to maximize theoretical insight, then, even though this book presents data on a variety of outlets, it treats the national media as a more or less homogeneous entity, while noting significant variations where they occur.

All parties to this process operate under uncertainty and pressure, with mixed motives and varying levels of competence and understanding. All are "cognitive misers"[40] who work in accordance with established mental maps and habits.[41] They are "satisficers"[42] who rarely undertake a comprehensive review of all relevant facts and options before responding. Few political leaders or journalists have the time to do that, and even fewer members of the public have the inclination.[43] The implication of these cognitive limitations is that what passes between levels of the cascade is not comprehensive understanding but highlights packaged into selective, framed communications. As we go down the levels, the flow of information becomes less and less thorough, and increasingly limited to the selected highlights, processed through schemas, and then passed on in ever-cruder form. The farther an idea travels between levels on the cascade, the fainter the traces of the "real" situation are—whether the actual perceptions, goals, and calculations of the president way at the top, or the true mix of public sentiments moving from the bottom back up to policymakers.

In summary, let us consider exactly how the cascade model builds on and supplements previous approaches. First, it acknowledges variation and hierarchy within each level of the system that produces foreign news. By no means always a unified or skilled actor, the administration includes a variety of players, and disunity or ineptitude can significantly affect media coverage.[44] Sometimes a congressional party (most often, the GOP) puts up a united front, other times it is all over the map (typically, Democrats). Internal disarray undermines a party's ability to successfully attack (or defend) the White House frame. Moreover, individual participants are hardly equal: some get attention for their ideas far more often than others. Second, the cascade model helps explain whether elite dissent materializes. As indexing theorists have shown, the news usually (not always) supports the White House line unless American leaders have begun attacking it. But we need to understand better why such wrangles arise in some cases and not others, and what role the media play in triggering or suppressing dissent. The model also incorporates the possibly growing impacts of foreign leaders on U.S. news. Third, applying the concept of framing within the cascade model helps us distinguish the important information from all the other data and noise flowing among policymakers, journalists, and citizens. The model generates important distinctions among different expressions of support or criticism in the news. It clarifies exactly which aspects of the White House frame attract dissent, which earn acceptance, and what difference this makes to politics and policy. This approach also encourages more systematic analysis of visual, not just verbal, information. Finally, the model illuminates the way news feeds information about citizens back to officials, and thereby influences foreign policy. Although public opinion does rest at the bottom of the cascade, the citizenry's perceived and anticipated reactions can significantly impinge on what leaders say and do. As is true throughout the system, it turns out to be crucial that information travels in the form of frames—in this case, selective representations (and misrepresentations) of public sentiment moving up the cascade to leaders.

How Activation Spreads

In the interest of economy of explanation and clarity, the cascade model highlights the interactions of four important variables that influence the activation and spread of the White House's preferred frame to other elites, to news texts, and to the public: *motivations, cultural congruence, power,* and *strategy*. This chapter considers motivations and cultural congruence, which work internally to "pull" mental associations into individuals' thinking. Power and strategy, on the other hand, operate from the outside to "push" consideration of frames, and these are discussed more fully in chapter 4.

MOTIVATIONS

Among the most important motivations for our purposes are the following:

1. Minimizing cognitive costs
2. Avoiding emotional dissonance
3. Monitoring for and reacting to threats against core values
4. Participating in public life and citizenship
5. Maintaining interpersonal relationships through discussion of current events and issues
6. Advancing career interests, a motivation pertinent mostly to elites, who seek political influence and substantive policy goals, and to journalists seeking professional success

These motivations establish a high threshold for attracting the attention of most citizens to foreign affairs.[45] News of an event or issue must represent a truly significant threat to values, or must generate so much news of such high magnitude and resonance that a distracted public actually notices. Significant threats arising from foreign affairs are not uncommon, but they do not happen every month either. September 11th was, of course, unusually threatening and resonant and passed the threshold of attention almost instantly, as did the start of the two wars in Iraq.

Presidents have no difficulty attracting the attention of journalists. But if they want to control the news message, presidents must package frames in ways that comport with the media's institutional and individual motivations. Scholars have subjected these motivations to intense scrutiny[46] so they need only be summarized briefly here. News organizations and personnel are driven by economic pressure and incentives; professional customs, norms and principles; and normative values. In the first category are the needs to appeal to the large audiences that advertisers seek, and to economize on the cost of gathering news; analogously, individual journalists weigh impacts on their own careers in composing the news. These shape such principles as objectivity, simplicity, brevity, and timeliness, which constitute the second category. In the third are the sincere desires to play the heroic role prescribed by First Amendment theorists, to help hold government accountable and inform the public. These latter, normative self-images may at times modify or overcome the restraining force of the economic pressures and professional customs. The motivating influence of all three institutional properties of newsmaking are illustrated throughout this book.[47]

CULTURAL CONGRUENCE

The substance of a news event or issue matters quite a bit to whether the White House will easily dominate interpretations or whether it will face a frame fight. This is where the cascade model most importantly supplements earlier theoretical approaches. Cultural congruence measures the ease with which—all else being equal—a news frame can cascade through the different levels of the framing process and stimulate similar reactions at each step.

The more congruent the frame is with schemas that dominate the political culture, the more success it will enjoy. The most inherently powerful frames are those fully congruent with schemas *habitually* used by most members of society. Such frames have the greatest intrinsic capacity to arouse similar responses among most Americans. On the other hand, for many events or issues, culturally dominant schemas suggest conflicting or unclear interpretations. Framing of such *ambiguous* matters depends more heavily on motivation, power, and strategy. Finally, when it comes to news of matters *incongruent* with dominant schemas, common culture blocks the spread of many mental associations and may discourage thinking altogether.[48] These distinctions can be arrayed along a continuum, with an imaginary "tipping point" where contradictions among dominant schemas start to become dissonant or perhaps too complex for most people to handle and therefore call forth a blocking response:

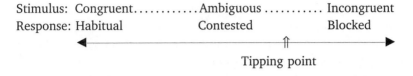

A good match between a news item and habitual schemas pulls a frame into people's thoughts with virtually no cognitive cost—with little time-consuming cogitation or costly searching memory for meaning or relevance. The September 11 terrorist attacks again provide an example. Terrorist hijackers were thoroughly familiar, as were other concepts, like skyscrapers (of which the World Trade Center would be a famous specific instance), firefighters, mayors (Guiliani), and so forth. It required almost no cognitive effort to make the connections promoted by the administration's frame of the event. Previous information had repeatedly activated most of the mental pathways connecting similar or identical concepts in the past. Research tells us that repeated use makes such mental associations or images more and more readily accessible;[49] this gives us an organic understanding of why practice makes perfect. Journalists, sources, and audience members sharing a common political culture think and talk about unambiguous events like 9/11 in congruent ways. Reporters readily construct associations in the news matching the public's habits of thinking. Journalistic motivations also help to solidify the sway of the conventional framing over the news. Conveying the congruent frame yields career-enhancing attention (or avoids career-damaging inattention and criticism) from editors, colleagues, and the public.

At the opposite extreme are culturally incongruent interpretations. Such ideas are blocked from spreading, typically due to their dissonance with dominant schemas.[50] Other factors that can undermine or block activation include unfamiliarity, complexity, and low apparent relevance to values. Responses to incongruent stimuli, rather than spreading along "logical" paths, cause a kind of mental short circuit, a detour that steers thinking down psychologically comforting pathways. Sometimes the easiest response is to ignore the matter altogether. In other cases people resolve the dissonance by applying schemas that yield more acceptable thoughts.

As an example, consider a culturally incongruent interpretation of the events of September 11 that was popular in some quarters outside the United States. It framed the hijackers not as evil terrorists but as freedom fighters striking a blow for justice against the arrogant, imperialist, and decadent American empire. Aside from its other deficiencies, such a message would be virtually incomprehensible—unthinkable—to most Americans, journalists included. Thus, although this version did receive attention from the media, it was not favorable, and those pushing this frame had scant success convincing Americans. It was far easier cognitively and emotionally to accept the dominant interpretation.

Other motivations to accept the White House frame of 9/11 and reject this counterframe are clearly relevant: monitoring the environment for threats to one's values;[51] interest in political events; participation in interpersonal networks on which such extraordinary news topics would come up (for citizens); and potential for career advancement (for elites and journalists). Americans would have risked ostracism if they came to work on September 12 and proclaimed little interest in what happened the day before. The motivations overcame the typical American's minimal interest in foreign affairs, as often happens during international crises. Remember, however, that how an event is framed determines whether most people interpret it as a crisis. Thus, for example, the Bush administration took great pains to downplay the North Korean challenge in early 2003 and avoided labeling it as a crisis. It wanted eyes focused on Iraq, and polls suggested this effort met with some success.[52]

Then there are the matters for which the political culture provides ambiguous guidance. Responses—by elites, journalists, and citizens alike—become less predictable when schemas bring up contradictory interpretations. As suggested earlier, ambiguity has become increasingly common in U.S. foreign policymaking.

If framing the attacks on the World Trade Center and Pentagon as evil terrorism engineered by the demonic Osama bin Laden registered easily given habitual thinking patterns, and if framing them as courageous strikes against the Americans would be blocked from spreading, what would be an example of framing in response to ambiguity? Consider the bombing of the Murrah Federal Building in Oklahoma City on April 19, 1995, which killed nearly two hundred people. In the immediate aftermath the media were full of speculation about the possible role of Middle Eastern terrorists. That was the familiar mental pathway: Islamic fanatics targeting innocent civilians. It took some time for the possibility to sink into the minds of leaders, then of the news media, and finally of the American public that a previously unfamiliar interpretation explained the bombing. Few Americans had heard much about the domestic "militia" subculture that spawned homegrown terrorists Timothy McVeigh and Terry Nichols. In the weeks following the bombing, a new schema took its place in most Americans' knowledge networks that knitted together ideas and feelings about *domestic terrorism*. Although perhaps mildly dissonant for many Americans, it fit with other motivations—it was not complicated, and it identified a genuine threat. In turn this stored interpretation of the Oklahoma City bombing influenced the earliest live coverage of September 11th—many correspondents repeatedly cautioned viewers against leaping to the conclusion that Middle Easterners committed the atrocities.

What the Cascade Model Suggests

Let us cast ideal visions of the free press in terms of this analysis. The cascade model suggests that the media should provide enough information independent of the executive branch that citizens can construct their own counterframes of issues and events.[53] It is not enough for media to present information in ill-digested and scattered morsels.[54] Rather, what citizens need is a counterframe constructed of culturally resonant words and images, one that attains sufficient magnitude to gain wide understanding as a sensible alternative to the White House's interpretation. This study seeks to reveal how much and what kind of counterframing information the media supply, when, why, and with what effects on democracy and foreign policy. By highlighting interactions among cultural congruence, motivations, power, and strategy, the cascade model produces new insights about the relationships between the White House's preferred framing and the frames that actually appear in the news. Five propositions arising from the model will be explored in the next five chapters:

> 1. *Presidential control over framing of foreign affairs will be highest when dealing with the culturally congruent or incongruent. In response to these situations, elites outside the administration tend to remain silent, and their quiescence allows the administration's claims to flow unimpeded, directly through to the media. In these instances, the predictions of the hegemony, indexing, and cascade models will be similar.*

When the White House frames an event or issue by invoking the match with clearly relevant and congruent cultural assumptions, motivations among elites, journalists, and the public usually fall right into line—especially when a foreign development threatens the country and its dominant values. In these circumstances, the administration's frame will pretty much completely control media coverage and indicators of public opinion. By the same token, when an event occurs that might cause dissonance because of its manifest incompatibility with dominant cultural thinking, other elites and journalists will cooperate with a White House frame that blocks dissonant connections from media texts and thus from influencing public opinion.

Chapter 2 explores the media's responses under such conditions. It examines the framing of two incidents that were substantially similar but culturally distinctive: the destruction of Korean Air Lines Flight 007 (1983) by a Soviet fighter pilot, and that of Iran Air Flight 655 (1988) by a U.S. naval cruiser. The first incident coincided with deeply habitual schemas about the Soviet menace, whereas Flight 655 was incongruent with America's self-image, and the news blocked certain connections. The comparison illustrates the four typical functions of substantive news framing and, more important, it reveals enormous differences in news of the two events, differences that closely reflected the administration's line. As the hegemony and index models would predict, presidential dominance of the news frames allowed little opportunity for journalists to convey or citizens to develop contrary interpretations of political consequence.

But many events and issues neither readily fit nor obviously clash with habitual, well-established mental associations, and schemas often conflict with each other. Such ambiguous circumstances open more space for elites and journalists to express dissenting views. Presidential success at winning contests over the framing of ambiguous matters depends on the motivation, power, and strategy deployed by the administration and other elites, and on journalists' own motivations. Hence the following propositions:

2. Journalists have strong professional motivations to include oppositional readings of foreign policy in their stories, and enjoy the greatest opportunity to satisfy these motives when the event or issue is ambiguous. Even when U.S. elites fail to challenge the White House, the motive leads journalists to convey a surprising amount of dissenting news.

3. Elites—especially members of Congress—have strong motivations of their own for political survival. This leads them to heed indicators of lopsided or intense public opinion. When a large majority appears positively inclined toward the president, other leaders tend to fall silent and coverage of opposing views is unlikely to generate a coherent counterframe. But, when public opinion appears split over ambiguous matters, elite motivations can spur opposition, and strategy and power come to the fore in determining who wins the frame contest.

Chapters 3 and 4 explore evidence for these points. Chapter 3 examines themes and visual images in the media's framing of U.S. interventions in Grenada, Libya, and Panama during the 1980s. With the partial exception of Grenada, the fading Cold War paradigm was irrelevant to these issues. Contrary to what the indexing or hegemony models might predict, each incident generated quite a lot of critical news coverage despite overwhelming public *and* elite support. The cases reveal the contours and ironic limits on both the media's capacity to maintain distance from the White House, and on their ability to promote democratic accountability in foreign policy. The source of the irony is the very responsiveness of officials to indicators of public opinion. The major reason that journalists' own efforts to bring up opposing information failed to blossom into useful counterframes is that elites were cowed into silence by indications that the public would not abide any carping. The result of the contrary push and pull of journalistic and elite motivations was reporting that combined critiques of the administration line with uncritical propaganda, sometimes in the very same story. The cascade model suggests that elite dissent and skeptical public majorities are not always required in enabling the media to contest the administration line. Here it was journalists themselves who constituted much of the opposition, but their efforts were diluted and, on their own, they could not spread dissent either upward toward officials or downward to the public.

America's response to Iraq's 1990 invasion of Kuwait was another issue for which the culture gave ambiguous guidance, and the ensuing debate provides the focus of chapter 4. The most significant differences here are that public opinion appeared divided and that respected, powerful leaders did clash openly over the White House's framing. Some agreed with President George H. W. Bush and wanted to begin war as soon as practicable, but others urged reliance on sanctions to compel Iraq's capitulation. Congress was almost evenly split between these options, and members on both sides actively jockeyed to contest or support the president. Debate over policy toward Iraq therefore offered an unusually fruitful opportunity to explore the relationship between elite disagreement and media framing. The indexing model would lead us to expect something like parity between the White House's and opposition's frames. In fact, media frames favored the Bush administration—in subtle but revealing and politically decisive ways. The cascade model illuminates the ways power and strategy combined to make this happen in 1990—and, as chapter 5 discusses, how similar forces shaped news of debates over Iraq in 2002–3. A president at the top of his game, and congressional opponents unwilling to use institutional powers strategically, undercut dissenters' ability to spread their ideas through the cascading system.

But more determined and skilled opposition from Congress and other elites—and journalists—can change this equation. What hegemony models miss in particular is that, under the right circumstances, leaders may have little incentive to support the White House, and they can use culturally dominant, habitual schemas to mobilize *against* the administration's frame. That leads to the next proposition:

> 4. *In the post–Cold War period, if the White House mismanages its relationships with other elites and journalists, especially if it cannot find compelling schemas that support its line, a president may lose control of the frame. For ambiguous matters, under some circumstances, elite opponents, journalists, and indicators of public opinion may together attain as much influence over framing as the administration.*

Chapter 5 assesses the evidence. Once the dust settled from the first Gulf War, the breakdown of the Cold War paradigm seemed to diminish the reliability of White House influence over the framing of U.S. foreign policy. As ambiguity came to dominate many foreign issues, the media's depictions of U.S. interventions in Somalia, Haiti, and Bosnia and Kosovo revealed increased slack in the framing process: opportunities grew for news organizations to compete with—and sometimes trump—the administration's line. The loss of frame contests, or even the prospect of it, may be sufficient to make the administration modify or abandon its policies. So, at least under some circumstances, the media themselves have become actors in the global political arena, promoting certain problem definitions and remedies and neglecting or derogating others. The findings testify that presidential power is sometimes limited by the sway of cultural schemas over elites, journalists, and the public. Just like everyone else, presidents are well advised to stay on the good side of these schemas.

Chapter 5 discusses how, when Bill Clinton attempted in 1994 to persuade American elites and citizens that the country had a vital interest in democracy for Haiti, he ran into such schemas as *quagmire* (fear of lengthy, costly, unsuccessful engagements) and *racism* (unspoken, perhaps unconscious assumptions that black suffering is less important than white). There were also recent memories of Somalia, where U.S. intervention in 1993 had been framed prominently and resonantly as a disastrous failure. The same schemas that discouraged and limited (without preventing) U.S. engagement in Somalia and Haiti worked against President Clinton's ability and willingness to even consider a serious preemptive intervention in Rwanda in 1994, when genocide loomed and ultimately occurred.[55] Minus the racism, similar processes operated in debates over intervention in Bosnia and Kosovo. Perhaps more surprisingly, as I suggest in chapter 5, after the glow of apparent victory over the Taliban and al-Qaeda in Afghanistan faded, President George W. Bush was unable to maintain continuous control over the framing of policies in the war on terror. The media promoted dissent over Bush's proposal to project America's military might into Iraq. However, in another turn of the screw, just as in the earlier Iraq war, superior administration power and strategy generally diminished the prominence and political effect of dissenting views in the news.

The role of the public in all this is no straightforward matter, and chapter 6 assesses the implications of the cascade model for democratic representation in foreign policymaking. The premises of the chapter are that framing is an inescapable feature of representation, and that this increases the political influence of the media. Surveys from the last years of the Cold War reveal that the public favored increases in defense spending at the same time they wanted more spent on many other programs—and decreases in taxes, *and* a balanced federal budget. Similar ambiguity characterizes public opinion data before both wars in Iraq. There is little guidance in such data even for leaders who sincerely want to represent the public will. It is mainly through the selective framing of public opinion indicators that the public can have an impact. Elites would be paralyzed if they tried to act simultaneously on all the available opinion data. Public opinion is therefore subject to framed interpretations that enter the fray where, just like other political communications, they may spread or fizzle depending on the motivations, strategies, and power of those playing the game. This suggests a final insight from the cascade model:

> 5. *The decline and disappearance of the Cold War paradigm has made the public's responses to foreign affairs less predictable, and this heightens the media's role in representation. In unsettled times, politicians and news organizations monitor indicators of public sentiment more carefully than before—indicators bound to frames in the media.*[56]

Elites gauge public opinion not only by looking at polls but also by using news frames to draw inferences of likely public responses. Furthermore, poll questions and wording, and thus the survey data available to politicians, depend heavily on the news. Chapter 6 explores these ideas in the context of public opinion on defense spending and nuclear arms control. I conclude that representation has been at best a haphazard thing, with the media playing a central but problematic (and insufficiently appreciated) role in transmitting interpretations of public sentiments on foreign policy up to officials.

Reviewing the cascading activation model, the findings, and the analysis, chapter 7 considers exactly how much media-assisted, independent public interpretation and input does occur, and how much is desirable. It acknowledges limitations on the media's abilities to fulfill the ideals of a free press—and the problems that the public has living up to ideals of democratic citizenship when it comes to foreign policy. My conclusion suggests that diversifying the *elite* public sphere may be the most realistic path to improvement, and I propose the creation of two new positions to help realize this vision. Both posts would be designed to publicize novel ideas more effectively than current practice allows. *Designated Statesmen or Stateswomen,* experts and former officials, would undertake the explicit assignment of activating and spreading innovative ideas along the networks and corridors of power in Washington. *Liaison editors* working for major media organizations would attempt to highlight connections and contradictions that tend otherwise to get neglected in the daily rush of news production.

These proposals are presented not as panaceas but as realistic incremental steps toward improvement. The empirical findings and analyses here suggest caution about the real-world potential for achieving much more democratic responsiveness and accountability in foreign policy. At the same time, the study indicates that making empirical judgments about the degree of actual government responsiveness to public opinion is inextricably bound up with forming normative judgments of just what constitutes responsiveness. The chapters that follow, in other words, suggest that empirical and normative analyses in the study of political communication must systematically inform each other.

The first step on this empirical and normative journey will be to clarify further the concept of framing. That is the purpose of the appendix immediately following this chapter. The material was placed in an appendix as a convenience for readers whose impatience to get on with the substantive findings outweighs their interest in conceptual matters.

Finally, the book was nearly finished when the Iraq war of 2003 began. As much as was possible, it incorporates available data and observations on the media's responses to the "major combat operations" (March 21–May 1) and to the immediate aftermath. Exhaustive studies of news about this projection of American power could not be undertaken, however, before *Projections of Power* had to go to the printer.

APPENDIX TO CHAPTER 1

• •

As suggested in chapter 1, developing an understanding of framing helps deepen our theoretical insight more generally into the political influence of the news media and into the relationships among elites, media, and the public. Here I explore in greater detail the objects of framing in the news, using the events, actors, and issues arising out of the September 11, 2001, terrorist attacks as examples. I then distinguish the concept of framing from others often used synonymously; my argument is that reserving the term "frame" to denote the specific concept outlined here, and using other terms for related concepts, will help build theory.

Objects of Framing

Frames in the news are typically a part of the reporting process for three different classes of objects: political events, issues, and actors (who may be individual leaders, groups, or nations). Often the same set of news stories simultaneously frame more than one object, providing framing information not just about an event, say, but also about a related issue or actor. This was certainly true in framing the Taliban rulers of Afghanistan after September 11th. Which framing function or object of discourse a text provides depends on where one draws the analytical lines. Using the grid displayed in figure 1A.1, we might find media coverage that provides, say, a clear problem definition in framing the event, a remedy in framing a related issue, and a moral assessment of an official involved. The coverage might neglect, for instance, to provide explicit evaluations of the related event or issue. The news frequently exhibits such voids in framing, gaps that audiences may fill by using tacit understandings (that is, their existing schemas) or that they may simply ignore. Whether those gaps are illogical or irrelevant is usually open to dispute. And crucially, whether the audience has a realistic opportunity to work out a fully developed counterframe to the White House line may depend on how well the coverage elaborates that counterframe. When counterframes are poorly developed, when news with alternative information exhibits serious gaps in several of the cells of figure 1A.1, the average citizen may have great difficulty developing a more independent interpretation and evaluation.

	Focus of Frame		
Function of Frame	Issues	Events	Political Actors (Individuals, Groups, Nations)
Defining problematic effects/conditions			
Identifying cause/agent			
Endorsing remedy			
Conveying moral judgment			

FIGURE 1A.1 *Functions and Objects of News Frames*

The cells in figure 1A.1 are useful to the extent they help us understand the framing process, but they should not be taken as mutually exclusive categories. For instance, one could consider the totality of framing news coverage of the September 11 attacks as focusing simultaneously on all three objects and thus providing a fully developed narrative frame—one with all twelve cells explicitly (even fulsomely) filled. The coverage framed an event as an "act of war," an issue (war against terrorism), and a political actor consisting of groups and their leaders (Taliban, al-Qaeda, Mullah Muhammad Omar, and Osama bin Laden). Figure 1A.2 illustrates how the problem in the actor frame is a more specific version of the cause in the event frame; that is, bin Laden, al-Qaeda, and the Taliban are the problematic actors, the specific manifestation of terrorism. Similarly, the remedy in this actor frame—namely, war—becomes the focus of the issue frame; and in this third frame, the causal analysis emerges from the event frame as a whole. War against the Taliban and al-Qaeda would not be necessary, would not be an issue, were it not for the September 11 act of war against the United States.

Habitual schemas are often organized into an overarching *paradigm,* or a meta-schema.[1] Paradigms are networks of habitual schemas that promote the application of analogies from previous major stories to new developments. Frames that tap into such paradigms are particularly influential. The paradigm of *terrorism* supplied analogies upon which journalists and elites as well as ordinary citizens readily drew in responding to September 11th.[2] It brought to mind a familiar set of prototypical *events* (suicide bombings,

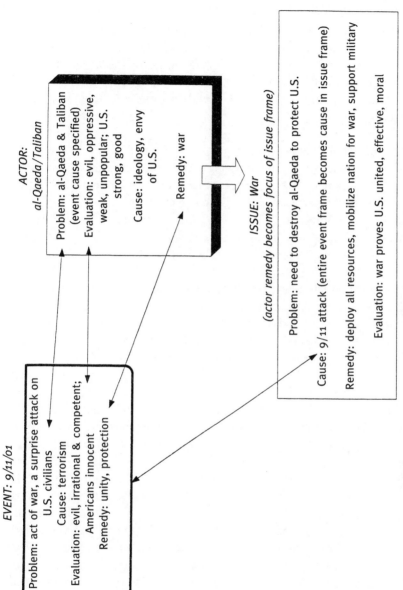

FIGURE 1A.2 *Fully Developed Frame for September 11th*

EVENT: 9/11/01

Problem: act of war, a surprise attack on
U.S. civilians
Cause: terrorism
Evaluation: evil, irrational & competent;
Americans innocent
Remedy: unity, protection

ACTOR:
al-Qaeda/Taliban

Problem: al-Qaeda & Taliban
(event cause specified)
Evaluation: evil, oppressive,
weak, unpopular; U.S.
strong, good

Cause: ideology, envy
of U.S.

Remedy: war

ISSUE: War
(actor remedy becomes focus of issue frame)

Problem: need to destroy al-Qaeda to protect U.S.

Cause: 9/11 attack (entire event frame becomes cause in issue frame)

Remedy: deploy all resources, mobilize nation for war, support military

Evaluation: war proves U.S. united, effective, moral

airplane hijackings), *issues* (sanctions versus military strikes), and *actors* (Islamic extremists, Iraq, Libya, Saddam Hussein). An event may activate paradigms in elites' and journalists' minds, stimulating their use of certain resonant words and images in constructing the news. These in turn encourage the public to make connections, perhaps leaping from an event like 9/11 to apparently similar matters like Pearl Harbor or the 1995 bombing in Oklahoma City.

Frames and Related Concepts

Some terminological matters require further clarification. The verb "to frame" (or "framing") refers to the process of selecting and highlighting some aspects of a perceived reality, and enhancing the salience of an interpretation and evaluation of that reality. Scholars from across the social sciences have used the term "frame" as a synonym for such concepts as schema (discussed in chapter 1), script, and image. All of these help people interpret their perceptions, but distinguishing them from frames could enhance the precision of scholarly understanding. Without claiming that this book's usage is the only correct approach, let us reserve the term "script" for standardized information processing rules that journalists use in covering certain categories of events, actors, or issues. Thus what scholars have referred to as the "conflict frame" and "human interest frame" would, in this book's terms, be stories told following the conflict or human interest *script*.[3] Their use of the label "frames" for notions that might be better termed "scripts" does not undermine the usefulness of these studies; my suggestion is simply that standardizing terminology and distinguishing frames from related but different concepts would improve scholars' ability to build on each others' work.

To say that journalists applied a conflict or human interest "frame" in reporting a dispute over taxes cannot tell us (or audiences) the particular problem definition, causal analysis, remedy proposal, or moral judgment (if any) that the text promotes. Often stories written through these scripts do not even obliquely promote a sensible interpretation or evaluation. What differentiates a frame from a script most clearly is this: framing directly promotes interpretations that lead to evaluations. The conflict *script* yields a particular type of story, one that journalists frequently produce by following habitual information processing routines when confronted by certain types of situations. When developing a story using the conflict script, journalists focus on the disagreements and jockeying among the sides, and this is what they emphasize, rather than the substantive basis of the dispute or the considerable overlap in positions that might actually exist. A good example of news following the conflict script was the coverage journalists gave to affirmative action, a hot-button issue in the 1990s.[4] Far from making probative arguments about problems, causes, and remedies, then, these and other nonprobative scripts that shape the news can create voids or distract the audience from the policy-specific attributes of political messages.

On the other hand, one other use of the term "frame" seems clearly appropriate because it does refer to substantive information in the communicating text that can promote particular interpretations and evaluations. It employs experimental and survey methods to demonstrate how different framing of issues and their remedies (policy options) can lead to very different responses even when the underlying facts are identical.[5] Typically the researchers vary only a few words and treat this small semantic difference as framing the matter differently. Usually such studies find what many researchers call "priming,"[6] by which they mean *activating an association between an item highlighted in the framed text and an audience's thinking about a related concept.* For instance, in a classic experiment, Kahneman and Tversky described a hypothetical public health crisis and proposed remedies. The solution framed in terms of lives saved was far more popular than the one framed in terms of deaths avoided, even though the remedies were substantively identical.[7] Apparently experimental subjects did not like remedies that explicitly encouraged associations to the concept of death. Kinder and Sanders found that whites' support for government policies such as tax breaks for business and increased spending for schools is significantly greater when framed in class terms (as benefiting the poor) than in racial terms (as benefiting blacks).[8] Another illustration of framing's impact from attitude research concludes:

> The effect of framing is to prime values differentially, establishing the salience of the one or the other. Framing thus tends to guarantee a disjunction between acts and (some) attitudes, not because the attitude is not sincerely held, but because it has not been primed while a competing value has. The consequence . . . is that a majority of the public supports the rights of persons with AIDS when the issue is framed to accentuate civil liberties considerations—and supports as well mandatory testing when the issue is framed to accentuate public health considerations.[9]

Framing operated in the latter instance by communicating the information about the dangers of AIDS spreading while omitting the civil liberties infringements that testing may cause. As in this case, the communicating text supplies most people with the considerations they will use in responding to interviewers who ask about the issue of AIDS testing.[10] In these and similar examples, again, the term "frame" seems applicable since the texts actually do possess the potential to prime interpretations and evaluations, typically by advancing problem definitions and remedies. The frames prime the audience members' responses by activating associations between the information highlighted in the text and concepts already stored in their schema systems.

Finally, the concept of image has been used in psychologically oriented studies of international relations.[11] The concept is a refinement and specification of "schema." An image is a type of schema that stores and processes analogies. Although distinguishing the concept of image from schema has proven useful in international relations theory, using the term "image" in place of "schema" in studying media would be confusing. In political communication studies, "image" is best reserved for nonverbal, visual illustrations.

2. GUILT AND INNOCENCE IN THE KOREAN AIRLINE AND IRAN AIR TRAGEDIES

On September 1, 1983, a Soviet Air Force fighter jet shot down Korean Air Lines (KAL) Flight 007, killing 269 people. On July 3, 1988, a U.S. Navy ship, the *Vincennes,* shot down Iran Air Flight 655, killing 290. In both cases, military officials misidentified a passenger plane as a hostile target; in both cases, the perpetrating nation's officials claimed that circumstances justified the attacks. This chapter explores the sharply contrasting news frames used by several important U.S. media outlets in covering these two incidents. For KAL, the news emphasized the moral bankruptcy of the guilty nation; for Iran Air, coverage deemphasized moral judgment and focused on the complex problems of operating military high technology.

In covering two tragic incidents where similar military mistakes killed hundreds of civilians, media framing varied dramatically, but in both cases closely followed the White House's cues—and the predictions of the cascade model. The near-perfect congruence between Ronald Reagan's interpretation of KAL and habitual Cold War schemas made for overwhelming domination of the news by the "murder" frame. On the other hand, the killing of civilian passengers on Iran Air by American forces, an incident reminiscent of KAL, was thoroughly at odds with Americans' national self-image. The dissonance was strong enough to block reasonable reservations about U.S. policy, and the White House's strategy was to guide thinking toward the acceptable and politically helpful "technical glitch" frame.

Comparing media narratives of events that could have been similarly reported helps to reveal the critical choices that framed the story and shaped its political impacts. Many framing decisions can appear to be "natural," unremarkable selections of words or images. This chapter reveals that such choices are critical to establishing the "common sense" of an event—the dominant interpretations among elites, in news texts, and in the indicators of public opinion. The frame of KAL identified the problematic event as murder and the cause as the Soviet government. This produced harsh moral condemnation and the remedy of heightened diplomatic and military opposition to the Soviets. The frame for Iran Air defined the problem as a tragic accident, the cause as human and technological fallibility. In this way, the framing rendered the question of morality pretty much irrelevant, and merely promoted slight changes in operating procedures as the solutions. Here I explore the way print and electronic media used consistently different words and images to frame these two similar events, and apply the cascade model to explain exactly how and why they did so, and with what effects. The chapter also constitutes a primer on how frames operate in a text.

Framing Similar Events Differently

My focus is on the two issues of *Time* and *Newsweek* following the KAL and Iran Air incidents, along with the *CBS Evening News* for the same two-week period. The newsmagazines[1] arguably summarize the dominant news and editorial emphases of the national media in the United States; their relatively leisurely deadlines usually allow them to canvass official sources (and other media) thoroughly, distilling the results in a narrative reflecting the principal themes in the news.[2] CBS can be safely treated as broadly representative of ABC and NBC broadcast coverage.[3] Data are also cited from an analysis of all articles on the events in the *New York Times* and *Washington Post,* perhaps the two most influential newspapers, for the same period. It might be improper to generalize to all mass media from these outlets; even within the group analyzed here, treatments differ a bit. But the strength of the findings, and previous research on the KAL flight alone,[4] suggest that most U.S. news media framed the events similarly.

Comparing the two stories does not require an assumption that the underlying facts of KAL and Iran Air were analogous to a fine degree. Both were complicated events open to varying interpretations, and no doubt part of the reason for the contrasting frames lies in aspects of each event that were unique to it. But there is no way to establish as a factual matter, for example, that the United States was any less morally responsible for the fate of the Iranians than the Soviet Union was for the KAL passengers, and therefore that the media's emphasis on Soviet guilt and denial of American was somehow compelled by the facts.

Consider that the *Vincennes* had only a few minutes to decide whether to shoot down the Iranian plane, which was flying over an area of the Persian Gulf that had just experienced combat. This context could morally justify the shooting. Yet one could argue that the U.S. Navy's awareness of civilian air traffic traversing the Gulf imposed a moral imperative to establish procedures for identifying passenger planes like Flight 655. In that perspective, the shootdown might appear morally indefensible. For its part, the Soviet Air Force had over two hours to ponder what to do about the intruding plane, in a context free of combat. While these facts could be read as condemning the Soviet action, the KAL jet was flying over highly sensitive Soviet military installations, around the time of a scheduled missile test and just after an American spy plane had entered the same area.[5] One could argue that by holding off firing for two hours in hopes of identifying the plane positively, the Soviets demonstrated moral sensitivity. Or one could blame civilian air traffic control systems and international aviation organizations rather than the governments and militaries of either country. The argument could go on indefinitely but, for analysis, the crucial point is to establish comparable potential framing.[6] Nothing inherent in the reality of the events themselves forced the starkly different frames that the media created.

Contrasting Magnitude

The *sine qua non* of successful framing is magnitude—magnifying those elements of the depicted reality that favor one side's position, making them salient, while at the same time shrinking those elements that might be used to construct a counterframe. Whatever specific words and images depict the event, it is important to first ask how much material on the event is available and how prominently is it displayed. The frame of a news portrait can be enlarged so that the reports penetrate the consciousness of a public with little motivation to pay foreign affairs much attention. Or the frame can be shrunk to miniaturize an event, diminishing the number and prominence of the words and images, rendering them, at the extreme, politically irrelevant. If a frame does not have magnitude, its content matters little; for this reason, my focus here and throughout this study is on those frames that attain prominence and repetition, and on comparing them with possible counterframes that received insufficient attention to influence politics. Magnitude in this way measures and helps determine a news event's political importance.

The media granted the KAL incident far more magnitude than Iran Air.[7] Table 2.1 displays some comparisons. CBS dedicated 50 percent more time

TABLE 2.1 *Coverage of KAL vs. the Iran Air Incident*

	KAL	Iran Air
Time/Newsweek	51 pages	20 pages
New York Times	286 stories	102 stories
Washington Post	169 stories	82 stories
CBS	303 minutes	204 minutes

Source: Author's analysis; CBS data from the Vanderbilt Television News Archives Indexes. Includes coverage during the two weeks following each incident.

to KAL than Iran Air (303 versus 204 minutes), and the print media devoted two or three times more attention to KAL. Beyond this, KAL led twenty-seven of the forty-three evening news shows on ABC, CBS, and NBC during the two weeks after the incident and received some coverage on every program. Iran Air led the news half as much—just fourteen of the forty-eight broadcasts. With one exception (CBS on the eighth day), KAL supplied the lead for nine consecutive days of the three network evening news telecasts. Iran Air served as the lead on all three major networks for just the first two days and two other (nonconsecutive) days.

If both events were tragedies, KAL was configured as larger, more important. To be sure, Americans would have reacted much more strongly to the deaths on the KAL flight (which carried dozens of Americans) than to Iranians' deaths even if the volume of reporting had been the same. But the magnitude likely made a political difference: Continuing high public awareness of KAL pressured Reagan's potential opponents to remain silent or hop on his "Evil Empire" bandwagon to confront the Soviets. On the other hand, lower public awareness of the Iran Air incident meshed with the White House's desire to discourage opposition by anyone tempted to gain political leverage from the miscue.

The circumstances did not automatically produce such dramatically disparate coverage given to these stories; the White House strategically maneuvered to achieve the desired magnitude.[8] This conclusion is suggested by the fact that the names of President Reagan and Secretary of State George Shultz appeared 697 times in the *Post*'s KAL coverage but only 111 times in its Iran Air reporting; for the *Times* the figures were 771 times and 150 times, respectively. KAL received about twice as much coverage; adjusting for this, references to the two top foreign policy officials appeared about three times more in KAL news.[9] The administration wanted to distance the president and secretary of state from the Iran Air tragedy, but sought to feature them centrally in the reporting on KAL. Given the media's focus on the presidency, the very presence of the chief executive's face and voice magnified the KAL story while his comparative scarcity shrank the political import of the Iran Air narrative.

Resonant Framing of the Problem and Its Causes

Beyond the frame's magnitude are the resonant words and images that constitute the specific event frames. The framing of KAL was saturated with morally judgmental words and images that arose directly and inevitably from the problem definition and causal analysis. In terms of spreading activation, once the cause of the event was established to be intentional murder on the part of the Soviet Union, the journey along the pathway to emotional, negative moral judgments was instantaneous. In cases like this, the problem definition, cause, and moral evaluation are completely intertwined and feasible remedies virtually predetermined.

The very different identification of problem and cause in the Iran Air coverage, on the other hand, pointed decisively away from moral evaluation. In that case certain mental associations were blocked, and the administration steered news frames and public thinking by inundating reporters with far more words and images about technology than about human responsibility. Dissonance engaged motivations among most participants in the framing process, from the president down to the common citizen, to block moral interpretations. It was easy for journalists to follow the administration's guidance on Iran Air, to adopt a focus on technical details of military machinery and decisionmaking rather than on human suffering and American responsibility for it. Again the problem, cause, and (absent) moral assessment were closely linked.

In both cases, initial cues arising from the specific words and emotional tone used by top administration authorities led editors and reporters to recall (probably with little conscious effort) habitual moral or technical concepts. Combined with continuing cues from the vocabulary and visual images supplied by government officials, this encouraged journalists to process information and frame stories through the consistent use of words and images that portrayed very different responsibility for *causing* the events and that led to the divergent *moral evaluations*.

CONTRASTING CAUSES: GUILTY AGENTS (USSR) AND TECHNICAL GLITCHES (IRAN AIR)

What causal force created the newsworthy event? By convention, the answer typically appears in headlines, and in these cases headlines bolstered the different frames. The first *Newsweek* cover after the KAL incident (12 September 1983) was headed "Murder in the Air"; the title on the lead article was "A Ruthless Ambush in the Sky." *Time*'s cover headline that week was "Shooting to Kill/The Soviets Destroy an Airliner"; the lead story, "Atrocity in the Skies/The Soviets Shoot Down a Civilian Airliner." The view propounded by these words was that the Soviet government knowingly acted to annihilate a civilian airliner. They defined the event as yet another instance of Soviet evil, a callous act of violence confirming established moral assessments of the USSR. The second week's coverage continued in this vein; for example, *Newsweek*'s cover (19 September 1983) was headlined "Why Moscow Did It/Inquest on Flight 007/The World's

Outrage/The Diplomatic Impact/The Soviet Stonewall." Notice who committed the act: not an air force pilot patroling the Siberian sky, but "Moscow" or the "Soviets," implying that the entire USSR government caused the incident.

In contrast, the *Newsweek* cover about Iran Air (18 July 1988) promised to disclose "Why It Happened." Construction was passive, causality obscured. *Time* relegated the Iran Air shootdown to the corner flap, which read, "What Went Wrong in the Gulf." Again, no mention of human responsibility, passive voice, abstract language—not who did wrong but what went wrong. (The *Time* editors judged the space program, the main cover story, more newsworthy that week.) In both magazines, the second week's covers failed to feature the Iran Air incident at all.

Beyond the covers and headlines of the newsmagazines, the KAL stories repeatedly attributed guilty knowledge to the Soviet leaders. The magazines and CBS made several references suggesting that Premier Andropov "must have" known or that the fighter pilots "knew" or "should have known" their target was a passenger plane. These suggestions culminated in the following statement in *Newsweek* (19 September 1983, 30): "By every law of Soviet psychology, 269 lives was not too high a price to pay for the assurance that the sacred borders were being well protected." Thus the report implied that Soviet decisionmakers knew not only that there were civilians aboard the doomed plane, but exactly how many.

Iran Air stories alluded to guilt quite differently. For example, when the *Time* story (18 July 1988) noted that the *Vincennes* did not maintain detailed information about civilian air schedules over the Persian Gulf, the reason given was that "[n]obody thought it necessary to do so."[10] The story contained no ethical assessment of this omission, no conclusions about the moral nature of U.S. military policy or the American psyche that could result in such an oversight. Instead, the story explained that the U.S. Navy "is just not used to operating" in the Gulf environment. Assertions that the *Vincennes* crew "should have known" the identity of the Iran Air flight did not appear; on the contrary, central to the narrative from the very first words about the incident on CBS was the understandable absence of guilty knowledge. The newscast opened with Admiral William Crowe, chairman of the Joint Chiefs of Staff, saying: "We believe that the cruiser USS *Vincennes,* while actively engaged with threatening Iranian surface units and protecting itself from what was concluded to be a hostile aircraft, shot down an Iranian airliner over the Straits of Hormuz."[11]

The magazines' cover art and the inside graphics also confirmed the causal framing for each event. *Newsweek*'s cover portrayed the center of a target pointing at the words "Korean Air Lines" on the 747, and both magazines pictured the fighter jet apparently close enough to read those words. The illustrations validated the Reagan administration's claim—which it quickly learned to be false[12]—that the Soviet government knowingly ordered destruction of a civilian airliner. CBS News visually depicted the incident similarly. Its initial graphic resembled that of *Newsweek,* showing a large KAL airliner with a target superimposed. In other graphics repeatedly shown over several days, CBS stories depicted the Russian and KAL planes in apparent close proximity, close enough for the Soviet pilots to have easily identified the civilian plane.[13]

The magazines and the television news program used corresponding logos to illustrate the beginnings of KAL-related stories, all featuring the hammer and sickle, the most widely recognized symbol of Soviet communism. As the central figure on the Soviet Union's red flag, it was as familiar and perhaps emotionally potent (though negatively so) as the U.S. stars and stripes. For instance, the logo for *Time* in the second week was a silhouette of the KAL plane inside a sickle. CBS's continuing logo was a large, side view of the KAL airliner, with the KAL corporate logo and "Korean Air Lines" visible, superimposed over flags with the hammer and sickle. By associating the event with the archetypal symbol of communism, the graphics suggested that the event was caused by the Soviet system itself.

In marked contrast, the *Time* cover mentioning the Iran Air case, albeit only on the corner flap, offered a picture so small it is difficult to interpret. It showed a man sitting before numerous control panels holding his head, apparently in exasperation and confusion. The illustration supported the administration's preferred causal analysis: the incident was traceable not to moral failure but to imperfections and complexities of high technology and the understandable if not inevitable shortcomings of humans struggling to manage it. Explicitly, the *Newsweek* cover neither affirmed nor denied the technical framing; it showed the *Vincennes* after it had shot a missile during maneuvers. But by not including a picture of an exploding passenger plane on the cover (as for the KAL incident), *Newsweek* defined the central newsworthy problem as revolving around the officers and technology on the *Vincennes,* not the Iran Air passengers.[14]

The graphics in the coverage by CBS even shifted responsibility to the *Iranians.* The animation of the flight path shown on three of the first five days depicted an oversized plane appearing to dive right at the *Vincennes.* A central part of the administration's initial framing strategy was to claim that the ship's instruments showed the Iran Air jet to be heading straight for them. Such circumstances explained and justified the shootdown and confirmed its moral neutrality. Although by the fourth day after the attack CBS did raise doubts about this false claim, the graphics belied the doubts.

Time's logo for the Iran Air incident was neutral: a small, red plane silhouette inside a black circle. The *Newsweek* logo again reflected the framing of the event as a tragedy of technology. It showed a stylized radar screen with a small, jagged, starlike splotch presumably indicating the explosion of the Iran Air plane, with the words "Tragedy in the Gulf." On CBS the continuing logo showed a largely head-on view of the plane, which obscured the Iran Air markings, superimposed over a map of the Persian Gulf region. In all three media, unlike in the KAL illustrations, the cause (the United States or its navy) was not symbolized at all, and the civilian identity of the aircraft was not clear, again obscuring human responsibility while subtly justifying the difficulty the *Vincennes* had in identifying the plane.

In sum, through choices of words and graphic images, the media reinforced the idea that the Soviet government and military committed intentional murder, with all the moral condemnation that implies. In covering Iran Air, they portrayed the U.S. military as committing an understandable blunder—with all the excuses that implies. Yet perhaps even more powerful was how the framing of Iran Air so frequently obscured human responsibility altogether and so inhibited any moral thinking at all. The framing for Iran Air blocked associations to schematic understandings that might have allowed for a cascading of deeper, more complicated thoughts and feelings among elites and ordinary citizens alike. A story of flawed technique that channels associations to the kind of dry details on naval operations that filled the pages of the two newsmagazines is one unlikely to stimulate much thought, or perhaps much notice at all—which was just fine with the Reagan administration.

Promoting Mental Operations That Solidified the Frames

Although the evidence for the effects of the causal framing on the audience's thinking is indirect, it appears quite strong and suggests at least three principal contrasts. Compared with the Iran Air frame, the KAL frame encouraged far greater *empathy* with those directly affected by the event; different *categorizing* of the event; and broad *generalizing* from the event. Frames may stimulate empathy by using words or images that allow audiences to see from the perspective of those who directly experience the problematic condition or effect. Frames categorize by using words and images that connect a matter to similar, familiar ones in the schemas of the audience. Evaluation frequently arises out of categorization even without explicit links to morality. Calling someone a "terrorist" is enough to activate negative associations, for example, without any further information. Frames may encourage generalizing by connecting the framed matter to larger categories—a specific event, say, to groups or nations.

EMPATHIZING

The verbal and visual messages humanized the victims on the KAL flight, encouraging empathy toward them. The Iran Air victims did not receive the same attention, and there was less affirmation of the humanity they shared with Americans. Deemphasizing the victims both reflected and helped establish the Iran Air story as a technical one. Thus, for example, two weeks in a row the magazines featured detailed drawings of the flight path, chase, and destruction of the KAL plane. They also engaged in a kind of verbal litany, describing and redescribing the shootdown throughout the coverage. Graphics of the flight path from the second week's issues took up a full page of *Time* and about three-fourths of a page in *Newsweek*. The magazines allotted fully 239 square inches to graphics of an exploding KAL plane. Such details were barely to be found in the Iran Air coverage, and only for the first week.[15] Only eighteen square inches illustrated the Iranian airliner in any guise, most of these filled by a photo of the nose and other wreckage of the jet. All the drawings of the Iranian airliner were about one-inch square or less. The *Newsweek* story depicted the actual impact of the American missile on the Iranian aircraft as a small, jagged starlike figure. The illustration implied an explosion, but the passengers' suffering diminished in salience, since the image did not even depict an airplane. *Time* had no picture of the Iranian airliner, only small lines ending in dots, about the size of a filled-in letter "o," tracing the intersection of the jet's route and the ship-to-air missile—no representation of an explosion, let alone a passenger plane.

The stark difference between a cover portrait and full-page graphics of an exploding KAL airliner, on the one hand, and on the other a tiny dot representing the Iranian aircraft offers a powerful demonstration of how thoroughly the frame suffused visual images and promoted empathy—and moral outrage—in one case but not the other. This finding also supports the notion that any measure of framing must take magnitude into account—making individual ideas more or less salient, in this case literally by making the KAL but not Iran Air victims' fate loom visually large in the graphics. The point also illustrates the importance of comparative frame analysis; without the comparison, the size of the airliner illustration might have escaped notice as an important framing device.

For its part, CBS showed repeated animations of the KAL flight path every day for a week after the incident but gave the Iran Air flight path much less time on screen. Both the magazines and CBS also offered pictures of named victims on the KAL flight and of identified grieving relatives. These visualizations of the victims as identifiable human beings or of their families did not appear in the Iran Air coverage.[16]

In the newsmagazines' verbal content, emphasis on the physical facts helped humanize KAL victims, and the absence of such details distanced Iran Air casualties. For one thing, the KAL reports offered copious descriptions of the weather, the cold sea, and other physical elements. The reports provided imagined details of what was going on in flight, encouraging identification with passengers. For example: "After reaching cruising altitude . . . many passengers took off their shoes, reached for pillows, and stretched out for sleep."[17] And the stories described the terrified passengers in the damaged airliner tumbling to earth for minutes. This rich detail contrasts with the spare and plain language describing the fate of the Iranian airliner. The actual shooting and aftermath were described in their entirety as follows by *Newsweek* (18 July 1988, 21): "Rogers gave the order to fire. Two missiles homed in on their target: At least one hit. The threatening symbol disappeared from the CIC screens and the Aegis [computer system] reported the target destroyed."

The coverage also used more resonant and humanizing words in representing the victims of KAL than Iran Air, the data for which are displayed in table 2.2. We can see that in the CBS coverage about 52 percent of the references to KAL victims were humanizing, compared with 22 percent for the victims of Iran Air. Humanizing terms implied or said explicitly that the victims were human beings; among the phrases were "innocent human beings," "269 stories of personal poignancy," "loved ones," and "269 people." Neutral terminology included such terms as "travelers," "civilians," "passengers," "those who died," and "269 lives." As table 2.2 reveals, across all the media, nearly half of the words reminded the audience that the KAL victims were human beings. This compares with only about one-fifth of references for the Iran Air victims in the magazines and on CBS. Though the newspaper accounts also humanized the KAL victims more, their terminology was less imbalanced, perhaps because they had so much more space to fill with details.

The reasons for these contrasts are varied. Notoriously ethnocentric, Americans appear to empathize far more easily with American than with foreign victims of disaster or violence.[18] Motivations arising from the practicalities of news production reinforced this tendency. Whereas pictures and descriptions of KAL victims were readily available from relatives in the

TABLE 2.2 *Use of Humanizing and Neutral Terms in Coverage of KAL and Iran Air Incidents*

	KAL			Iran Air		
	Humanizing	*Neutral*	*Total*	*Humanizing*	*Neutral*	*Total*
Time and *Newsweek*	44.7%	55.3%	100.0%	20%	80%	100.0%
n	17	21	38	4	16	20
CBS	51.9%	48.1%	100.0%	21.7%	78.3%	100.0%
n	27	25	52	10	36	46
New York Times	48.4%	51.6%	100.0%	39.3%	60.7%	100.0%
n	149	159	308	44	68	112
Washington Post	47.5%	52.5%	100.0%	41.1%	58.9%	100.0%
n	105	116	221	53	76	129

Note: Cell entries register the total times that terms deemed humanizing or neutral appeared in coverage describing the victims of the two incidents.

United States, U.S. journalists enjoyed no such access to Iran Air passengers' families.

CATEGORIZING

By placing the event in the category of criminal evil, the highly resonant and emotional KAL descriptors promoted moral judgment—even outrage—at the incident and its perpetrators. Employing a more abstract and technical vocabulary, news coverage of the shooting down of the Iranian airliner categorized the event as a no-fault accident.

In referring directly to the acts themselves, the words most commonly used were "tragedy" and "attack." Table 2.3 displays the different terms. The print media all described the KAL incident most frequently as an attack, the Iran Air incident as a tragedy. In fact, as the first row of the table shows, *Time* and *Newsweek* did not use the word "attack" even once for Iran Air, whereas for KAL they chose "attack" about 64 percent of the time. Although the Iran Air shooting was every bit as much an attack, the print media downplayed this word, with its implication of aggression and responsibility. CBS news stories actually used "attack" and "tragedy" about equally for KAL and Iran Air, suggesting television's commercial motivations may spur the evening news to energize and emotionalize language as a way of attracting viewers; an unintended consequence could be that television attains slightly more independence from the administration's preferred vocabulary[19] than print news.

The Soviets were subjected to further calumny through journalists' use of other, more resonant nouns to represent the event. These words firmly

TABLE 2.3 *Use of Words "Attack" and "Tragedy" in Coverage of KAL and Iran Air Incidents*

	KAL			Iran Air		
	Attack	Tragedy	Total	Attack	Tragedy	Total
Time and *Newsweek*	64.4%	35.6%	100.0%	0.0%	100.0%	100.0%
n	38	21	59	0	23	23
CBS	52.6%	47.4%	100.0%	44.4%	55.6%	100.0%
n	10	9	19	12[a]	15	27
New York Times	67.3%	32.7%	100.0%	48.4%	51.6%	100.0%
n	99	48	147	30[b]	32	62
Washington Post	60.6%	39.4%	100.0%	37.5%	62.5%	100.0%
n	66	43	109	24[c]	40	64

Note: Entries are numbers of appearances of the words "attack" and "tragedy" in coverage of the two incidents.

[a] Two quoting or citing Iranian responses.

[b] Seven quoting or citing Iranian, Soviet, or Libyan responses.

[c] Ten quoting or citing Iranian responses.

placed the KAL events in the category of intentional and therefore evil acts (see table 2.4). Of the forty-one labels the magazines used for the incident, 95 percent implied that the Soviets acted with deliberate cruelty. The most frequent words were "atrocity," "crime," "kill," "massacre," and "murder." In virtual mirror image, for Iran Air the magazine stories implied 87 percent of the time that the United States had made a mistake, and the two suggestions otherwise came from Iranians. The *Washington Post* and *New York Times* stories also emphasized Soviet guilt and American innocence.[20] CBS too presumed Soviet culpability, and although it seemed to cover Iran Air a bit more evenhandedly, the attributions of U.S. guilt all came from hostile sources.

In *Time* and *Newsweek,* forty-four adjectives or adverbs modified the descriptions of shooting down the Korean plane. Among these the most common were forms of the words "wanton," "brutal," and "barbaric" (each used five times). All but three of the forty-four modifiers again implied Soviet guilt by placing them in the category of inhuman violence. The description contrasted with the twenty-two adjectives or adverbs describing the shooting down of the Iran Air flight. Among these the most common were "ghastly," "tragic," "fatal," and "understandable." Six of the descriptors implied U.S. guilt of criminal wrongdoing, but all came from Iran or the Soviet Union.

The contrast was similar in the *Washington Post* and *New York Times.* In

TABLE 2.4 *Use of Assertions Portraying Soviet Action in the KAL Incident and U.S. Action in the Iran Air Incident as Deliberate or a Mistake*

	KAL			Iran Air		
	Deliberate	*Mistake*	*Total*	*Deliberate*	*Mistake*	*Total*
Time and *Newsweek*	95.1%	4.9%	100.0%	13.3%	86.7%	100.0%
n	39	2	41	2[a]	13	15
CBS	100.0%	0.0%	100.0%	53.8%	46.2%	100.0%
n	6	0	6	7[a]	6	13
New York Times	92.9%	7.1%	100.0%	23.1%	76.9%	100.0%
n	79	6	85	15[a]	50	65
Washington Post	76.1%	23.9%	100.0%	24.5%	75.5%	100.0%
n	51	16[b]	67	13[c]	40	170

Note: Cell entries are numbers of assertions that conveyed the sense that the actions taken by the military forces in each incident were either deliberate or unintentional. Percentages add horizontally within KAL and Iran Air categories.

[a] All citing or quoting Iranians or other hostile foreign sources.

[b] Five citing or quoting Soviets.

[c] Twelve citing or quoting hostile foreign sources.

the 169 *Post* articles, the most commonly used modifiers for the KAL incident during the sample period[21] were forms of the words "barbaric," "deliberate," "murderous," "brutal," and "wanton." Similar words led the list in the *Times*.[22] In the *Post* and *Times* articles mentioning Iran Air, "murderous," "wanton," and "brutal" did not appear at all, although a few other words connoting guilt did, almost all quoting Iranians, Libyans, or Soviets. The most common descriptors for the Iran Air incident in the two papers were forms of the words "mistaken," "tragic," "justified," and "understandable."[23] CBS's coverage exhibited similar patterns.[24]

GENERALIZING

The moralizing frame in the KAL reports was also reinforced by explicit generalization from the attacks to conclusions about the guilty actor's political system and leaders. KAL news coverage frequently attributed the act not simply to a Soviet pilot or the Soviet military but to the (immoral) Soviet Union or government as a whole.[25] Stories treated the action as a symbol[26] of much larger and unpleasant truths about the Soviet government and culture. Generalization about the United States was essentially absent from coverage of the Iran Air incident.

The KAL stories generalized first through their identification of the actor that shot down the plane. The magazines contained sixty-two references to the actor, thirty-three implying that the Soviet government or nation as a whole was responsible and twenty-four implying responsibility only on the part of the individual pilot or fighter planes. (The Soviet military as a whole was implicated four times, and once, then-Premier Yuri Andropov was actually described as having shot down the plane himself.) Reflecting the rarity of assertions about a causal agent, the Iran Air reporting included only eleven uses of a term denoting the actor. Just two attributed the act to the U.S. government or nation as a whole, both quoting an Iranian general. The other nine references were to the "*USS Vincennes,*" the "U.S. Navy," or "Captain Rogers of the *Vincennes,*" all narrower, more precise attributions.

A second way the frames promoted or inhibited generalization arose from explicit judgments of the nations implicated in the events. In the KAL case, the newsmagazines conveyed fifty-three judgmental generalizations about the Soviet Union, fifty-one of them negative.[27] The following examples give the flavor: the Soviets suffer from "national paranoia" and "a national gospel of secrecy and suspicion";[28] the "Soviet Union . . . is essentially evil" and "[t]hey place highest priority not on human lives but on preventing penetration of their airspace."[29] The Iran Air case offered just three judgments of the United States, of which one was positive and two (from Iranians) negative. If the magazine stories had drawn conclusions about alleged American paranoia and inhuman priorities from the Iran Air mishap, which occurred nowhere near U.S. airspace, judgments might have been equally harsh—and equally problematic. CBS News offered sixteen generalizations about the Soviet Union, all unfavorable, and no generalizations about the United States.

Subverting the Impact of Contradictory Information

The two cases that are the focus of this chapter admittedly were chosen in part because they exemplify one-sided framing that offered few diverse views and generated little elite or public dissent. Yet it is important to recognize and explore the contradictions to the dominant frame that did appear. In this section we find that frame dominance does not banish all contradictions and challenges to the White House line. However, the form of presentation can subvert the political relevance of such information. Only those with expertise in international relations and bureaucratic politics (or with previously internalized oppositional schemas) could have used the contrary information to fashion a nonconforming event schema for KAL or Iran Air. For the vast majority of citizens, the isolated reports that challenged the logic of the dominant frame likely sputtered out without spreading activation of a contrary interpretation—if they were noticed at all.

One telling example of subverted contradiction involved a challenge to the attributions of moral responsibility for the KAL tragedy. The second story of *Newsweek*'s second issue (19 September 1983, 24) revealed that the Soviet interceptors might not have approached closely enough to identify the KAL plane as civilian. The text also mentioned that Andropov and other top officials not only were unaware beforehand but would have had compelling reasons for preventing such a diplomatic and humanitarian disaster; the story traced the incident in large part to "military confusion and bureaucratic rigidity" (22). But *Newsweek* did not cite this second story as contradicting its cover graphics and claims of the previous week—which had said that the Soviets committed "murder in the air" (12 September 1983). Nor did it link this bureaucratic interpretation to its lead story in the very same (19 September) issue, which included the familiar charges that the Soviets committed deliberate murder and did not care about human life. In fact, the headline on the cover of this second issue read, "Why Moscow Did It"— despite the information inside showing that "Moscow" did not.

The later story did not explicitly challenge the frame but instead reinforced stereotypes about the Soviets' "national gospel of secrecy and suspicion" and bureaucratic inefficiency. Although these stereotypes of the old Soviet government were accurate, that is not the point here. Instead, this example illustrates several more general properties of subverted contradiction and reveals how a dominant frame can obscure the meaning and drain the political potency of contrary information.

The new information obtained little magnitude. Far from appearing on the cover and leading off the coverage, which some might expect since the story contained truly novel interpretations starkly contradicting the dominant line—it was a real "scoop"—the revisionist item appeared well inside *Newsweek*. Also, the report appeared a couple of weeks after the initial frame had been implanted in the media texts and after the event schema had been set in both journalists' and audiences' minds. Challenging first impressions is difficult, particularly when they are vividly supported by emotional language and visual images of threat.[30] Given that negative information tends inherently to have more salience than positive, particularly for a threatening, stereotyped "other" (the Soviets), a late, low-magnitude challenge to the negative associations unleashed by the first reports would be even less salient. Finally, far from configuring the new material as an overt challenge to conventional wisdom on KAL and using it to construct a counterframe, this report failed even to make a connection with the rest of the stories. This of course is hardly surprising. Few editors would publish a story that explicitly concluded something like this: "And all of this means that the cover headline and lead story in this very issue, along with all the reporting in last week's magazine, are deeply problematic if not completely misleading."

To take an example of subverted contradiction from the Iran Air case, both *Time* and *Newsweek* offered individually signed essays sympathetic to the Iranian victims. But the items neither attributed moral responsibility to the United States nor criticized U.S. leaders' failure to apologize for the incident.[31] Instead, the essays, consistent with the dominant frame, obscured causal agency. Thus even while implicitly straying from the technical framing by considering the event in moral terms, the essays reflected blocked schematic processing, the resolution of dissonance by making easier mental connections. The essay in *Time* was titled "When Bad Things Are Caused by Good Nations." Placed after all the news reports, this piece said: "Grief stricken voices were distressingly few, and there was almost no compelling sense of shame" (18 July 1988, 20). A sophisticated essay, it argued that the limited expression of guilt in the United States was probably due to cognitive dissonance and "conflict with the nation's self-image." Still, in what appeared itself to be a dissonance-reducing move, the author repeatedly insisted that U.S. intentions were good. For example, "Sometimes—in a disorderly world—grand intentions produce grotesque results." His description of the intentions of the U.S. military presence in the Persian Gulf during 1988 as "grand" rationalized a policy whose purposes were highly controversial even among U.S. elites. The major thrust of both opinion pieces was to blame the public at large for moral insensitivity. The irony was that the newsmagazine coverage itself contributed to the absence of empathy in the many ways already discussed.

Scholars and journalists often interpret such examples of mixed messages or "polysemy" in the news as evidence that audiences have an adequate opportunity to learn multiple sides of an issue and resist any single dominant government line. The cascade model suggests that such inferences are problematic.[32] For most audience members, who have little motivation to engage in careful deliberation, the contradictory information would possess far too little salience to activate new thoughts.[33] Exceptions would be found among those few individuals highly motivated to engage in what Petty and Cacioppo term "central processing," that is, active cogitation that might yield more independent interpretations.[34] Isolated morsels of challenging information do not add up to an opportunity for most people to develop a novel interpretation. And because so few citizens were likely to fully process the stray bits and develop oppositional event schemas, even elites who did understand the substantive import of the information had little political incentive to react to it. Elites intuitively expect that most audience members will only engage in "peripheral processing."[35] Such thinking relies on a few salient pieces of information (unusual words like "barbaric," the president's angry tones and facial expressions,[36] images of a civilian airliner burning) to activate habitual associations and arrive at a quick judgment.

Dominating the Frame Yields Political Benefits

Several political outcomes indirectly but strongly suggest the significance of the dominant frames for both stories. The House and Senate both voted unanimously to denounce the KAL shootdown as a "brutal massacre," the result of a "cold-blooded barbarous attack," and "one of the most infamous and reprehensible acts in history." This elite consensus was probably traceable in part to politicians' fear of seeming soft on communists in the highly charged political environment that the news frame engendered.[37] In addition to the rhetoric of its denunciation, Congress took concrete steps by authorizing production of both the MX missile and nerve gas, intended as messages of warning to the Soviets. Before the shootdown, neither of these policies had been expected to pass.[38] At about the same time, the momentum of the nuclear freeze movement, which had been building, dramatically slowed or disappeared, and chances for Senate passage of a freeze resolution apparently died too (see chapter 6).

The KAL story apparently convinced the public. A poll showed 52 percent saying Reagan's responses were not tough enough, 37 percent saying they were tough enough, and only 3 percent saying they were too tough, suggesting that almost everyone with opinions accepted the Soviets' moral guilt and hardly anyone rejected it.[39] The 52 percent who said Reagan was insufficiently tough actually bolstered his position; such "criticism" could hardly damage his hawkish image and made the administration's responses seem reasonable rather than overzealous. Dallin[40] reports that "the Gallup Poll showed the Soviet Union at its worst ranking in American opinion since 1956." A poll also found that 61 percent thought the government was holding back information people ought to know,[41] but this skepticism did not prevent acceptance of the harshly anti-Soviet line. Most people apparently thought that it was legitimate for the U.S. government to keep some information secret[42] but felt that they knew enough to answer the question about the toughness of the administration's response with hawkish gusto.

In the Iran Air case, news coverage helped block mental associations that might have unraveled support for American policy or created dissonance with the country's self-image. The frame deemphasized information suggesting that the (controversial) benefits from U.S. presence in the Gulf were not worth the human cost by reducing its salience in the text and making it harder to discern in the onrush of news. A *Washington Post*–ABC poll found that 71 percent believed the naval cruiser was justified in shooting down the plane; 74 percent believed Iran was more to blame than the United States; and 82 percent wanted to maintain U.S. military presence in the Gulf. Perhaps most tellingly, 65 percent approved specifically of the Reagan administration's Persian Gulf policy—the highest proportion since the question had first been asked in May–June 1987.[43] Thus, rather than causing a deterioration in support of the administration's policy, the incident was followed by a surge in public backing. These responses suggest that large majorities accepted the technical explanation and rejected any analogy to the KAL incident.

OTHER INTERPRETATIONS

It could be argued that political socialization rendered news frames in these two instances superfluous. In this view, the killing of Americans by the Soviet Union, in 1983 the long-demonized and primary national enemy of the United States, inevitably produced mass outrage. By the same token, the Iran Air tragedy was so threatening to the national self-image that a well-socialized public and news corps would naturally fail to consider its disquieting implications.

Yet public outrage after the KAL downing was not preordained. Rather, here and generally, the public's responses were susceptible to a range of media frames. If the KAL incident had occurred in *1988*, for example, the administration's initial rhetoric might well have encouraged a technical frame. The administration knew in 1983, shortly after the incident, that the Soviets, hampered by inferior radar technology and poor lines of communication, truly thought the intruder was a spy plane.[44] By 1988, administration policy was to avoid demonization of the Soviet Union and to deactivate the old Cold War schemas. This might have been tricky in light of those old habits, but if anyone could have pulled it off, it would have been the card-carrying Cold Warrior himself—Ronald Reagan. Far from pumping the crisis to heighten tension,[45] the administration might have employed it in 1988 to promote the value of its revised policy thrust, which was by then to reach arms limitation and other agreements with the new Soviet premier, Mikhail Gorbachev.

As for the Iran Air shootdown, elite opponents have in the past used moral rhetoric to undermine public support for U.S. policy. Although denial and rationalization in the face of dissonance would arguably have blocked negative associations about the United States, elite opponents (including the 1988 Democratic presidential candidate) might have had some success with a morality-based critique of Persian Gulf *policy* based on this incident had it not been for the further barrier presented by the dominant frame in media coverage. Both cases suggest in different ways that a news frame can help make resistance by elites futile and politically foolhardy, that it can stamp out any potential spreading of opposition.

As further, though more indirect, evidence for the power of a frame in the media's and audience's information processing, consider the deliberate bombing of Pan American Airlines Flight 103 over Lockerbie, Scotland, on December 21, 1988, in which 270 died (188 Americans). Almost immediately it became clear to U.S. officials that this was an act of terrorism; and soon thereafter the United States learned that it had been the work of Libya, Syria, or Iran. But for diplomatic reasons the government decided not to make a major issue of an actual instance of premeditated murder—this time mostly of Americans, not Koreans—by enemy forces.[46] Informal observation suggests that reporting did not reach the same volume or pitch as in the KAL affair. For example, in the two weeks following the incident, Flight 103 made the cover of *Time* or *Newsweek* only once, and the total pages devoted to it in the four issues came to seventeen, just one-third the total for KAL.

Conclusion: Winning the Frame Contest

Having explored in detail the framing of these two tragic events, let us return to the question of explaining the outcome of framing contests. The central goal of all the political maneuvering over news frames is simply *to generate support or opposition to a political actor or policy*. Some White House frames—such as those described in this chapter—succeed in winning acceptance of their problem definition, cause, remedy, and moral assessment. From all the evidence, these frames led audiences to develop a matching schema that they used in processing information about the events.

The framing of a given matter over a defined time period can be arrayed along a continuum from complete dominance by one frame to a complete standoff between competing frames. Sometimes, one among the potential frames of a situation so thoroughly dominates the media that developing alternative readings becomes difficult for most people. As in the two cases here, the dominant frame produces extraordinarily one-sided opinion poll results and these in turn discourage dissenting politicians from speaking out, thus cementing the hold of the one frame. Complacent views of America's free press notwithstanding, especially in covering foreign policy the news often exhibits a single overwhelmingly dominant frame.

Frame Dominance . . . . Frame Contestation . . . . Frame Parity

Frame parity describes the condition that free press theories prefer: two (or more) interpretations receiving something like equal play. Parity requires not merely that the news provide bits of unrelated information critical of the administration's frame scattered throughout the coverage.[47] To reach frame parity, the news must offer a *counterframe* that puts together a complete alternative narrative, a tale of problem, cause, remedy, and moral judgment possessing as much magnitude and resonance as the administration's. Availing themselves of such diverse, clashing, and equally well-developed understandings, a democratic citizenry can in theory freely and intelligently come to its own interpretation. But, as already suggested, frame parity is the exception, not the rule. More frequently, frame contests occupy the left sector of the continuum, falling somewhere between complete frame dominance and a degree of contestation.

The Cold War paradigm powerfully shaped responses to the KAL attack among elites, journalists, and citizens. Based on the U.S. government's initial descriptions of the KAL downing, and on habitual understandings shaped by the Cold War, journalists quickly developed a new event schema[48] for "the KAL attack." The schema encouraged them to perceive, process, and report further information about the event in ways supporting the administration's basic interpretation. To be sure, all journalists did not possess identical event schemas, and as the story evolved, many sought information that challenged certain aspects of the dominant story line. But in general, when reporting KAL, journalists' cognitive habits (and those of their organizations), combined with heavy dependence on elite sources, led them to make frame-confirming data more salient in the news—and to deemphasize contradictory data.[49]

Conversely, the facts of the Iran Air were so provocative, so potentially threatening to most Americans' understanding of their own country—especially coming less than five years after the United States denounced the Soviets for doing the same thing—that the cascade model predicts blocked associations. In practice this means that journalists would pass over some logical connections and leave gaps in the narrative that discouraged the spread of certain negative associations. Ironically, it may have been precisely because the event was so powerfully evocative in supporting criticism of Reagan's Persian Gulf policy that elites feared to raise it energetically. It was too incendiary a matter to use in mainstream politics; even making the relatively innocuous link between the tragedy and the need to pull out of the Gulf threatened to spill over into dangerously dissonant mental territory.

In both cases, the dominant frame made opposing information more difficult for the typical, inexpert audience member to discern and employ in developing an independent interpretation. This does not mean that every American interpreted the two incidents identically and in the ways promoted by the dominant frame, but it does suggest that, when a single frame thoroughly dominates—when it occupies a spot close to the left end of the frame contestation continuum—politically impressive majorities will come to congruent understandings. In such cases, for all practical purposes, the public is relegated largely to the role of passive spectators whose managed consent serves mainly to legitimize the president's policy and political objectives, and to dampen any impulse toward dissent that might arise inside the foreign policy establishment.

3. SUPPORTING AND OPPOSING PROJECTIONS OF POWER: GRENADA, LIBYA, AND PANAMA

• •

This chapter probes three projections of U.S. military power that took place during the decade after Vietnam. These three small military actions of the 1980s served as a prelude and to some extent a laboratory for military—and media—strategy in the massive mobilizations for the Gulf War (1990–91) and, since September 11, 2001, for the war on terrorism. Unlike the KAL and Iran Air cases in the previous chapter, media responses to U.S. actions in Grenada (1983), Libya (1986), and Panama (1989–90) were not virtually predetermined by the sway of habitual schemas or the blockage of dissonant thoughts. These three wars offer examples of framing the ambiguous issues that became increasingly common as the Cold War wound down. In only one of these cases could the administration plausibly even attempt to link the problem to the communist menace (Grenada)—and that claim came under media attack. In the other two, as in all the cases since, the Cold War paradigm simply did not apply. In the news coverage of these ambiguous matters, propaganda and disinformation coexisted with stinging challenges to the White House. But this is not a tale of a text whose meaning is so open that each individual could interpret it in unpredictable ways. It is a tale of news more resistant to the administration line in some respects than the hegemony or indexing models would predict, but the texts nevertheless cannot be simply categorized as outright propaganda, as reporting by an aggressively "free press," or as a postmodern pastiche.

As the cascade model suggests, ambiguous events present more opportunities for players outside the administration, including the media themselves, to affect framing. This chapter demonstrates that the administration's control over different aspects of framing varied. When it came to *defining the problem,* the media overwhelmingly favored the administration, but they provided considerable basis for doubting the administration's *remedies.* The high degree of policy opposition in the news appeared despite the near-absence of the congressional disputation that is so crucial to indexing models. Moreover, grist for negative evaluations of the administration's leadership appeared frequently—though on procedural rather than substantive grounds. The latter results illustrate the importance of distinguishing between process-oriented news that criticizes technique and reporting that could spread debate on the issue itself.

Here I present evidence from quantitative content analyses and from a qualitative interpretation of the texts. The content analysis compares the well-respected *New York Times* to the less venerated but highly influential network news. The chapter also applies the same basic coding protocol to the *visual* messages of *Time* magazine's coverage. The qualitative exploration clarifies the counts, yielding a clearer sense of the nature and limits of opposing information in the news.

To justify the U.S. invasion of Grenada, in October 1983, the Reagan administration asserted that a coup had brought to power a pro-Marxist regime that posed an imminent threat to American citizens studying medicine in Grenada and a longer-term peril to national security. The administration warned that the island might serve as a forward base for the spread of Cuban communism throughout the Caribbean. It launched a military invasion that overthrew the new junta and created a pro-American government. To defend America's bombing of Libya in 1986, the administration charged that its leader, Mohammar Qaddafi, was organizing terrorist strikes on Americans and U.S. interests abroad, specifically citing an attack on a disco in Berlin that killed two U.S. servicemen. The U.S. Navy sent ships into parts of the Mediterranean Sea that Libya claimed as territorial waters. Military hostilities ensued, culminating in a bombing attack on Libya proper that killed (among others) one of Qaddafi's daughters. The final case is the U.S. invasion of Panama during 1989–90, which the Bush administration ordered because that country's corrupt president, Manuel Noriega, participated in drug trafficking. Following some embarrassing delays, the invading force succeeded in arresting Noriega and installing a new government.

Quantitative Content Analysis Finds Support and Opposition

This section analyzes *New York Times* index entries covering each crisis and transcripts of network evening news broadcasts (CBS for Grenada and Libya, ABC for Panama).[1] The White House frame shows a similar thematic structure in each war, facilitating the analysis: the problems motivating the U.S. intervention in the three nations involved their export of instability or terrorism, their rule by an evil antidemocratic dictator, and the physical threats they posed to American lives. (Details on coding and the content of the frames are posted at the author's website, http://www.raceandmedia.com/pop.)[2] The results show lopsided support for the White House's definition of the policy problem, but a negative balance on the policy remedies as well as on leadership technique: each war was subjected to substantially more disparagement than backing in these respects. However, that is not the whole story, as we shall see.

Table 3.1 summarizes the results of the *Times* analysis, breaking down support and opposition by appearance on page one or on inside pages. Inside-page items are separated into news and editorial. In each case, the administration's frame of the problem garnered substantially more support than opposition, though the degree differed from war to war. The first row of the table ("problem positive") reveals that the administration's problem definition achieved support by wide margins, ranging from 64–36 percent in Grenada to 88–12 percent in Libya.

The *Times* did question the Grenada problem definition, although mostly on the inside pages rather than on page one, and rarely on the editorial pages. On the front page the paper supported the administration's problem framing by a 3:1 ratio. On Libya and Panama the administration's problem definitions went essentially unchallenged on page one and largely unquestioned inside the paper (including the editorial pages). The television data in table 3.2 reveal broadly similar findings, with the administration's problem definition favored by over 80 percent for each intervention. There are too few coded assertions to support any generalizations from the differences among the wars. What does seem clear from the evidence is that neither elites nor the media made much effort to dispute the administration's definition of the problems allegedly facing the United States.

One explanation might be that these definitions were indeed unassailable—that Grenada (population eighty-nine thousand in 2000) posed serious security risks to the United States and its allies, that Libya and Qaddafi were the epicenter of world terrorism threatening the United States in the 1980s, and that then-Panamanian president Manuel Noriega was a keystone of the drug traffic devastating many American communities. Even at the time, though, some serious doubts were raised about such notions, and in retrospect the claims seem even more problematic. This is not to say they were without all merit, or even that they were more wrong than right; it is simply to suggest that a vigorous, evenhanded discussion on the problem definitions was theoretically possible for each war.[3]

Turning to the framing of the administration's preferred policy remedies and leadership technique, we find quite a different story: there is in each case a predominantly negative emphasis. Note in table 3.1, however, that front-page coverage is close to being even; the negative balance piled up on inside pages. For instance, the *Times* gave the policy for Grenada positive

TABLE 3.1 *Framing of Grenada, Libya, and Panama in the New York Times: Support for Problem Definition but Criticism of Policy and Leadership*

	Grenada				Libya				Panama			
	p. 1	p. ≥ 2	Edit	Total	p. 1	p. ≥ 2	Edit	Total	p. 1	p. ≥ 2	Edit	Total
Problem positive	76.9%	58.1%	50.0%	64.4%	95.2%	85.0%	85.7%	88.2%	81.0%	80.6%	70.0%	79.1%
n	20	25	2	47	20	34	6	60	17	29	7	53
Problem negative	23.1%	41.9%	50.0%	35.6%	4.8%	15.0%	14.3%	11.8%	19.0%	19.4%	30.0%	20.9%
n	6	18	2	26	1	6	1	8	4	7	3	14
Policy positive	54.2%	39.1%	50.0%	43.8%	44.1%	29.5%	58.3%	36.8%	45.5%	36.8%	56.3%	43.4%
n	13	27	6	46	15	28	14	57	10	14	9	33
Policy negative	45.8%	60.9%	50.0%	56.2%	55.9%	70.5%	41.7%	63.2%	54.5%	63.2%	43.8%	56.6%
n	11	42	6	59	19	67	10	98	12	24	7	43
Leadership positive	26.7%	4.8%	31.6%	20.0%	33.3%	50.0%	25.0%	33.3%	75.0%	23.1%	0.0%	23.1%
n	4	1	6	11	1	2	2	5	3	3	0	6
Leadership negative	73.3%	95.2%	68.4%	80.0%	66.7%	50.0%	75.0%	66.7%	25.0%	76.9%	100.0%	76.9%
n	11	20	13	44	2	2	6	10	1	10	9	20

Note: Cell entries are numbers of stories supporting or opposing the administration's framing, coded from the *New York Times Index* entries. Percentages add vertically for problem, policy, and leadership.

TABLE 3.2 *Framing of Grenada, Libya, and Panama on TV Evening News: Support for Problem Definition but Criticism of Policy and Leadership*

	Grenada	Libya	Panama
Problem positive	83.7%	81.4%	87.6%
n	82	92	85
Problem negative	16.3%	18.6%	12.4%
n	16	21	12
Policy positive	60.9%	40.9%	49.5%
n	56	70	47
Policy negative	39.1%	59.1%	50.5%
n	36	101	48
Leadership positive	25.0%	0.0%	38.5%
n	7	0	5
Leadership negative	75.0%	100.0%	61.5%
n	21	11	8

Note: Cell entries are numbers of assertions, coded from transcriptions of network coverage. Percentages add vertically within problem, policy, and leadership categories. Grenada and Libya: CBS; Panama: ABC.

evaluations in 54 percent of front-page stories, 44 percent for Libya, and 45 percent for Panama. Though procedural evaluation of leadership does not by itself undermine the substantive framing, the administration took indisputably strong hits here, especially on Grenada and Panama, for which nearly 80 percent of evaluations were negative. However, there were not very many of these assertions, especially when it came to Libya and Panama. These stories denounced the administration for violating international law or the U.S. War Powers Act, for imposing press restrictions, for putting forth shifting or unclear policy rationales, or for bungling oversight of the invasions. The *Times,* with much greater space to convey verbal information for its more elite audience, constructed a more critical view of policy than the television networks, especially on inside pages. But as table 3.2 shows, television news broadcasts did not merely offer propaganda for the White House's policy and competence either.[4]

Despite all the criticism that appears, polling results for the three policies indicate wide support. This outcome suggests an important qualification to the results: the source of many critical assertions was foreign. In the *Times,* for example, the following percentages of the assertions that countered the administration line came from foreign sources:[5]

	Grenada	Libya	Panama
Problem definition	30%	75%	43%
Policy remedy	59%	64%	51%
Leadership technique	20%	20%	20%

On television too, a large number of the challenging assertions (whether on problem, policy, or leadership) were sourced to foreigners—people whom Americans might well discount, mistrust, or ignore entirely. The overall percentages were: 41 percent for Grenada, 64 percent for Libya, and 49 percent for Panama. In fact, a significant proportion of the critique arose not merely from foreign nations but from hostile ones: Cuba, the Soviet Union, or the targeted countries themselves. Nor is it clear how much more credibility attached to allies or to the mixed category (which encompasses the UN, Organization of American States, or vague references such as "foreign reaction"). The political culture encourages Americans to disregard foreign criticism of the United States,[6] and surveys indicate that is what happened in the wake of these three interventions.

Presumably the more credible sources would be American officials. Yet, toting up the critical reactions to the White House line, Congress was conspicuously absent from television news and had but a weak presence in the *Times,* especially on page one. On television, congressional members proffered just nine critical assertions during Grenada, three during Libya, and five during Panama. Foreign sources contributed far more to the policy critique than members of Congress—in the most extreme case, that of the Libya action, by a ratio of about 28:1 (television) and 22:0 (*Times*).[7]

Taken together, these findings suggest both the sensitivity of members of Congress to a public opinion they apparently read as strongly favoring the administration, and journalists' significant independence of debate among U.S. elites, even on television, the most audience-driven medium. If coverage in these three cases had been closely "indexed" to the public discourse of American elites, considerably *less* criticism of policy and leadership would have appeared. Public dissent among American elites appears to offer only part, albeit a significant one, of the explanation for critical media coverage.

That open debate among U.S. elites did not break out is important. Because journalists had almost no sources to quote who cast doubt on the administration's framing of the *problem,* media-generated critiques of the *remedy* dangled awkwardly, lacking a firm cognitive foundation. This gap weakened the potential for applying the "quagmire" schema or other anti-interventionist considerations. Citizens could not connect the policy critique that did appear with the thicker network of mental associations that an alternative definition of the problem (or at least detailed rebuttal of the administration's version) might have stimulated. In a self-perpetuating circle, elites and journalists in turn, detecting no evidence of a public appetite for more dissenting information, kept mum. Thus the administration's domination of the problem framing made its inability to prevent news critical of its policy and leadership technique less significant than it might otherwise have been for public opinion and foreign policy. Still, the heavy representation of criticism belies the predictions of the hegemony and indexing models, and points to the importance of the media's own motivations to provide some degree of balance in their coverage of ambiguous issues.

Visual Images Support the Administration

Research on framing and on news of foreign policy has paid scant attention to the visual dimension of media coverage, even though many scholars suspect it has substantial influence.[8] The major reason for the dearth of attention is presumably the difficulty of developing a coding scheme that measures the images' cognitive and affective content, a difficulty compounded by the absence of any well-developed general models of how visual images affect political thinking and feeling.[9] These problems do not, however, seem sufficient reason to neglect visual content; as Newhagen and Reeves suggest, visual images may have more potential than words to activate mental associations:

> Television images are the same as the real objects they depict to the degree that in a dense, analog symbolic representation like the human visual system, internal states correspond to objects in the external world. . . . Photographic images are explicit indicators of the objects they depict, and the emotions they arouse in the viewer are psychological effects in the strictest sense, while words must be elaborated to extract their symbolic meaning to have an "effect."[10]

The following analysis can only be suggestive, but the danger of somehow misleading readers or distorting the "real" messages or impacts of the visuals seems outweighed by the potential insights generated in plunging ahead—with due caution. In this section I grapple with how one might develop understanding of visual messages, and with how the visuals might reinforce or contradict the verbal framing. One substantive point also serves as a methodological and conceptual warning: visual messages are multidimensional, and possess many potential interpretations as they interact with the keywords of the frame.

First the numbers. All visual images, including photographs, drawings, diagrams, and cartoons, appearing in *Time* magazine's coverage of the three wars were analyzed. Unfortunately, videotapes of television network coverage were unavailable; the applicability of the findings to television will be considered later. The *Time* images are assumed to convey meaning in conjunction with their captions, so the unit of analysis is the visual with its written caption. Each unit was evaluated for whether it conveyed information that reinforced, questioned, or was neutral or mixed with respect to the administration's preferred problem definition and policy.[11]

For example, *Time* ran a half-page photo of Panamanian ex-president Manuel Noriega, whose removal was the chief goal of the Panama operation, clothed in a tee shirt and looking grim in a mug shot, holding a sign headed "U.S. Marshall, Miami, FL" and showing his prisoner number (15 January 1990, 24). That picture was coded as bolstering the administration's problem definition. Lacking a caption, it supported quite vividly the preferred administration theme that Noriega was a drug-dealing common criminal, not the legitimate leader of a sovereign nation. Bolstering this interpretation is the recognition that an administration exerting tight control over press access to the Panama operation would not have released the photo had it not believed it to be politically beneficial. (The credit line on the photo read "U.S. Marshall Service," and the same issue carried another picture of Noriega in the physical custody of two lawmen, with a credit line for the Department of Defense.)

Table 3.3 displays the results of this exploratory analysis of visual images. Photos and captions that illustrate military machines or men in successful action or that depict the destruction of military targets are examples

TABLE 3.3 *Visual Depictions in* Time *as Reinforcing White House Line*

	Grenada	Libya	Panama
Visual images supporting administration's problem definition (*n*)	100.0% (14)	100.0% (23)	100.0% (7)
Visual images undermining administration's problem definition (*n*)	0.0% (0)	0.0% (0)	0.0% (0)
Visual images supporting administration's policy (*n*)	60.9% (14)	90.9% (20)	84.6% (11)
Visual images undermining administration's policy (*n*)	39.1% (9)	9.1% (2)	15.4% (2)

Note: Cell entries are numbers of visual images (photos, drawings, or cartoons) coded from *Time* magazine coverage of each U.S. intervention. Percentages add vertically within problem definition and policy categories.

of policy support—visual information that claims the success or wisdom of the mission. Visuals bolstered the administration's problem definition in each case, most notably for Libya. Many demonizing images of Qaddafi appeared, along with several portraying victims of terrorism. An example of a visual image that might have engendered negative associations with the administration's problem framing is a picture of then–vice president Bush shaking hands with a well-dressed Noriega, captioned as having been taken during the years when Bush treated the Panamanian leader as a reliable ally. No doubt such images did appear in some media outlets, but none found their way into *Time.*

As for policy framing, an example of visual images undermining the administration's policy is a photo of looters in Panama City that was captioned "When Noriega's troops were gone, no one replaced them. Looters flooded Panama City's streets. The U.S. estimated it would take at least a week just to pacify the capital" (1 January 1990, 22). This was coded as a policy challenge because it showed that the results of the invasion were not entirely positive; the postinvasion chaos in Panama was one theme of the verbal criticism. Overall, news of Libya and Panama contained little challenging imagery, although Grenada coverage did contain quite a few negative visuals.

It is worth considering the Grenada illustrations in more detail. This discussion will illustrate the difficulties of coding and again put the reader on notice about the tentative nature of the findings. The nine negative images (bottom row of table 3.3) encompassed four pictures of injured or dead U.S. soldiers; two photos of destroyed U.S. helicopters; one of a mental hospital mistakenly bombed; one of a Belgian demonstration denouncing the U.S. invasion; and one cartoon comparing Grenada and Vietnam. In each case, coding must rely, quite problematically, on assumptions about the average American's response to the image. It is certainly not clear that photos of dead American soldiers actually challenge support of policy by reminding audiences of its human costs. Casualties are expected in wartime, and the reported number—nineteen in all—was relatively low.[12] (There were no photos of dead U.S. soldiers from Panama, presumably because press access was more controlled than during Grenada; the two American deaths in the Libya action occurred in an airplane so their bodies could not be photographed, although *Time* did include snapshots of the airmen taken earlier.) The same would hold for pictures of the downed U.S. helicopters, since some equipment loss is unavoidable. The Belgian demonstration photo might well have annoyed more Americans than it pushed toward opposing American policy—especially since the picture and caption depicted the demonstrators burning an American flag. Indeed, one might argue that if anything the photo supported the administration frame by making foreign critics seem anti-American rather than genuinely concerned with Grenada. The cartoon's comparison to Vietnam could have appeared extreme to many readers, and the surrounding text was an essay by the hawkish Charles Krauthammer devoted precisely to denouncing the analogy.

Finally, the image of the bombed mental hospital, with a nurse looking at the rubble, was the most complex. The photo reminded readers of an unfortunate by-product of the policy, but in several ways the implied importance of this result was low. The photo was small—perhaps a fifth of a page, in an issue (14 November 1983) containing many more photos supportive of the administration, fifteen in all, most of them larger. (Two other opposing visuals, the Belgian demonstration and the Vietnam cartoon, also appeared in this issue.) The caption read "Ruins of the mental hospital wing bombed by U.S. aircraft during the invasion; skilled paratroopers, heroic helicopter pilots and some tragic mistakes." The illustration did not show civilian bodies or grieving relatives, while the caption failed to mention the number of dead or injured, or their names. Those committing the "tragic" act were labeled as skilled and heroic. With its caption, this photo was equivocal: Some might consider it a sanitized justification, others a clear sign of the invasion's human costs. In any case, as these nine Grenada examples should illustrate, coding erred on the side of categorizing visuals as anti-administration.

Judging by *Time*—a newsmagazine that stresses illustration far more than newspapers—visual images seemed more thoroughly in the administration's command than verbal themes. The most obvious explanation is that the administration's power to exercise strategic control of information was heightened through its tight restrictions on photojournalists' access to these actions. Most of the pictures were taken by the U.S. military or by photographers allowed at a scene only with the military's permission. Not being admitted to certain places at certain times precluded certain images. Perhaps responding to the inconveniently critical visuals that entered the Grenada coverage, the White House and Pentagon later limited the press's access to the Libya and Panama operations even more strictly.

More important, perhaps, those making anti-administration statements normally supplied no photographs or diagrams. Their themes were inherently difficult to visualize. In this sense, however clever their strategies might have been, the inability of elite sources outside the administration to create compelling visual images severely limits their ability to stir up opposition along their own networks or those of journalists or the public.

For example, one theme of criticism in each war was violation of international law or treaties. Such claims are not easily illustrated; images would have to be "talking heads." And *Time* did not even offer opponents much talking-head room. Despite the widespread opposition to all three missions among U.S. allies, only four pictures of critical allied leaders were shown, all in one composite shot after Libya, where each leader's head occupied less than one square inch (28 April 1986, 28). The one allied supporter, Margaret Thatcher, appeared in two small photos in that issue. Meanwhile *Time* offered twenty shots of Ronald Reagan and ten of the secretaries of state or defense during Grenada and Libya. Thus the magazine's failure to illustrate opponents was not entirely due to an aversion to talking-head shots. George H. W. Bush's picture appeared just once in coverage of Panama, perhaps because, as Brit Hume reported on ABC (see below), the White House deliberately portrayed Bush as not "biting his nails" over (that is, not deeply invested in running) an operation that floundered for a while before achieving its stated objective of removing Noriega.

As with the KAL and Iran Air coverage, it is unlikely that photo editors and others thought about the ways pictures or the lack of them contributed to frames. Rather they were simply illustrating dominant verbal themes and the powerful, familiar U.S. officials who described and largely controlled the policy decisions—along with the military action. The names and faces of the European or Latin American opponents were unfamiliar, although for that very reason, photos of them could have very slightly enhanced readers' interest.

In other cases, opposing visuals are easier to imagine and potentially more interesting, but their use would violate normal professional practice or rules. The very potency of visuals could make inclusion of images undermining the administration frame appear as illegitimate editorializing. To show as many pictures of dead civilians' bodies as of heroic U.S. armed forces would seem inappropriate to the elite consensus and reported mood of public celebration. In fact, not one picture of a dead civilian appeared, although the written texts did report on civilian deaths and sometimes raised questions about whether the civilian toll was worth the gains. As another illustration of a striking potential contrast between written and visual texts, consider that to balance the pictures of a demonized Qaddafi with ones of him, say, kissing the adopted baby daughter who died in the raid would likely have seemed an outrageous violation of journalistic propriety, a transmission of blatant anti-American propaganda.[13]

Although we cannot generalize from the newsmagazine to television, the most visual medium, these examples of absent and impermissible images suggest that the visual dimension of network news probably resembled *Time.* The previous chapter on KAL and Iran Air coverage showed that television's images paralleled those of *Time* and *Newsweek,* and the next chapter makes the case that the same was true in coverage of the 1990–91 debate surrounding war with Iraq. The networks probably showed more talking heads of foreign opponents, judging from the sound bites in the transcripts, but otherwise the verbal texts hint at no major departures from the pattern exhibited by the newsmagazines.

The rules of photographic and visual engagement for most news organizations tend to minimize empathetic images of enemy nations, reflecting and reinforcing Americans' lack of emotional connection with foreigners, especially those outside western Europe. The U.S. public's unfamiliarity with foreign nations and cultures, the tendency to assimilate foreign realities to American cultural schemas, and the social demand to "support our troops" in war also discouraged stories that bolstered any verbal opposition with visuals.

Finally, it seems quite possible that journalists unconsciously believe they can "get away" with reporting as much opposing information as they do only by understating the critique so that it does not become overly explicit. In the main, reporters avoided the heightened salience that might accompany the use of vivid or controversial illustrations to buttress critical words. In this sense, the very act of putting in oppositional words may compel journalists to undermine their salience and thus diminish their ability to form a counterframe. At the minimum, journalists would need the assistance of powerful political elites voicing coherent, counterframing ideas.[14]

Interpretive Analysis Reveals Propaganda and Critique
Because a review of the news reporting for any one of these wars could fill a chapter, this section focuses on aspects of the coverage that appeared for all three, in the verbal text of network television reports. The analysis demonstrates how journalists served as more or less loyal conduits of U.S. government propaganda in wartime—yet also provided, sometimes in the very same news program or even story, independent information that challenged the White House line. However, the analysis suggests, the opponents' points never coalesced into readily useable counterframes.

PROPAGANDA COMMON
Television sometimes conveyed unadulterated propaganda—messages that had a shaky or no basis in facts, and that employed distorted or essen-

tially emotional data to promote ill-informed assent to U.S. policy. A study that looked at only selected dimensions of the coverage could easily conclude that television reporters served as little more than flacks for the government. While the data overall do not support that conclusion, neither did TV scrupulously avoid this role.

During each of the wars, the networks passed along without qualification claims later shown to be bogus—assertions that were problematic on their face and might have aroused immediate skepticism. Most appeared to come from intelligence or military sources with propaganda axes to grind. As long as the assertions were new, and supported the administration frame in a colorful or dramatic way, they seemed legitimate grist for the news.[15] As Grenada developed, for instance, Lesley Stahl reported (27 October 1983): "Government intelligence sources tell CBS News they now believe a large number of Cuban troops, as many as two battalions, were sent into Grenada . . . shortly before the assassination of Prime Minister Bishop. The sources believe the Cubans were growing impatient with Bishop and sent the troops in to encourage the takeover and to build a Cuban military outpost." This was shortly shown to be entirely untrue (CBS itself broadcast the news on November 1 that no more than about fifty Cubans on Grenada were military personnel). It made little sense that Castro would oust Bishop, since prior to the coup the Reagan administration had been fingering the Bishop regime precisely as a dangerous outpost of Castroism, and Bishop and Castro were in fact close.

In covering Libya, David Martin of CBS said (14 April 1986):

> Meanwhile, more details of the evidence linking Qaddafi to last week's Berlin disco bombing became public. A well-informed Pentagon source said messages between Tripoli and the Libyan People's Bureau in East Berlin spoke of making arrangements for a quote, "wedding." On the night of the bomb blast a message said to read the newspapers tomorrow morning for news of a, quote, "great success." . . . subsequent messages went out to other Libyan People's Bureaus telling them to follow the example set by East Berlin.

At the time, Martin could not have known that these purported messages would later be shown to lack documentation.[16] Still, given the tendency of government to contrive self-serving vignettes, a tendency well established since at least Vietnam,[17] Martin might have suspected that Pentagon sources were using him to further demonize Libya and Qaddafi. And Panama news too featured unqualified, widely repeated reports that Manuel Noriega practiced voodoo and stored a vast amount of cocaine in his home, later revealed to be deliberate falsehoods planted by the U.S. government.[18]

COMBINING PROPAGANDA AND OPPOSITION

More frequently, the news coverage of the events in Grenada, Libya, and Panama contained a dizzying mix of propaganda *and* skeptical challenge. This material reflects the contrary motivations tugging on journalists, the tensions between chronicling the actions and frames of the powerful, and providing skeptical, independent analysis.

Consider this broadcast after the Libya bombing (16 April 1986):

> Dan Rather: When Americans go into combat this nation stands together and pulls for them, of course. Forty-eight hours ago that's what many in the U.S. were doing. TV spectators, not sure exactly what was happening but knowing the teams. It was the U.S. against Qaddafi. Now, two days later, citizens are beginning to examine more about why we fought, what the U.S. won or lost.
>
> There is the question, is Muammar Qaddafi the terror master or just one of many? Not necessarily the most vicious, just the loudest. To hear a lot of analysts tell it you could look just as well at Iran and Khomeini, better yet perhaps, Syria and Assad. . . .
>
> Paul Kreisberg (Council on Foreign Relations): We probably won't even notice Qaddafi's absence, in terms of total terrorism in the course of a year, if he's not there.
>
> Rather: And even if Qaddafi supplies all the bullets terrorism experts say he doesn't call all the shots.
>
> Gary Sick (terrorism expert): Not all terrorism is state sponsored by any means. . . . Two people, operating by themselves, with a stick of dynamite or a sub-machine gun can do a tremendous amount of damage. . . .
>
> Rather: So why are we hitting so hard at Qaddafi? . . . Syria and Iran, why not attack them?
>
> Paul Wilkinson (terrorism expert/CBS News consultant): Because they saw Libya as a more accessible target with less risk to them involved in taking military action. It would not be feasible to take that kind of action against Iran and Syria. . . .
>
> Sick: It provides an answer for those people who have been saying to the Administration, are you all talk and no action? And they can now honestly say that—that—the—it's action as well as talk.

This story questioned the administration's rationale for the Libya bombing by raising doubts about the definition of the Libyan problem (Libya as keystone of international terror), and implied the administration deliberately misled the public about the real calculations behind the bombing. Yet Dan Rather used the term "we" for the U.S. government and military, a classic rhetorical move that denies the existence or legitimacy of domestic dissent and incorporates the citizenry's perspective into that of the administration. At the story's outset Rather said overtly that the nation "stands together," though he immediately qualified that by saying only that "many" Americans were doing this. But the experts then questioned the motivation or effectiveness of the action, and the final quote from Gary Sick suggested the main reasons for the bombing were psychological and political.

Evidence from the texts of their reports shows journalists as considerably more active and independent of U.S. elite discourse than previous theories might lead us to expect. Notice, for example, that Rather's story assembled three different quotes from unofficial elite sources; presumably few if any members of Congress were promoting a similarly analytical attack on Reagan's policy. While this is a mark of active journalism, the absence of an official, congressional imprimatur on the challenging interpretation may help explain its lack of political influence. Although able to convey oppositional information not provided by U.S. officials, news organizations at least during the 1980s were too dependent on the administration for information and language to escape its frame entirely or consistently. It may be noteworthy that although the Cold War paradigm was clearly on the wane by 1986, it retained influence in one sense: the engrained habit of deference to the White House persisted.[19] It was, after all, a habit maintained save for brief interludes even during the contentious days of Vietnam,[20] one spawned by decades of unrelieved anxiety about American vulnerability to nuclear annihilation and communist subversion. During Grenada and Panama too, confusing meldings of propaganda and challenge were common. With the implosion of the Cold War paradigm and conclusion of the anomalous Gulf War, however, deference became mixed with a more actively critical demeanor, as discussed further in later chapters.

Journalistic Motivations Limit Counterframes

Despite the efforts to gain some distance from the White House frame, journalists failed to activate much in the way of open opposition among U.S. elites or the public. This can be traced to the many routine, motivating features of the news business that constrain the impact of the strong "watchdog" motivation to include criticism of the White House line. The lack of muscle is not the media's or anyone's "fault." Nor does it betoken a "hegemonic" news system, which would have cleaned up the contradictions far more efficiently.[21] The more important causes probably include:

- News definitions that emphasize action and predicted action rather than policy reasoning, and stress yesterday, today, and tomorrow, not last year or next year.
- The principle (or ritual)[22] of objectivity, which discourages journalists from offering their own, fully elaborated, *overtly* challenging substantive interpretations in most news stories.
- The absence of a coordinating mechanism designed to achieve overall frame parity by detecting contradictions and imbalances among all the separate news reports.
- The organization of journalism into beats that do not necessarily communicate with each other, which fragments narratives.
- Daily deadline pressure from new developments that often prevent reporters from following up contradictions to what has become old news.
- The severe limitations imposed by the public's short attention span and sparse knowledge base, which discourage reporters from providing detailed context, especially on television or page one of most newspapers.
- Reliance on administration sources who strategically provide and withhold information and who, if offended, can cut off communications with individual reporters, editors, or news organizations—each of which operate in highly competitive conditions and suffer seriously when frozen out of the loop.
- The virtual absence of opposition from the putatively checking and balancing legislative branch in the face of surveys indicating impressive public support.

To expand on this last point, Democratic House Speaker Thomas P. "Tip" O'Neill issued some tepid criticism immediately after the Grenada invasion. He was quoted on the *CBS Evening News* (28 October 1983) as saying: "In my heart I truly feel that the President has been looking for a period of two years to do what he did the other day and that's gun note—boat dip—diplomacy and that's wrong." Although O'Neill said the action was wrong, and vaguely suggested Reagan was politically motivated, the quote offered no coherent argument beyond the category "gunboat diplomacy," an historical allusion that many audience members would not understand and others might even see as linking Grenada positively with America's muscular history of interventionism. O'Neill's inarticulate, stumbling rhetoric may have further undermined any impact of his opposition. In any event, he shortly changed his tune after polls showed the public rallying behind Reagan. In addition, a quote from Democratic senator Joseph Biden (Del.) preceded O'Neill's: "I do not get too tied up on legalistic notions about what is right and wrong when in fact the evidence becomes clear. The action that's being taken [by Grenada] in our back yard is directly and clearly inimicable (sic) to our security interests." It's clear the opposition party hardly put up a united or even disunited front of opposition.

And here is O'Neill quoted on CBS (15 April 1986) after the Libya bombing: "I—I—if the child is killed then the—all this started because of the evil heart of a bad man. Every time he escalates we have to strike. He ha—he has to be brought to his knees on a thing like this. He has to—he has to learn his lesson." Rhetorical timidity and verbal disorganization also seemed to characterize O'Neill's successor after the Panama intervention. On ABC's *Nightline,* Democratic Speaker Thomas P. Foley said: "[T]here are U.S. citizens involved in Panama who I think the President very sincerely felt were in great danger. Noriega declared war on the United States. Whether that was intended to be a formal declaration or not, it was the kind of incitement to violence and heightened rhetoric of threat that this very brutal and murderous man has implemented before, and for which I think the President needed to take seriously as a threat to Americans." It might be stretching to suggest that the act of opposing the president's war policy was so intimidating to the two Speakers that it tied their tongues, but in any case the quotes clearly reflect the paucity of organized opposition for the media to index, and therefore the considerable independent work journalists had to do to present oppositional themes to the public.

Democrats were responding to poll results revealing overwhelming support for apparently successful short-term military ventures.[23] According to Kernell, with respect to the invasion of Grenada—just as predicted by the cascade model under ambiguous situations—initial polls showed the public "confused and ambivalent." Some Democrats attacked the invasion, most "temporized." Then, as optimistic media reports of policy results rolled in, polls showed public enthusiasm; Kernell quotes one senator as saying "'Most people [that is, senators], once they saw the polls come out, went underground.'"[24] For example, CBS reported (28 October 1983), in the same story quoting O'Neill, that 82 percent of poll respondents who listened to Reagan's Grenada speech believed Cuba intended to turn Grenada into a military outpost, and 65 percent believed the medical students were in danger before the U.S. intervention.[25] Tip O'Neill's reversal to support was covered with front-page stories in the *Times* and *Post* as a response to public opinion said to be undergoing a "wave of patriotism."[26]

In fact, contrary to expectations raised by both the hegemony and indexing models, the rhetoric of at least some of the mainstream media themselves—as voiced on editorial pages—was more intensely and convincingly oppositional than anything generated by U.S. political elites.[27] On November 10, 1983, for example, the *New York Times* (at A26) ran an unsigned editorial headed "Grenada, by O'Neill, by Orwell," that attacked the problem definition and remedy with rhetorical guns blazing:

> . . . Although 1984 is at hand, hardly anyone dares confront the Orwellian arguments by which this grave action has been justified.
>
> **To Save the Students.** The testimony that American medical students in Grenada felt endangered comes either from students most frightened by the invasion itself or from officials who need to justify it. Contrary testimony, from the school's management, has been revised under the tutelage of U.S. officials who now control the school's assets. No hard evidence has been produced.
>
> But assume, like a delegation of Congressmen did, that the students faced a "potential" risk of being harmed or taken hostage. Why would the Marxists who had just seized power from other Marxists want to threaten Americans? The only reason could be to protect themselves from a feared American invasion. The pretext for the invasion, then, was a presumed danger posed by invasion. . . .[28]
>
> **To Stop the Cubans.** . . . That the Cubans and the weapons finally counted in Grenada were a danger to the United States is far from proved. If they were, then the motive for invasion was a good hunch— and a quest for evidence to justify invasion. Without . . . a record of proof and warning, people around the world who do not automatically assume American virtue are left to conclude that the United States is either a bully or a paranoid—quick to attack where it can do so safely or when it feels compelled to demonstrate muscle.
>
> That's why Speaker O'Neill's final judgment may be the most shamefully motivated of all. "Public opinion is what's behind things here," explained Representative Torricelli of New Jersey. . . . "[P]eople feel their frustration relieved, and members of Congress sense that."
>
> . . . So the invasion is finally justified because Americans needed a win, needed to invade someone. Happy 1984.

It is difficult to imagine a more vigorously worded evisceration of the White House line along with a fierce attack on Democrats for political cowardice.[29] Thus we have journalists taking politicians to task for being responsive to indicators of public opinion—indicators shaped by the media's own cooperation with the administration's frame! The absence of a counterframe in turn is traceable in major part to the silence of the potential congressional opposition. Note the irony and ambiguity for advocates of democratic representation: through its exquisite responsiveness to indicators of public opinion, Congress helped the administration manage public opinion, or at least perceptions of it.

Indicators of Public Opinion Are Malleable

One reason for apparent public support for the actions in Grenada, Libya, and Panama may have been the shortness of each operation and the low U.S. casualties; high or highly salient casualties do spur opposition to policies in the polls.[30] The poll results suggest three points. First, the policy and leadership criticism that did appear in the media failed to generate significant public opposition. For all intents and purposes, the policies enjoyed near consensual approval. As suggested by the *Times* editorial and other coverage of Grenada quoted above, large survey majorities intimidate elites, creating strong motivations to avoid open opposition and stopping the spread of challenging ideas. Second, approval of the specific action seemed to spill over into more general polling responses. And third, these results raise questions about any broad conclusion on the public's independence in forming opinions.

When it comes to Libya, for instance, according to Hinckley,[31] 69–79 percent of the public approved of the raid in various polls taken after the bombing, and approval remained high months later. Thus it would appear that the occasional outcroppings of opposition in media texts, as exemplified by Dan Rather's story discussed above, never coalesced into a counterframe that could stimulate politically significant opposition to the policy. Not only was the policy itself popular; it also appeared to generate other changes favorable to the administration. Thus, in January 1986, administration polling had found 51 percent of the public opposed to U.S. military retaliation for terrorism, with 48 percent supporting it. By June 1986, however, this general question yielded approval on the part of 61 percent, with 39 percent opposed, in apparent response to the publicity about terrorism and to the seemingly successful raid against Libya.[32]

On the matter of "success," no good evidence was available initially that the Libya bombing achieved even the stated goals. There was no way to tell in the immediate aftermath if terrorism would be significantly curtailed. And the whispered goal of killing Qaddafi obviously remained unattained.

Indeed, the White House would later accuse Libya of ordering the 1988 destruction of Pan American Flight 103 over Lockerbie, Scotland, allegedly in retaliation for the U.S. strike on Libya. The Lockerbie assault killed many more Americans than died at terrorists' hands during the entire two Reagan terms.[33] Thus by some lights the Libya raid was a disastrous failure. Perceptions of policy "success" often do not rest on objectively measurable conditions, but rather must rely on selective interpretations and evaluations—on framing.

Similar patterns arose with respect to Grenada and Panama. Kernell[34] reports that polls taken November 3–7, 1983, the week after Reagan's Grenada justification speech, found an increase from 42 to 55 percent in approval of President Reagan's handling of foreign policy generally. It was also during this period that Reagan first began opening up a significant lead over Democrat Walter Mondale in polls on the 1984 election.[35] This increasing public support is especially noteworthy in light of the bombing of the U.S. Marine barracks in Beirut, which killed nearly three hundred Americans, only two days before the Grenada action. Beirut raised obvious questions (and considerable elite criticism) over the wisdom of the administration's policy in Lebanon. Intentionally or not, the Grenada triumph crowded out what might have been much more negative impressions of Reagan's foreign policy prowess.

As for Panama, polls would show that the operation markedly improved Bush's somewhat wavering image.[36] Surveys revealed massive support for the invasion, and increases in general presidential approval ratings as well. For example, Brace and Hinckley[37] report that before the invasion of Panama, Bush's popularity rating was 68 percent; after the invasion and surrender of Noriega it reached 80 percent, although four months later it was back down to 65 percent. Still, as they point out, "[f]or any president concerned with the polls, four months can buy time to derail press stories about the administration being in trouble or to discourage people looking for more trouble."[38]

These outcomes suggest that indicators of public opinion can be highly malleable. If large segments of the public were either reframing for themselves or disregarding the dominant frame, it is difficult to explain, for example, how a victory as small in scale as Grenada could outweigh a policy debacle as costly as Lebanon in evaluating President Reagan's foreign policy performance.[39] Also, as illustrated in figure 1.2, polling is enmeshed in the networked system of cascading activation; it too responds to the words and images embodied in the White House's framing of the events, which in a sense institutionalizes the malleability of what elites *perceive* as the public's opinions. As is true of visual images, so with polls: questions must appear balanced and avoid anything that smacks of editorializing or taking sides. Thus surveys rarely ask a question such as "If it were true that the medical students could have been safely evacuated without military intervention, as the new Grenadian government offered to do, would you support Reagan's policy?" Or "If evidence shows the Cubans were not establishing a military base on Grenada . . . ." Or "If investigation reveals that President Reagan trumped up the danger in Grenada in order to distract Americans from the deaths of many Marines in Lebanon . . . ." Such questions might well have shown a more ambivalent, less supportive public as interviewees reacted to different cues and weighed other "top of the head" considerations before answering.[40] This is not to argue that we can know what public opinion "really" would have been if people had been properly informed or if pollsters had only asked the right questions. The point rather is that the dependence of polling as an institution on the administration's frame can heighten the ability of the White House to manage perceptions of public opinion; more on this in chapter 6.

Notice again the circularity characteristic of the cascade model (fig. 1.2), underlining the fact that the arrows of influence run in both directions even if the predominant flow is from the top down. When many Americans respond favorably to poll questions worded in accordance with the president's problem definition, the pressure for Congress to go along heightens. That means media are less likely to convey a counterframe and that polling results are less probable to reveal politically significant opposition. Here then is a major explanation for the activation (or deactivation) of elite opposition to the White House's policies. Indications that public opinion lopsidedly favors the president tend to dampen elites' inclinations to mount open challenges. Of course the spiral can run in the opposite direction too. Elite opposition can spur more reporting that contests the White House frame, and that can undermine perceived or actual public support of the president, further emboldening the critics.

Does Responsiveness Undermine Journalistic Autonomy?

The survey results introduce complexities into normative visions that call for responsiveness to public opinion by government and the media. Had they been more responsive to a public whose desires were embodied in polls that relied heavily on news frames and elite discussion (or its absence), the media might have reported or highlighted even *less* critical information. And the congressional opposition's hypersensitivity to apparent public approval made the media's goal of reporting independent of the White House line even more difficult. As it was, many journalists worked to include oppositional material in their reports, without much support from public reaction (although it is worth reiterating that reporters—and scholars—only knew as much about that reaction as pollsters cared to ask about) or from elites.

If anything, the evidence suggests members of the public seek to avoid dissonance by refusing to confront the implications of journalists' criticism. Indeed polls suggest, time after time, public hostility to complaints from news organizations about restrictions on their ability to cover the military action.[41] This implies the public does not really care to have doubts or complications raised when the news has told them that the United States is enjoying military success. Accommodating the public's tastes further diminishes the media's ability to activate policy opposition, and buttresses journalists' tendencies to cloak and soften oppositional information.

One manifestation of this tendency is the use of historical allusions or other rhetorical devices that are too elliptical or obscure to inform the average American. An example is the CBS News story in which David Martin suggested Reagan really wanted to assassinate Qaddafi by comparing Reagan's obsession with the Libyan leader to Kennedy's with Castro: "[N]ot since John F. Kennedy took on Fidel Castro has an American President been so obsessed with getting rid of a foreign leader" (18 April 1986). Kennedy's approval of efforts to assassinate Castro are documented in reports issued during the mid-1970s and in books of history and biography, but these are not widely part of the Kennedy legend. Martin avoided directly calling Ronald Reagan a liar by this device, flashing a narrative wink at sophisticated audience members that Reagan protested his nonlethal intentions too much. Martin thereby salvaged some professional pride, but he was unlikely to get his conclusion through to most of the audience. To be fair, a more sympathetic reading of this quotation and others like it is possible. Perhaps Martin, himself educated and sophisticated and used to dealing with similar people, simply overlooked the fact that the mass audience does not carry the same store of historical context in long-term memory, available for ready application to new information.[42]

Another media practice that was apparent in the coverage of Grenada, Libya, and Panama, and in much other reporting, is the division of sources' pronouncements into "public" and "private." Thus, to take one of many examples, CBS's David Martin (14 April 1986) said: "U.S. officials have said publicly they would back off if Qaddafi ceases his support for terrorist attacks against Americans. Privately, these same officials say they see no evidence Qaddafi is ceasing his terrorist campaign." The notion that Martin was guiding the audience into the backstage area[43] of private elite discussion is of course belied by the assertion's very presence in the news. These officials could not be saying such things very privately if they reach a CBS correspondent. The distinction between public and private does tell the audience that diplomacy and foreign policy consist of multidimensioned and strategic signaling, and does convey a warning not to take administration pronouncements at face value. Yet there is little evidence that this approach encourages sophisticated policy assessment among audiences. Instead, this kind of "inside baseball" reporting on process may invite audiences to observe the game, to judge how convincing the administration's staged performance seems to be rather than how wise its policy is. Moreover, the rest of the report undercuts Martin's warning. For example, in the very same story, Martin praised the attack as a "great success" and passed along the Pentagon's unsubstantiated and later denied claim (discussed earlier) that Libya ordered the Berlin bombing.

Panama provides a final example of reporting on policymaking as a public relations game. Brit Hume reported on *ABC World News* that the White House was "doing everything they can to portray him [Bush] as a man not staying up late biting his nails over this operation." Hume suggested that this may have been only a portrayal rather than a reality, but, because he provided no further information, the audience had no basis for guessing whether Bush really was sanguine or was genuinely concerned with the Panama invasion's progress. Of course Hume could not have known Bush's real state of mind, and he deserves credit for at least raising the possibility of image manipulation. But he left the audience without cognitive closure. If anything, the audience learned a kind of helplessness. If journalists disclose their own uncertainty and frustration, how can the average American, with much less access to information and decisionmakers, hope to participate? Such cynical reports could reinforce the public's uncertainty about their ability to separate (at acceptable cognitive cost) reality from public relations and could chip away at their fragile motivations to pay attention to foreign affairs.[44]

Conclusion

In covering the events in Grenada, Libya, and Panama, journalists were hampered by their inability to sustain substantive critiques on their own, their vulnerability to the administration's release, withholding and framing of information, and other limitations. Yet they were still able to weave in their own doubts, as well as those of foreign sources and experts, about the White House's policy. This finding upholds the second proposition from the cascade model, which is that reporters and editors have motivations to contest the White House's frame of ambiguous matters. What journalists could not do on their own in these cases was put together a genuine oppositional narrative, a fully developed counterframe, and as a result their independence had minimal political or policy repercussions. The media's critique was somewhat shapeless compared to the White House line, with stories full of unresolved and subverted contradiction, featuring floating bits of data lacking narrative glue. Coherence characterized only the administration line. An ambivalent public was left without much in the way of cognitive resources to build opposition to these specific interventions out of their considerable general skepticism toward foreign adventurism. What Americans did receive, courtesy of a strategically adroit White House, was a coherently presented and documented frame compatible with their other, more interventionist leanings. Thus even when journalists enjoy the relative flexibility provided by ambiguous issues, the administration's control over the dominant frame in the text remains high—assuming the White House manages its media relations, as Reagan and Bush did, with strategic skill, and that elite opposition is disorganized and timid.

The cascade model predicts the greater degree of autonomy exercised by journalists here than in cases that involve habitual and blocked mental associations, but these three wars also help to clarify the limits of that autonomy, which are rooted in the way the White House's power and strategic moves interact with elites' and journalists' motivations. The cascade model's third proposition highlights officials' motivation to obey strong indications of public opinion. Meanwhile, journalists' professional motivations produce a narrow, process-oriented definition of "news" that, when combined with skilled strategic news management by the administration, trumps reporters' watchdog instincts. Together, these interactions produce a tendency for an *elite* "spiral of silence"[45] to operate. The spiral metaphor helps answer one question raised by indexing studies, which emphasize the crucial importance of openly voiced elite dissent to the news but do not fully explain why discord arises, or fails to, in the first place.

The sequence works something like this: the administration commits to an intervention and frames it for the media; oppositional elites may respond in some number and with some intensity; media cover any initial debate. All this occurs quickly, and it is at this point, during the initial round of criticism, that power and strategy become most critical. By itself, media enterprise may bring useful new information before the public a day or two later, but without the push from continued, strategically adroit opposition by anti-administration leaders, potential counterframes receive insufficient magnitude and resonance to yield much learning or questioning by the public. The low salience to the public interrupts any tendency for oppositional thinking to spread further among elites, which in turn reduces its ability to cascade down repeatedly into prominent news reports and cohere into a counterframe. The paucity of publicly voiced opposition among U.S. elites discourages journalists' attention to critical views, both by depriving reporters of raw material (quotes) for use in substantive criticism, and by keeping the proliferation of public opposition below the threshold of political significance. On the other hand, if the president's power is shaky, if public opinion indications are negative, leaders may feel free to challenge the president. Disunity within the administration and among its partisans in Congress is especially significant. If elites from the president's own team criticize the White House, its frame may weaken early on, emboldening still more elite opposition and leading to a spiral of expression rather than of silence, a process that is illustrated in chapter 5.[46]

Bolstering this spiral rooted in politicians' electoral motivations[47] is journalists' strong tendency to define news (although not editorials) as action described and predicted, rather than as ideas analyzed. This predilection guides the focus of much critical news toward the procedural rather than substantive.[48] The principle of objectivity normally prohibits journalists, at least in the news pages or broadcast news reports, from conveying their own evaluations of policy substance.[49] On the other hand, for reasons that need not concern us here, they feel quite free and even obliged to engage in evaluation of the president's success in applying power, and of other technical aspects of leadership.[50] Procedural criticism often arises not merely from opposing politicians' attacks but from journalists' own enterprising reporting and analysis. But procedural or technical evaluation does not fit the rest of the frame logically, does not rely on an interrelated problem definition, cause, remedy, or moral evaluation. Of course, the public may perceive process criticism as sufficient grounds for questioning a frame. In this sense, aggressive criticism of the administration's leadership competence should not be dismissed as irrelevant, as it can undercut the president's legitimacy.[51]

Yet from the perspective of democratic theory, the problem with relying heavily on evaluation of techniques is that administrations can often shape or alter them to silence any critics without having to adjust policy itself. Indeed, presidents may engage in some strategically chosen rituals (consulting congressional leaders, holding diplomatic meetings) or even in deliberately controversial techniques (such as controlling reporters' access to combat) as ways of distracting journalists from the substance of policy. Controlling substantive framing tends to be more consequential for the ability to manage policy choices and outcomes, as the best-case test in the next chapter reveals.

4. DEBATING WAR AGAINST IRAQ

● ●

The preceding chapter shows that even during the 1980s, before the Cold War paradigm evaporated and even without vigorous elite dissent to "index," journalists conveyed critical assertions about some elements of U.S. foreign interventions. To be sure, these were highly selective and in many ways limited, yet their existence shows that media are not merely hand-maidens to the White House press office. But in the absence of powerful American leaders voicing opposition, journalists failed to sustain a frame contest on their own. This chapter explores media coverage of a policy that elites did debate energetically in 1990–91: war against Iraq.[1]

As the first instance of U.S.–Soviet alliance since World War II, the Gulf issue fell into the ambiguous category. The Cold War paradigm did not apply, and habitual schemas contradicted each other. Favoring quick military intervention (President George H. W. Bush's preferred option) were, to put the schemas in shorthand, "Oil," "U.S. dominance (the sole super-power must take charge)," and "Munich (democracies must not appease aggressive dictators)." On the other side, the "quagmire" schema (fear of protracted, costly involvements, which some have called the Vietnam syndrome) pointed toward the congressional opposition's remedy: reliance on diplomacy and sanctions. The contradictions gave members of Congress political elbow room, activating an unusual mixture of motives that emboldened normally cautious politicians. Members applied power and strategy to openly challenge the president's policy, and public opinion appeared split. Here was a best-case opportunity for frame parity.

The dispute erupted in full force after President Bush announced installation of an offensive capacity in the area on November 8, 1990, and it lasted until just before the war began on January 16, 1991. Democrats and Republicans agreed on the broad outlines of the problem definition, cause, and moral judgment, so the frame contest centered mainly on the remedy. Though in some senses limited, this was the ground on which the frame contest took place, and the decision was no small matter—it was literally a life or death choice, and the distance between the two sides on what to do was substantial.

Other aspects of the situation made the prewar debate on Iraq nearly ideal for framing news that more comprehensively contested the White House line:

- The decision to go to war was not carried out immediately, in an urgent crisis atmosphere, as with Grenada in 1983 or Afghanistan in 2001. There was time for elites to debate and for journalists to investigate.
- Not only were legitimate, prestigious figures in the foreign policy establishment strongly and publicly criticizing the administration's move toward war after November 8, 1990. Revealing the relative equality in forces on both sides, even as late as three days before combat commenced, the final congressional vote authorizing war (January 12, 1991), was close, especially in the Senate (52 to 47). Thus if media coverage reflects the degree of elite conflict, this was a period when reporting should have yielded parity between the competing frames.
- The public also seemed evenly divided. Conditioned by the Vietnam experience to fear American involvement in high-cost, low-benefit quagmires, Americans evidenced much more initial skepticism about administration policy toward Iraq than they did in the preliminary stages of the earlier war.[2] In contrast with the political environments described in chapters 2 and 3, no overwhelming public consensus appeared to pressure elites or media organizations to curb critical analysis of government policy. Three CBS–*New York Times* surveys in December and early January, for example, found the public divided almost exactly in half on whether, if Iraq failed to withdraw from Kuwait by January 15, 1991, the United States should start military action.[3]

In this chapter I trace the media's response to the unusual opportunity afforded by the Gulf War debate to construct frames in parity. The analysis focuses on two crucial nine-day periods when critical voices would be expected to peak: November 8–16 (Period 1), when opponents reacted to President Bush's announcement of the massive troop increase; and November 27–December 5 (Period 2), when Congress held hearings on Iraq policy that featured critical voices from unexpected and even startling sources. In harmony with the best-case approach, highlighted results are from the *New York Times* and *Washington Post,* papers with large foreign news staffs, high prestige and sophistication, and a record of willingness to take on the government. Coders rated hundreds of assertions from their stories, using a quantitative analytical protocol. For data from an outlet of wider public circulation, the same protocol was used to code transcripts of *ABC World News* programs. But as chapters 2 and 3 revealed, traditional quantitative content analysis cannot fully disclose whether information possesses enough salience to give the oppositional views truly equal standing in the frame contest. Therefore, evidence from an interpretive analysis is deployed as well. Illustrations and a broader context emerge from a careful reading of all *New York Times* editorials and op-ed pieces during the full November 8–January 15 period.

Findings

The analysis reveals that coverage of the debate overall appears nearly balanced, with criticism of the Bush administration slightly more frequent than support. However, the most pertinent critical information tended to be displayed less prominently than support, and much of the reported criticism was procedural rather than substantive. The news offered few fundamental criticisms of the administration's problem definition, which meant discussion of remedies was limited to just the choice of war or sanctions. An option largely absent from the news pages but seriously considered among European elites was negotiating with Saddam Hussein. On what basis did journalists decide how to allocate attention among competing remedies? The data suggest they based prominence in the news on predictions of how much power each side would exert over the final policy choice. Since few journalists saw negotiating with the demonized Saddam as a politically viable option for American officials, that meant gauging the likelihood that those seeking to initiate war soon would prevail over those preferring sanctions. This power-calibrating norm typically reinforces the White House's place at the top of the cascading discourse system. The qualitative analysis of the newspaper's responses to the congressional hearings illustrates how that norm and other motivating forces undermined genuine frame parity—despite forceful opposition from many elites, and despite editorials in the nation's two leading newspapers slanting against Bush's leadership and policy and urging (in this book's terms) frame parity.

HIGH VOLUME OF CRITICISM

During the periods studied, a substantial amount of news criticizing the administration's policy and behavior appeared. In both newspapers, critical assertions substantially outnumbered supportive; ABC, though tending more toward support, also offered considerable criticism. The content analysis coded all assertions that explicitly or implicitly expressed support or opposition to the Bush administration's preferred problem definition, causal analysis, remedy, and moral evaluations. The codes were for (1) explicitly critical, (2) implicitly critical, (3) mixed or ambivalent, (4) implicitly supportive, and (5) explicitly supportive assertions. Table 4.1 displays the aggregated results, with all but the last two columns listing numbers of critical assertions on news pages or editorial pages, supportive assertions in news or editorial items, and totals.[4] Of the total 1,633 coded assertions, 55 percent were critical and 45 percent supportive of the Bush administration.[5] As the rightmost columns show, during Period 1, 63.2 percent of *Times* and 53.6 percent of *Post* assertions that offered an evaluation criticized the administration. Period 2, overall, shows roughly similar proportions. During both times, however, ABC television news offered more support than criticism. And if we look at the news pages alone, the papers actually conveyed an almost equal balance between criticism and support; the critical margin piled up on the editorial pages of the *Times* and *Post*. On balance, from these data, Iraq policy debate would appear to offer something approaching frame parity, as might be expected given the vigorous elite debate. But closer examination suggests a more complicated result.

CRITICISM LESS SALIENT AND FREQUENTLY PROCEDURAL

Zeroing in for a closer look at the critical assertions clarifies the limits to counterframing in the Gulf War debate. The key point here is that placement in the news obscured the information needed to activate and spread a counterframe. The coverage accorded the opposition's remedy prescription significantly less magnitude than attached to the administration's.

This held in two key senses. First, coded assertions tended to be relatively sparse on page one, the most prominent spot. Table 4.2 shows data for page-one assertions—those with the most magnitude and salience—only,[6] divided into substantive and procedural. The *Times* featured a total of 755 relevant assertions, of which just 13.5 percent (102) appeared on page one; in the *Post*, 13 percent (89 of 687) were similarly placed. Although these figures are in part a result of the simple physical reality that most material in newspapers cannot appear on page one, they do have theoretical significance, because information printed inside tends to receive much less attention. Most of the discourse on policy during these times of dramatic elite argument was relegated to less-noticed portions of the newspapers.

Second, much of the anti-administration content focused on procedural matters. Substantive assertions were those considered clearly relevant to audience members' understanding and acceptance of a policy remedy: the administration's "war soon" or the opponents' "sanctions first." These asser-

TABLE 4.1 *News and Editorial Support and Criticism during Gulf War Debate*

	Critical News (n)	Supportive News (n)	Critical Editorials (n)	Supportive Editorials (n)	Total Critical (n)	Total Supportive (n)	Total Assertions (n)	Proportion of All Assertions Critical (%)	Proportion of All Assertions Supportive (%)
Period 1									
New York Times	175	140	124	34	299	174	473	63.2	36.8
Washington Post	156	166	81	39	237	205	442	53.6	46.4
ABC	40	69	0	0	40	69	109	36.7	63.3
Total	371	375	205	73	576	448	1,024	56.2	43.8
Period 2									
New York Times	109	110	44	19	153	129	282	54.3	45.7
Washington Post	109	98	24	14	133	112	245	54.3	45.7
ABC	36	46	0	0	36	46	82	43.9	56.1
Total	254	254	68	33	322	287	609	52.9	47.1
Both periods									
New York Times	284	250	168	53	452	303	755	59.9	40.1
Washington Post	265	164	105	153	370	317	687	53.9	46.1
ABC	76	115	0	0	76	115	191	39.8	60.2
Total	625	629	273	106	898	735	1,633	55	45

Note: Cell entries are numbers of coded assertions criticizing or supporting the administration on news or editorial pages; last two columns list percentages of total assertions criticized or supported; for Periods 1 and 2 separately and overall.

TABLE 4.2 *Procedural and Substantive Criticism, Page-One or Lead TV Stories*

	New York Times[a]		Washington Post[a]		ABC[b]	
	Substantive	Procedural	Substantive	Procedural	Substantive	Procedural
Period 1						
Critical	27.0%	77.4%	64.0%	85.7%	31.4%	58.3%
n	10	24	16	18	11	21
Supportive	73.0%	22.6%	36.0%	14.3%	68.6%	41.7%
n	27	7	9	3	24	15
Total %	*54.4%*	*45.6%*	*54.3%*	*45.7%*	*49.3%*	*50.7%*
Total n	37	31	25	21	35	36
Period 2						
Critical	65.5%	80.0%	42.9%	62.5%	34.2%	42.3%
n	19	4	15	5	13	11
Supportive	34.5%	20.0%	57.1%	37.5%	65.8%	57.7%
n	10	1	20	3	25	15
Total %	*85.3%*	*14.7%*	*81.4%*	*18.6%*	*59.4%*	*40.6%*
Total n	29	5	35	8	38	26
Grand total %	*64.7%*	*35.3%*	*70.4%*	*29.6%*	*54.1%*	*45.9%*
Grand total n	66	36	69	29	73	62

Note: Cell entries are percentages and numbers of assertions in page-one news stories during each period, for the three media outlets. Percentages in roman add vertically for each period, for critical vs. supportive assertions. For instance, the first four rows and first column of the table show that the *Times* during Period 1 published 37 substantive assertions on page one. Of these, 10 (27%) were critical and 27 (73%) supportive. Percentages in italics add across for totals of substantive vs. procedural in each outlet, for each period. Thus, the fifth and sixth rows of figures show that, during Period 1, 54.4% of page-one assertions (n = 37) in the *Times* were substantive, 45.6% (n = 31) procedural and virtually identical percentages held for the *Post* (54.3% substantive, 45.7% procedural).

[a] Page 1 stories.
[b] Lead stories only.

tions either directly stated support or opposition to the policy, or assessed the costs and justifiability of the policies (and thus encompassed problem definition, causal analysis, and moral judgment by discussing the degree of danger to U.S. forces if war ensued, and justification of the ultimate policy objective of ejecting Hussein). Assertions counted as procedural if they evaluated behavior by those involved in the framing contest, that is, by Bush and the administration or members of the (domestic) opposition. In the Gulf War debate these involved specifically the need or failure to explain administration policy; attribution of political motives to Bush (or his opponents); Bush's need or failure to consult Congress; other aspects of Bush's leadership; and assertions focused on public opinion and support from other elites.[7]

The nature of critical assertions changed notably from Period 1 to Period 2. During Period 1, criticism focused more on the procedural than the substantive, especially for the *Times* and ABC. There were many attacks on the president and hardly any support, for example, concerning his failure to explain the policy clearly and his duty to consult Congress. But table 4.2 also shows that the administration maintained a healthy flow of highly visible claims supportive of its substantive policy during Period 1, the critical juncture immediately after the large troop deployment. In the *Times* and on ABC, substantive support outweighed opposition by better than 2 to 1. If we accept a corollary of the cascade model that is well supported by research in psychology—that early coverage is the most important because it shapes audience reactions to succeeding information—the heavy predominance of substantive support in the elite paper of record and on the (then) most watched network during Period 1 was an especially critical achievement for the administration. The *Post* was an outlier for Period 1, registering a predominance of substantive criticism over support. Adding all three outlets together, though, supportive assertions still dominated over opposing (62 to 38 percent). And close analysis (below) of the *Post*'s coverage during the congressional hearings reveals that the paper was anything but consistent in pushing an anti-administration frame.

The administration was able to reduce procedural criticism in Period 2 without altering the policy that received so much supportive press during Period 1. By explaining the policy better, by making a great public show of consulting Congress and obtaining U.N. approval[8] during Period 2, the administration reduced the overall amount of criticism, as revealed by the bottom half of table 4.2. Whereas the *Times* included thirty-four critical assertions on page one during the first period, it offered only twenty-three during the second; comparable figures for the *Post* were thirty-four and twenty. And this occurred despite the congressional hearings, the opponents' major attempt to contest the administration's frame. With procedural objections answered, the criticisms that remained did focus more on the substantive during Period 2, especially in the newspapers. Still, in the nation's two leading newspapers, substantive criticisms barely outnumbered plaudits (34 to 30). This means that each paper averaged not quite two substantive criticisms per day on page one. And ABC favored the administration on substantive matters by a 2:1 ratio during Period 2 just as it had during Period 1.

The network offered just thirteen substantive criticisms in lead stories during the second period. Thus, for example, when two former military chiefs of staff endorsed sanctions over war in congressional testimony on November 28, ABC found room for only one sound bite:

> War's not a need, it's not tidy and once you resort to it, it's uncertain and it's a mess. (Admiral William Crowe)

After two equally spare prosanction sound bites from Democratic leaders, the story provided longer quotations from two pro-Bush sources (his press secretary, and former Secretary of State Henry Kissinger) and concluded with the White House's cynical interpretation of the dissent:

> The Administration sees political mischief in Democratic advice that would keep U.S. forces in the desert through summer while the standoff keeps fuel prices up and the U.S. economy down. The hope here is that if the U.N. authorizes force, the U.S. Congress will too. (Brit Hume)

As for the newspapers, it is worth noting that editorial pages were heavily skewed against the administration. During the first period, for example, critical assertions in *Times* editorials and op-ed pieces outnumbered supportive by almost 4 to 1 (124 to 34). If the *Times*'s editorial expressions have special significance for officialdom, the paper might have actually spread activation of elite dissent rather than merely reflecting it. And in terms of proportionality, if we assume that Congress (as measured by the final vote on war) and the public (measured by polls) were about evenly split, the *Times* and *Post* heavily overrepresented critical views on their editorial pages. But it was procedural criticism that received the most emphatic treatment in the *Times*'s own voice.[9] During the entire November 8–January 15 prewar phase of the Gulf crisis, the *Times* ran twenty-five unsigned editorials concerning Iraq. Of those, five focused on the theme that Congress should be consulted on any decision to go to war (16 November and 15 December 1990, and 3, 7, and 13 January 1991). This consigned the newspaper's arguments against war to shaky ground once Congress voted to authorize force. Indeed, the *Times* devoted its harshest language, concerning President Bush's "Double Insult" (16 November 1990) and "unconscionable" dodging of the issue (3 and 7 January 1991) by Congress, to procedural issues rather than to the necessity or horrors of war. The theme that Bush should better "explain" or "give reasons" for his policies was featured in four editorials (14 November and 2 December 1990; 1 and 2 January 1991), and the idea that allies should get a bigger voice in policy took up one editorial (11 December 1990). Thus, though the *Times* editorials were the most strongly and consistently critical voice in this sample, fully ten of the twenty-five editorials, or 40 percent, were devoted to procedural matters, and these were generally the most forcefully worded.

To emphasize the importance of substantive discourse does not deny all significance to procedural criticisms. Such complaints about official behavior and of shaky public support do place pressure on administrations—ever tempted by the twin lures of secrecy and unchallenged policy control—to consult Congress. Consultation, if public, requires the president to share (some of) his thinking and intentions, heightening the possibility that informed opposition might spread. But fulfilling this potential requires that the press pay sustained attention to the substance of the ensuing debate. Otherwise a credible and memorable counterframe remains inaccessible to an easily distracted public—and for that reason, less politically relevant to elites.

By focusing the most salient criticism during the crucial early days of Period 1 on procedure, media coverage tended to soften the advancing edge of opposition, diminishing its ability to connect with anti-interventionist schemas, and obscuring the major issue: was going to war soon in fact the wisest course? Procedural reproaches, even if decoded as disguised attacks on the policy itself, provide little cognitive basis for counterframing. The paucity of well-supported substantive criticism may help explain why most of those citizens initially opposed to the Bush policy changed their minds once the war approached and began. They had little foundation for continued opposition once proper procedures had apparently been followed and the U.N. and Congress gave their blessing to war.[10] Nor would the average citizen's motivations encourage thinking about reasons to oppose the war once "our troops" were in harm's way, and especially after they appeared to be winning a low-cost victory—low-cost, that is, to most Americans, but not to families of U.S. or Iraqi casualties.

Coverage of the Hearings Protected the Administration

During Period 2 (November 27–December 5, 1990), Democrats mounted an organized effort to publicize dissent through media events and thus to activate and spread opposition along the elite and public networks.[11] Closer examination of the media's responses reveals and explains the administration's ability to reduce the magnitude (and salience) of substantive criticism.

In his hearings, Democratic Senator Sam Nunn of Georgia brought together a series of former military officers and other experts who testified that sanctions should be given time to work. Consider the *Post*'s reporting of these hearings. On November 28, it featured a front-page story headlined "Democrats Urge Caution on Gulf." Only in the continuation, back on page 31, did the story quote Nunn's statement noting the "fundamental shift" in policy represented earlier that month by Bush's doubling of American troops in the Gulf. That point was buried beneath a story on U.N. wrangling over the Palestine Liberation Organization and dwarfed by a Christmas tree ad. Such treatment suggests how the administration's emphasis on gaining approval from the U.N., where Bush actually had more clout than in Congress, helped it steer the news focus away from the hearings—and from the ramp-up in troop deployment.[12] It also indicates how the news routine of focusing attention on the administration's actions and pronouncements frequently winds up deemphasizing key, substantive anti-administration arguments. As suggested in the previous chapter, presidents who create action, almost any kind of action, can draw journalists' attention away from mere ideas. The continuation page was also where the *Post* relegated the surprising assessment of James Schlesinger, the normally hawkish, Republican former defense secretary and CIA head, who argued that sanctions were very likely to be successful within about a year.

The next day's lead headline in the *Post* read "Ex-Chiefs Chairmen Urge Reliance on Sanctions." Despite this headline and two other front-page stories on Iraq, the news on page one discussed nothing but processes: partisan and institutional wrangling over control of policy and public opinion, predictions of likely events relevant to that control, and assessments of Iraqi reactions. Again, page one did not detail what might be seen as the key and most surprising news: professional military leaders expressing opposition to Bush's war policy. Admiral William J. Crowe, for example, formerly chairman of the Joint Chiefs of Staff (JCS) under Reagan and Bush, pointed out the many problems that would remain in the Middle East after vanquishing Saddam Hussein. Crowe noted the sacrifices and uncertainties of war and casualties, and argued that "we should give the sanctions a chance before we discard them."[13] The second former JCS chairman, General David C. Jones, said the deployment of more forces could lead inexorably to war and that sanctions should be given time.[14] Quotations from these and other witnesses, words illustrating the substantive themes mentioned in the page-one headline, appeared obscurely near the end of the story, back on page 46. Such treatment heightened readers' information costs, making it more difficult to notice oppositional arguments.

On the third day, November 30, the banner-headlined story, "UN Vote Authorizes Use of Force against Iraq" pushed aside the hearings. Only on page 30, in the middle of a process story headed "No Plans for Recalling Congress," did the *Post* note that Ronald Reagan's former secretary of the navy, James H. Webb, had joined the "parade" of military witnesses criticizing administration policy. Far more prominent—headlined on page one, continued and extensively excerpted (with a photo) on page 21—was "Quayle Cites 'Moral Costs' of Waiting." Vice President Dan Quayle had not previously been considered an authoritative voice on American foreign policy, yet the *Post* lent his speech the sort of gravitas and magnitude usually reserved for presidential addresses. The paper granted about as much attention to his remarks alone as it accorded Crowe, Jones, Schlesinger, and Webb combined (twenty-one assertions for Quayle, twenty-two less prominently displayed assertions for the others).

From there on it was downhill for coverage of critical testimony in Nunn's hearings. The *Post* of December 1 recorded the launch of new diplomatic actions that functioned as a major public relations counterattack. The resulting headline, at the top-right of page one, read: "Bush Proposes Mission to Iraq As Final Bid to Preserve Peace," with the subhead "Legislators Hail Decision to Seek Talks." Later events indicated that the administration had no interest in negotiations and only reluctantly scheduled the token meeting between Secretary of State James Baker and Iraqi deputy prime minister Tariq Aziz in Geneva.[15] Some of the coverage suggested journalists thought as much, but this did not prevent them from allowing the initiative—again, concrete action—to push hearings featuring ideas and analysis into obscurity. A front-page box headed "Bush Speaks Out" contained a photo of a determined president accompanied by lengthy quotations. Inside were long continuations of the stories and voluminous excerpts from Bush's news conference. The headlines treated his initiative as if it were unambiguously a peace mission, though Bush did not propose to negotiate but merely to reiterate his demand for unconditional withdrawal, a demand repeatedly rejected by the Iraqis. The paper discussed the hearings on pages 21 and 24. The institutional power of the presidency can help an administration reduce the magnitude of critical media coverage even when dissidents are as strategically skilled and respected as Nunn and the hearing witnesses.

Throughout Period 2, the *Times* handled matters quite similarly to the *Post*. For example, on December 4, the *Times* (like the *Post*) put the congressional testimony by Defense Secretary Richard Cheney and Secretary of State James Baker in its most prominent page-one position ("Cheney Sees Need to Act Militarily Against the Iraqis"), and devoted almost the entirety of page 12 to extensive excerpts from their testimony. The honor of this level of coverage was not accorded any of the critical witnesses.

For Period 2, overall, the administration won the contest to control frames in the newspapers, and thoroughly dominated ABC.[16] The one ABC sound bite quoted above from the Jones and Crowe appearance, for example, came in a story providing no reasoned basis for audiences to believe sanctions might actually work. Although most scholars would expect little else from network news, that the nation's two leading newspapers diminished the hearings in comparison to the pronouncements of the administration is more surprising. They did this despite the hearings' extraordinary newsworthiness: not only were they the chief forum for the nation's solemn debate, but they featured the "man bites dog" appeal of well-known hawks taking a dovish stand.

Yet, making their news decisions all the more intriguing, as already noted, the two papers did not promote the administration line on their editorial pages. Editorials in the *Times,* for example, said that the administration was going "Too Far Too Fast in the Gulf" (11 November 1990) and asked "What's the Rush?" (29 November 1990). In the *Post,* a column by Haynes Johnson called the hearings "vital" as a "national forum" (30 November 1990). Nonetheless, the *Post* itself that day virtually ignored the testimony in its news columns. As was true particularly in the case of U.S. involvement in Grenada (chapter 3), the editorial page hosted vigorous denunciations of the very framing that the papers treated so respectfully on page one.

This finding violates the indexing model's emphasis on the close connection between elite debate and media content. The cascading activation model helps explain the disjunction. Even within specific news outlets, control over the activation of mental associations is hierarchical. Editorial staffers are far less constrained than reporters in the associations between ideas they can draw and the texts they can construct. Beyond the obvious difference that their job is to express "opinion," editorialists have more time, for instance, simply to read their own newspaper and thus to note contradictions or gaps in the administration line. Freed from the kind of hectic workdays reporters put in—playing phone tag, leaving the building to conduct in-person interviews or cover events—editorialists and columnists also enjoy a chance for more reflection on the bigger picture. Their relationships with elite sources tend to be more symmetrical, because editorial and column writers do not typically have to rely as heavily as reporters on ingratiating themselves with interviewees they may need to call again and again.[17]

What those working on the editorial pages do not enjoy is the power to demand a change in news coverage—news editors and reporters would view that as a violation of objectivity.

ATTENTION CALIBRATED TO POWER OVER POLICY

Looking over the Iraq news after November 8, including not just reports of hearings but all other Iraq-related events and pronouncements, it is apparent that administration officials' action and talk received the greatest attention. This may have been a result of another motivation that seems to drive journalists: helping audiences predict future events. By focusing more on actions, plans, and statements of the most powerful than on the assertions of those who have less power to affect future action, then, the media help audiences economize on the time they spend with the news. The unintended consequence is that the administration's opponents obtain secondary treatment even when what they say is substantively important. So—in accord with the cascade model, which predicts stratification in ability to activate thoughts—during the Armed Services Committee hearings, witnesses received unequal treatment. The criticisms and other remarks of congressional Democrats were given more prominent attention than statements of Schlesinger, Crowe, Jones, and others, but all received much less fanfare than the rebuttals of those who occupied the highest level of the Washington power hierarchy—Bush, Cheney, Baker, and even Quayle. And testimony by those completely outside officialdom, such as Gary Milhollin, a prominent peace researcher, was essentially ignored. Even the legendary former secretary of state, Henry Kissinger, obtained just seven lines of text in the *Post* (plus one line in the photo caption) at the very end of a hearings story. The fact that Kissinger's remarks favored Bush supports the notion that calibration to power rather than ideological bias explains the lower prominence accorded administration critics.

The predominance of administration figures emerges with particular clarity from simple counts of how often their names appeared, either as subjects or sources of news. During Period 2, in the *Times* and the *Post* taken together, President Bush's name was by far the most frequently invoked— 1,086 mentions, over half (54 percent) of the 2,012 total names mentioned. The next most cited were James Baker (17 percent), Richard Cheney (5.8 percent), and Colin Powell (4.3 percent). Together with Dan Quayle and Brent Scowcroft, the administration's six top leaders accounted for 84.8 percent of all names mentioned.[18] Aside from Nunn himself (seventy-one mentions), most members of the Armed Services Committee were rarely or never cited. All the critics who testified before the Nunn committee were named throughout the period a total of 129 times, accounting for 6.4 percent of all names. Bush-supporter Kissinger, with thirty-eight citations, rounds out the list of most-cited figures. The coverage increased the information costs to citizens seeking independent perspectives on the issue, while dampening the pressure that perceived public involvement might have applied to Congress. As one measure of this effect, Delli Carpini and Keeter report that only 25 percent of the public could name an official who was critical of Gulf policy, and only about one-third knew that the Democrats were more critical (before the war) than the Republicans.[19]

FEW FUNDAMENTAL CRITICISMS

Few of the reported criticisms challenged the administration's problem definition and goal. For example, only 13.4 percent of the coded assertions ($n = 73$) for the *Times* and *Post* in Period 2 focused even implicitly on the wisdom and justice of the underlying policy goal of forcing Iraq out of Kuwait, and 81 percent (59) of these were supportive, only 19 percent (14) critical. Virtually all reported voices in the "great debate" over peace or war with Iraq shared certain basic assumptions with the Bush administration.[20] In particular, nearly all reported critics as well as supporters agreed that Iraq had no legitimate grievances and therefore had to be unconditionally dislodged from Kuwait, by force if necessary. The arguments put forward by Nunn, Crowe, Jones, and others did not contest the problem definition, causal analysis, or moral assessment propounded by the Bush administration. That meant they accepted the goal of dislodgement and the remedy of force, and only questioned the immediate necessity.

Perhaps the most telling illustration of the strict limits on counterframing was the virtual absence from the news columns of a third policy option: negotiating with Iraq over what Saddam Hussein considered the injustices that led him to order the invasion.[21] Only on the editorial pages, where journalists are most independent of elite sources, did this potential remedy receive attention. Among the eighty-one Iraq-related *New York Times* op-ed pieces and editorials that appeared between November 8, 1990, and January 15, 1991, and that dealt explicitly with U.S. policy, twenty-one favored negotiations and/or substantive compromise with Iraq. The rest favored continued reliance on sanctions, at least for a time ($n = 40$), or imminent use of force ($n = 20$). Although not one editorial voice in the *Times* clearly took Iraq's side against Kuwait or argued against U.S. involvement, at least a few voices for negotiation were present on the op-ed page; they were all but absent from the news pages, where only the two options the administration preferred to debate gained admission to the frame contest.

Conclusion

In this best-test case of the media's ability to activate and spread a counterframe, then, in the face of ambiguity and assertive elite opponents, news organizations came up short. Confronting an ambiguous issue that did not automatically call to mind schemas supportive of war, during a period of unusually vocal and lengthy elite dissent, support for the administration policy toward Iraq was reported about as frequently as criticism on the news pages, and, on ABC television, more frequently. Supportive assertions, as documented especially in the closer look at Period 2, received more prominent treatment and administration officials received much more attention in the news than those outside the executive branch. With support for the White House frame possessing greater magnitude, elites and ordinary citizens tending to oppose "war soon" had a harder time finding concrete reasons to do so than those favoring it. Furthering the difficulty of opponents, a significant part of the criticism was procedural rather than substantive. The reasons are traceable to the interaction of journalistic motives with the play of power and strategy between the Bush administration and congressional opponents. The skilled strategic moves of the Bush administration outflanked congressional Democrats' own media management efforts, which ultimately foundered on the latter's unwillingness or inability to deploy the institutional powers of Congress against those of the executive branch.

This is a good point to step back briefly and consider in a bit more detail the two variables of power and strategy, which were introduced in chapter 1 and have been mentioned in passing in chapters 2 and 3 as partial explanations for framing. Then I consider the implications of this chapter's data and analysis for the cascade model.

POWER AND STRATEGY

Whereas motivations pull mental associations into the minds of elites, journalists, and citizens, power and strategy are the external forces that may push the activation of a particular set of mental connections. Power to influence other elites and the media varies among different presidents and at different times, depending particularly on their perceived popularity and effectiveness.[22] Sooner or later all presidents contend with the fact that Congress members and staffers, and experts and former officials, do have a capacity to push opposing frames because they too enjoy a (smaller) degree of legitimate access to news organizations. Journalists assemble their narratives by weaving together information provided by the administration and this elite source network. Sometimes—especially when the matter calls to nearly all minds the same habitual mental associations—this chorus will sing the same song, providing a push to one-sided framing. At other times, however, those elites outside the administration (and occasionally some brave or foolhardy dissenters inside the tent) exploit the opportunity to use different words and images to promote a counterframe. Although journalists have less ability to shape news frames than members of the administration or elite networks, they do have some independent power, arising from their capacity to ask questions and to decide precisely which words and images to assemble and transmit. As we saw in chapter 3, this and their motivations to fulfill the "watchdog" role often lead journalists to seek out and publish dissenting views from foreign leaders even when American elites fall silent.

As for *strategies,* deliberate, planned activation of mental associations is the province mainly of elites. Word choice, information distribution and withholding, and timing are among the elements of strategy that help lend the White House and executive branch greater control over framing than congressional or other elites, although they too engage in strategic manipulation, as we saw in the case of Senator Nunn's hearings. Deciding how to frame the event is itself based on both individual leaders' substantive views[23] and on strategic calculations about domestic political advantage and international diplomatic benefits and risks.[24] As is detailed in the next chapter, strategically less adroit administrations, such as the Carter (1977–81) and Clinton (1993–2001) White Houses, found news frames spinning out of their control. Poor strategy creates a power vacuum that opposing elites and journalists may enter with their own interpretations. On the other hand, cunning presidential strategy can endow frames with extra energy to penetrate down through elite networks to news organizations, journalists and their texts, and finally to the public.

Journalists do go through some strategic thinking in deciding on how to frame their stories, though their goal is rarely to exert power over outcomes. Rather they seek to produce "good stories" that protect and advance their careers and that accord with their self-images as independent watchdogs who must provide a degree of balance to stories.[25] An important if partial exception involves pundits and editorial writers, who may strategize in shaping their opinion columns, with effects that merit more thorough study.[26]

Strategic adoption and adaptation of frames rarely occurs among members of the public. Citizens infrequently strategize in deciding what mental associations to arouse either within themselves or on their interpersonal networks. They respond "naturally." And that puts them at a substantial disadvantage. They can resist or they can choose to accept the dominant frame, but either way, as the only participants not self-consciously taking a position based in some part on self-interest, citizens may do so at the peril of their own needs and values.[27]

IMPLICATIONS

Even under conditions far more favorable than during the crises discussed in chapter 3, media motivations converged to limit the spread of a fully realized counterframe. It is a familiar story, for example, that the media tend to rely heavily on official sources.[28] They do so, in part, because of the ease of regular access to officials, the dependable supply of news the officials provide, the need to cultivate such sources over time, and the usefulness of citing legitimate, authoritative sources, all of which serve important commercial needs for these businesses.[29] In particular, as Cook proposes, the existence of regular beats encourages the overrepresentation of administration views.[30] The beat system also probably reinforces the procedural element in the coverage, since reporters share a career interest with sources on the beat in making sure the process includes an influential role for the institution covered. Shared interests would help explain journalists' complaints about insufficient consultation with Congress, the institution outside the executive branch best represented in the beat system.

These practices interacted with the different strategic and power exertions by the two sides in the contest. It appears that the media calibrate news judgments rather precisely to the clout of those whose remarks or activities are covered: the higher their apparent power to shape newsworthy actions and outcomes, the more attention they receive. The lower the power, the less attention, even if their substantive ideas are novel and—like the surprisingly dovish stands taken by hawkish defense experts at the hearing—possess considerable news worth by the stated standards of journalism. The Bush administration used its power strategically to maximize its control of the frame—orchestrating the U.N. vote, launching substantively empty but newsworthy diplomatic initiatives, not to mention continuing the buildup of troops and materiel on the ground. In addition, the Bush administration faced little challenge during the long period between Iraq's invasion of Kuwait August 2 and the start of the prewar debate in November. During this time, the administration repeatedly compared Saddam Hussein with Adolph Hitler in a partly successful attempt to activate and connect an important cultural schema or public memory from World War II—highlighting the terrible cost of appeasing aggression—to overcome quagmire fears.[31] All this made Congress reluctant to use its institutional power to halt the war plan by passing laws or cutting off funding. Journalists realized that all congressional opponents were ever likely to do was talk. Congress's hesitancy to act more decisively both reflected and helped cause the media's preferential treatment of the administration's frame. Thus does media power interact with elite power and strategy.

Despite the sincere devotion to democratic deliberation they evince when expressing their own views on the editorial pages, encouragement of knowledgeable citizen involvement seems to rank near the bottom among the motivations that influence day-to-day construction of news and its frames. If they had defined their roles more self-consciously as activating independent public thinking, the news media might have deliberately given opposition voices, no matter what their institutional roles or power, equal play with administration leaders. Perhaps they hesitated to do so for fear of seeming to editorialize. But the outlets sampled here did emphasize Cheney's testimony and Bush's announcements and even Quayle's speech apparently without worrying about editorializing, most likely because they believed a chief purpose of news is to help audiences predict future events. Editors felt it proper to focus on the most powerful officials. They apparently failed to recognize that altering these practices might have promoted the more robust democratic debate that their papers endorsed editorially.

The disconnect between editorial positions and "straight" news coverage, at least in the cases explored in chapters 3 and 4, leads to a strange disruption of spreading activation within the news text itself. In his classic study of media and Vietnam, Hallin found the same divorce between the more independent and arguably factual discourse on the editorial pages, the purported outpost of mere opinion, and the often-misleading content and silences on the putatively factual news pages.[32] In the *Times* and *Post,* even as Iraq editorials made logical and sometimes emotional arguments critical of the administration, the framing of the news persistently downplayed that logic. With a kind of postmodern, ironic nod to objectivity, journalists describe the play of power accurately but sacrifice accuracy when describing the real stakes and substantive options in policy disputes. Of course it is also true that different people edit the news and editorial pages, and that the production processes and professional subcultures are quite distinctive. Reporters are far more tied to reporting the views and activities of sources. Still, from the vantage of cascading activation and democratic process, the spectacle of newspapers blithely conveying at face value assertions they denounce as false, misleading, or dangerous on the editorial pages sends confusing signals to audience members as it tacitly gives permission to officials to manipulate reporters.

All of which raises the question: even without a Cold War, does the administration inevitably dominate the framing of foreign affairs news? In a word, the answer is no. As the cascade model suggests, under the right circumstances the media can and do promote counterframes that challenge the White House's control not only of the news but of policy itself. Chapter 5 explains how.

5. INDEPENDENT FRAMING AND THE GROWTH OF MEDIA POWER SINCE THE COLD WAR

• •

The Cold War paradigm made it relatively easy for presidents to manage the news. That is not to say they always had their way, but spreading opposition required an unusually vigorous push from elite power and strategy. The end of the Cold War allowed journalists themselves greater leeway to challenge the White House. This chapter examines more fully the consequences of liberating journalists—and elites and citizens—from the habits of Cold War thinking.[1]

Taking a leaf from Kuhn,[2] we might say that the period of the Cold War was characterized by a dominant paradigm or meta-schema that organized "normal" elite thinking, media coverage, and public response to foreign and defense policy. The problem was communist aggression and intention to conquer the world; the cause was an ideology melding atheism with ruthless totalitarian dictatorship; the remedy was constant vigilance and struggle on ideological, diplomatic, economic, and military fronts; and the evaluation tended toward moral condemnation of the communist side and idealization of "free world" allies. Virtually any problematic situation that arose in the world could be, and was, assimilated to the Cold War paradigm.

What exactly is meant by "breakdown" of the Cold War paradigm?[3] In terms of the cascading activation model, it betokens the growth of ambiguity in foreign policy events, issues, and actors, as habitual schemas laid down and continually reinforced during the Cold War fell into disuse.[4] The habits did not become entirely irrelevant: segments of the knowledge networks that once applied to the international communist conspiracy were, after September 11th, transferred to a new focus on the international terrorist conspiracy. The George W. Bush administration deployed its power and strategy to cleverly build on the remnants of habitual schemas, attaching new events, issues, and actors to notions that previously bolstered Americans' willingness (in John F. Kennedy's famous Inaugural words) to "pay any price, bear any burden, meet any hardship, support any friend, oppose any foe" to eradicate this new global threat.

Evidence from the 2003 Iraq war suggests that after initial hesitation, much of the media and public began—with reservations—accepting the new paradigm, or at least its applicability to Saddam Hussein. During the decade before 9/11, however, the United States confronted what appeared to be, at most, indirect threats. U.S. involvement in the 2003 Liberian civil war suggested such problems would likely remain common well into the twenty-first century. Where novel matters fail to fit a dominant paradigm, news media can activate counterframing ideas on their own, challenging the White House's problem definitions, causal and moral analyses, and remedies.

This chapter proposes four hypotheses that describe conditions obtaining early in the twenty-first century. They are not presumed to be permanent; in the new, uncertain epoch we should not expect permanence. The validity of the analysis requires testing and refinement; the chapter is an initial foray based on uncertain and mutating relationships among human participants, institutional constraints, and unforeseeable developments. The chapter uses news of interventions conducted under Clinton and George W. Bush to probe these interrelated hypotheses:

1. With the disappearance of the Red Menace, invoking patriotism to block opposition becomes more difficult, opening space for more independent influence by the media in defining problems and suggesting remedies.

2. Unmoored by a consensual paradigm, journalistic motivations impose a double bind on presidents: a simultaneous demand for assertive, interventionist leadership by "the world's only superpower," and chastisement of U.S. leaders when interventions turn costly or give signs of turning into quagmires.

3. With the familiar Cold War clichés and vocabulary stripped of relevance, the words and concepts needed to explain foreign issues become more complex. This heightens the influence of visual information in the construction of frames, images that media using the latest technologies can sometimes select more independently than when choosing words.

4. We can no longer generalize easily about "state" power over the media—if we ever could—because that power depends on which party inhabits the White House (and ultimately controls application of military force). For several reasons, including core ideological precepts that legitimize disciplined government control and thus media management, the Republicans usually enjoy more success dominating news frames than Democrats.[5] The critical difference between Republican and Democratic administrations helps explain the media's seeming swing from feisty independence during the Clinton administration toward general (though not complete) cooperation with the George W. Bush administration by the time of the second war in Iraq.

The Fading of Demons and Patriotism Augments
the Potential for Media Influence

The demise of the Cold War created a void, an absence of problem-defining, habitual associations to threats against the United States that communism automatically provided. If Somalia is overrun by deeply malevolent "warlords," Haiti or Liberia by antidemocratic despots, and the Balkans by evil Serbs, what is it to Americans? Why exactly should these be *problems* for the United States? Demonization becomes more difficult when regimes pose no direct threats to U.S. security and no longer activate automatic anxieties about the communist conspiracy.

For clarity's sake and following Sobel's suggestion, we can assume that two major paradigms have tugged at each other within American political culture: an extroverted interventionism fed by World War II and then the Cold War, and an introverted if not isolationist tendency that has risen, fallen, and risen again throughout U.S. history.[6] Demonization was the engine of interventionism and it had quite a run after World War II. The dearth of threatening demons disrupted journalists' and the public's associative links to the *benefits* of intervention. The quagmire schema, in which costs and risks of intervention occupy a central place, feeds the tendencies toward introversion and became more salient for most Americans after Vietnam and the Cold War.

The White House of William Jefferson Clinton could not call intervention in Somalia, Haiti, or the Balkans a patriotic duty. Even when it proposes U.S. military force against weak foes unable to inflict heavy casualties, the White House cannot as reliably invoke patriotism to block thoughts about the costs and risks of intervention. In part, patriotism consists in suspending what is common in domestic policy: habitual disbelief or at least skepticism of government. Without the dangerous direct enemies and certainties of the Cold War, foreign policy becomes more likely than previously to stimulate the kind of contests long dominant in domestic politics. Elites are emboldened, able to criticize problem definitions and policy options without seeming unpatriotic. In Somalia, Haiti, and the Balkans, the Clinton administration never could construct a frame that both defined problems as relevant to the United States and cemented the logic of its preferred policy options. And when George W. Bush decided that after Afghanistan, the next goal in the war on terrorism would be ousting Saddam Hussein, the White House line encountered considerable resistance. In these cases, counterframing that emphasized cost and risk was accessible and expressible by elites and journalists no longer fearful of adverse public reactions to what once would have seemed unpatriotic and disloyal.

A possibly extreme example can be found in newsmagazine coverage of America's 1999 intervention (with NATO) in Kosovo, when little but criticism of the Clinton administration appeared in many reports. *Newsweek's* initial coverage of the NATO bombing of Kosovo and the associated controversy was featured on consecutive covers of the magazine (5 and 12 April 1999). The tone was typified by this sarcastic assessment in the magazine's "Conventional Wisdom" section for April 5: "For weeks the CW has been saying that there is no good end game in Yugoslavia. Turns out there was no good beginning game, either . . . this thing is smelling like a fiasco." The cover headline of this issue was "War in Kosovo: Where Will it End?" Not one full paragraph in this issue praised Clinton's leadership or endorsed his problem definition and remedy. Again and again, the narrative challenged Clinton's assumptions, discussed the risks and costs of the intervention, and cast doubt on the possibility of a positive outcome. This approach reached its height in a two-page essay by former secretary of state Henry Kissinger, headlined "Doing Injury to History," which took apart the rationale and execution of Clinton's policy in Kosovo.

The April 12 issue featured a picture of three beaten American servicemen who were captured in Macedonia. The headline: " 'We're Trapped'/HORROR AND HOSTAGES: HOW AMERICA STUMBLED INTO A NO-WIN WAR." A photo essay led off the coverage, with a headline extending over four pages of pictures: "A Tragic Exodus . . . And No Exit" (ellipsis in original). Beyond focusing in great detail on the suffering of the three American prisoners (ultimately released banged up but in satisfactory health), the coverage again emphasized criticism of the policy and of Clinton's leadership. The only piece in either issue that defended the intervention was an essay by Holocaust novelist Elie Wiesel, like Kissinger a nonofficial member of the elite source network, a spokesperson selected by the media outlet itself. Wiesel defended the idea of attacking Slobodan Milosevic's regime, although he did not provide detailed justification of Clinton's policies. And Wiesel's piece was followed by a three-page story on "How We Stumbled into War," and a one-page essay devoted to slamming Clinton (as had Kissinger the previous week) for misreading history, calling his actions "foolhardy."

The point is not that Clinton's policy deserved gentler treatment. Rather, it is that *Newsweek* (and, impressionistically, much of the other national media as well), far from allowing the White House to dominate the framing of the Kosovo intervention, failed even to provide a balanced view. It tilted decisively *against* the administration. The indexing model might have predicted at least a more equal contest between the administration and its critics. New here was that the media, freed of Cold War constraints, themselves chose sources and composed and activated a counterframe, one that seemed to swamp the administration's line.

When Clinton's policy actually did succeed at evicting the Serb army from Kosovo and returning the Kosovar refugees home to a semblance of peace, the administration received remarkably little praise for its victory. The Kosovo success did not even make the *Newsweek* cover (which depicted "Stress" on 14 June 1999), and the lead story on Kosovo was headed "Victory, but at a Price"—not exactly a celebratory note. *Time* also chose a nontimely feature about "Heroes and Icons" for its cover, and put a similarly sour headline on its lead Kosovo story. Such treatment demonstrates again far less certain White House control over the media. Having imposed their own skeptical frame on the situation, one in which they defined the key problem not as the danger to Kosovars facing ethnic slaughter but as the peril to Americans facing combat, newsweeklies—which might in other times have reveled in an emotional story of American victory and humanitarian rescue—played it down. Trumpeting the achievement might have required *Newsweek* and the others to admit they had been wrong just weeks earlier in saying that the United States was "trapped" in a "no-win war." So Clinton's decision to intervene yielded essentially no political credit, and little incentive for future statesmanship.

Clinton's experience may be traceable in part to post-Lewinsky bitterness and the ambiguity of Kosovo issues, but it also suggests the important role that demons and enemies play in the administration's gaining credit for success. The leaders and armed forces of the former Yugoslavia posed only the remotest threat to the United States. Unlike Saddam Hussein, Kim Jong-Il, or others who have engaged in menacing rhetoric toward America, Slobodan Milosevic sought only to dominate a small, rather remote area of Europe, and he never seemed particularly interested in the United States. Consequently, when the U.S. forces defeated Milosevic, the media interest was fleeting. Rather than vanquishing a personified enemy endangering American interests, the intervention succeeded in serving more abstract humanitarian and democratic aims, and that made for a tepid victory narrative. From the lackadaisical coverage of Clinton's success in the Balkans, presidents who crave political recognition and glory can draw this lesson: statesmanship is less important than constructing villains and turning up the rhetorical heat on enemy states. Presidents who do that have a better chance of seeing American success translated into an emotionally satisfying and politically beneficial tale of triumph.

Contradictory Culture Produces Double Binds on Leadership

Journalists can impose a double bind in their framing of leaders' policy choices. National media outlets seem to provide among the most consistently interventionist voices in post–Cold War America, and frequently support firm U.S. action and the use of force. Facing no electoral constraints and no worries about diplomatic credibility or military budgets and losses, many pundits and foreign policy reporters pressed insistently for intervention in Somalia, Bosnia, and Kosovo. Then, many of the same media outlets urging that the U.S. project its power increasingly tended to criticize interventions when they actually occurred. Even as they pushed an interventionist agenda, many top journalists tended to blame administrations for the inevitable reverses and sacrifices. They demanded immediate and coherent responses to crises, and quick if not instant evidence of success— and clear indications that no quagmire loomed.[7] Where potential benefits of intervention appear low, news organizations seem especially likely to highlight the dramatic visual details of any U.S. casualties—images of unacceptable cost that can trigger isolationist leanings of ordinary Americans and create perceptions that majorities oppose involvement.[8]

Listing in chronological order *Newsweek* cover headlines on Somalia provides an example of the alternating, double binds of interventionist pressure and negative judgment by many elite media. Newsmagazine covers are particularly useful because they typically summarize the dominant framing of major foreign and domestic policy issues:

- "Somalia's Agony: Time to Send in the Troops?" (7 December 1992)
- "Going In/Should America be the World's Policeman?" (14 December 1992)
- "Into Somalia/But for How Long?" (21 December 1992)
- "Firing Away: Playing Cop in Somalia and Bosnia" (21 June 1993)
- "Somalia: The Messy Future of War" (28 June 1993)
- "GloboCop: Does America Have the Will to Fight?" (23 August 1993)
- "Trapped in Somalia" (18 October 1993)

The same points could be illustrated with *Time* covers. Consider, for example, "The Agony of Africa" (7 September 1992), depicting a little boy apparently wailing and adding to the media chorus in favor of intervening;[9] and "What in the World Are We Doing?/Anatomy of the Disaster in Somalia/Behind the Scenes in the Battle for Mogadishu" (13 October 1993). The botched mission to capture a rebel Somali leader that led to eighteen American deaths—memorialized in the 2002 film *Black Hawk Down*—

was disastrous for those involved. But few military operations in history have been conducted without just this kind of tragic bungling. The difference is the overwhelming media focus on the one relatively minor incident—and the sense that benefits of American intervention were so slim that even a small number of casualties was too high a price.

Or consider this simple listing of cover headlines in *Newsweek* during the first few weeks of U.S. intervention in Haiti:

- "Haiti: Is This Invasion Necessary?" (19 September 1994, upper right banner)
- "'Your Time Is Up'/Special Report/THE HAITI SHOWDOWN/Getting the Generals Out—And the Risks of Restoring Order/The Inside Story of How Clinton Stumbled into a Crisis" (26 September 1994)
- "CRISIS IN HAITI/WHO'S IN CHARGE HERE?/Carter's Lone Ranger Act/ Haiti's Rotten Cops/Why Democrats Can't Do Wars" (3 October 1994)

The dominant framing of Haiti in *Newsweek* (and elsewhere) questioned the administration's rationale, emphasized the costs and risks of its policy, and derogated Clinton's competence. Yet some of the writings deeper into the same coverage suggested that as the only superpower, America had to avoid becoming a "neurotic lion," overly "skittish" about committing to war.[10] One might forgive Clinton for indeed becoming skittish in the face of these conflicting pressures. It appears that journalists themselves, as we might expect, became as ambivalent, inconsistent, and theoretically rudderless after the Cold War as other Americans. This shaky understanding did not make the media less aggressive in holding Clinton administration officials, whom they often viewed with skepticism if not contempt, accountable for failing to find quick, low-cost solutions.

As a final illustration of the sometimes strident interventionist strain, consider a typical set of quotations on Bosnia. *Newsweek* headed its May 10, 1993, issue "Bosnia/Clinton Gets Tough—At Last/Will Air Power Be Enough?" The cover depicted an injured child, and the lead story was titled: "City of the Dead." Subheads read: "The accumulated horrors of the Bosnian war finally became too awful to ignore. . . . America would sit by no longer. The world's last superpower vowed to use its might to end the savagery in the Balkans." Another story (p. 22) was headed: "Getting Tough at Last," and subheaded: "Why should America take a stand in Bosnia? Because to enjoy the benefits of global leadership, we have to bear the costs, too." The story extolled the benefits of acting "as a force for good." It argued that the United States derived "tangible benefits from the perception that we're a country that stands for more than its own petty self-interest; it enhances our authority to call for free trade in Tokyo." It went on to dismiss any "public squeamishness about casualties." After this came a long story about military plans and practical problems of intervention. This material did hint at doubts about the intervention endorsed in the previous stories. But reinforcing the dominant framing was a long sidebar (p. 28) that concluded: "It's up to Clinton to show that this time around, if the Serbs don't mean business, he does."

In point of fact however, the Clinton administration largely deferred to European allies and the U.N. forces in the Balkans for about two years; fearful of a quagmire and domestic political damage, the United States took a secondary role and limited its involvement to air strikes. Then events took a turn for the worse and by mid-1995, the media pressure, very much combined with a complex of diplomatic forces and military calculations, became irresistible. The latter are beyond the scope of this book, but Robinson's detailed study demonstrates how the media's use of emotive rhetoric and visual images played an independent role in shaping U.S. policy.[11] The critical event was the fall of Srebrenica, which produced horrific human suffering and graphic images saturating the airwaves. What Robinson calls "empathy framing" highlighted the horrors. He quotes a *New York Times* report as typical: "The air was filled with anguished cries as the Bosnian Serbs loaded the first 3,000 women, children and elderly refugees on buses. . . . The refugees were dropped off . . . [and] forced to walk the last six miles across the front lines." At the same time the media were full of stinging critiques of the Clinton administration's failure to avert the disaster; coverage was suffused with words connoting failure: "spinelessness," "too little, too late," "absence of will," "impotence," "ineffectual."[12] Editorials in the *Times* and elsewhere repeatedly demanded action. These depictions both pushed the Clinton administration to take over leadership of the NATO efforts, which meant more direct involvement of U.S. forces, and helped it convince allies to go along with Washington's decisions. None of this is to say that the media alone caused U.S. actions. But Robinson makes the case, supported by evidence from interviews with the decisionmakers themselves, including then vice president Al Gore, national security advisor Anthony Lake, and Clinton himself, that news frames had a major effect.[13] One interesting impact arose *inside* the Clinton administration. Administration officials shared the common experience of seeing "horrific" visual images from the Balkans. Reactions to these provided leverage to those administration insiders who were urging intervention—both on substantive and moral grounds, and on grounds the media coverage would have negative political ramifications if the president did not act.

On the other hand, the media were also ever-ready with extraordinary emphasis on the costs and risks of intervention. The experience of just one pilot, Scott O'Grady, shot down and then rescued after a bombing mission, was grist for cover stories in the newsmagazines and lengthy reports on television and later even inspired a major motion picture, *Behind Enemy Lines* (2001).[14] In 1995, when Clinton made the decision to commit ground troops to enforce a peace agreement, he faced nothing like the unequivocal media support one might have expected given all the previous insistence on using American muscle. One reason marks an important difference from the 1991 war in Iraq, where, as discussed in chapter 4, the Democratic-controlled Congress did not back its critique of Bush's war plans by threatening legislative action. The newly elected Republican majority in the House, led by indomitable Speaker Newt Gingrich, actually passed a bill that would have prevented funding for U.S. troop deployment. Although the bill never became law, it did ensure the opposition was newsworthy, which meant a more even framing contest. In addition, some Democrats and liberals, normally allies of the president, spoke out against military involvement. Nearly half the members of the House signed a letter urging against deployment of troops, although ultimately Congress went along. Based on an impressionistic survey, the national media did not allow Clinton to dominate the framing of the risky decision to commit ground forces; on the contrary "risk" was a major theme of the coverage. Neither did Clinton receive much praise when the action succeeded with minimal losses to the U.S. troops.[15]

One might argue that the double binds arise out of the media's inability to resolve the logical contradiction between interventionism and isolationism. They fill the void through a logic emerging from journalists' and news organizations' motivations and limitations. It is absurd to demand both vigorous interventionism and instant, cost-free success. But the media need narrative, and they shape it according to motivations embodied in news norms and values. Given the penchant for procedural evaluation of officials—that is, journalists' constant search for evidence of the president's competence or incompetence, popularity or unpopularity—and such news production rules as simplification and dramatization,[16] it actually makes perfect sense for them to impose mutually exclusive demands on the White House. One could hardly expect reporters to ignore the heart-rending shootdown of Scott O'Grady or the amazing saga of his survival in the woods and eventual rescue—irresistible fodder for media outlets competing to keep audiences. Yet such an emphasis made the costs and risks of U.S. involvement far more salient than the benefits.[17]

What the media must have is good stories, and they believe these by definition include drama, conflict, and human interest. Media narratives cannot easily encompass nuance or irony. They cannot readily acknowledge intractable contradiction without blaming political authority. For example: the contradiction that the United States had to intervene in Bosnia and Kosovo to be true to its humanitarian, democratic principles, but that it could not do so without violating the same principles (and others), such as responding to the majority of Americans who told pollsters they opposed intervention.

Notice the striking switch: in these cases, the media did free themselves from dependence on the White House frame, but in its place provided confusing, contradictory interpretations that may have met journalistic needs for drama and sensation, but did not actually yield frame parity. Instead, frames fashioned by journalists and elite opponents ruled the text. However, outcomes can differ when a president employs culture, power, strategy, and motivations to convincingly portray a significant threat to the United States—as George W. Bush arguably accomplished in justifying his war in Iraq. (More on that shortly.)

The Visual Shift

The ability to transmit powerful visual messages has been heightened by technical advances in satellites, photography, and color reproduction.[18] Couple this with elites' tendencies to assume that visual images have major impacts on public opinion, and the result may be more influence exerted by news organizations.

The absence of a tightly wound verbal paradigm with familiar framing words may elevate the relative power of pictures. Showing a dead American soldier dragged through the capital of Somalia was as powerful in its effect as any written account could have been. The picture activated the anti-interventionist, quagmire schema and brought it into Americans' thinking where polls picked it up. But words still exert defining power. That image of a desecrated American body *could* have set off intensely angry retributive responses—fight rather than flight—with the proper verbal frame. It probably would have done so had the enemy forces been connected to the Cold War or terrorism. Just such a reaction to images of brutalized Americans in New York City on September 11, 2001, provoked a fight response, as did pictures of injured American prisoners of war in 2003. But for Somalia such framing was absent because there was no way to attach it to any compelling schema promoting intervention.

It is not that the media are unaware of the problematic power of visuals.

They just cannot help themselves, given motivations arising out of production and commercial imperatives. Indeed, they find themselves ensnared in contradictory pressures similar to those they impose on leaders. For example, a *Time* cover story headed "In Feeding Somalia and Backing Yeltsin, America Discovers the Limits of Idealism" asserted that emotions and "generous feelings" had been driving American foreign policy. This emotionalism arose "from pictures, either still photographs or television clips, that are mainlined directly into the democracy's emotional bloodstream without the mediation of conscious thought" (18 October 1993, 37–39). Perhaps so, but just to the left of this assertion appeared a one-and-a-half-page picture of a young Somali boy holding the pants of a presumably dead U.S. soldier. And a large caption read: "Images like this one are mainlined directly into the democracy's emotional bloodstream."

Whether critics are right to worry about foreign policy driven by simplistic emotional responses to pictures is less clear than it may seem on the surface.[19] The implication is that a public relying on words alone will be more informed, more thoughtful. Yet to take one counterexample, the public's surveyed support for the 1986 decision to bomb Libya relied only marginally on pictures. It was based on a months-long campaign to stoke fear of terrorism, packed with false verbal details about the villainy of a terrorist attack on a Berlin disco that killed American servicemen, allegedly on the orders of Libyan leader Qaddafi. The words here were powerful, and powerfully misleading.[20]

Republicans' Media Advantage

Although the discussion so far points to an apparent growth in the media's own influence over the framing of national defense policy during the 1990s, experience after the Clinton administration suggests that the party controlling the White House makes a difference. Republican presidents seem able to exert more reliable control over framing than Democrats.

The Clinton administration's failure to control framing was partly due to the way elite discourse structurally differs depending on partisan control of the White House. The Republicans, and many Democrats in Congress, freely contested the White House's shifting problem definitions in Bosnia, Somalia, and Haiti. These clashes helped shape the public's survey responses even as they also reflected elites' and journalists' readings of Clinton's shaky standing in presidential approval polls, chronic disunity among his advisors, and his administration's occasional strategic blunders. For an opposing frame to pervade the media, the opposition party must understand its function precisely as producing a counterframe.[21] That means asserting and repeating mutually reinforcing linkages to familiar schemas, resonant slogans, and symbols the media can pick up and reiterate. Republicans, ideologically more unified on foreign policy and more amenable to following disciplined leadership, generally supply counterframes more effectively than the fractious Democratic coalition. Democrats seem to have a harder time than Republicans reconciling internally contradictory ideological impulses between protecting human rights and upholding international law on the one hand, and pursuing American self-interest and needs for dominance on the other. This causes vacillation and internal fights that weaken Democrats' ability to execute successful media management strategies.[22] These tendencies were vividly on display in congressional Democrats' thoroughly disjointed response to George W. Bush's Iraq war plans. The party's top leader in each house of Congress—who happened to be running for president at the time—aligned with Bush, against their own rank-and-file members. As the cascade model suggests, spreading activation can be undermined by gaps in the chain of connections. When a party's elite "nodes" fail to fire in unison (that is, neglect to use the same framing themes and words) it disrupts the flow of mental connections that journalists might otherwise make. Repetition across the network of party sources provides raw material for news frames, and unity in proclaiming the same themes also works as a signal of the leadership's power and effectiveness, which makes the themes more newsworthy.

A key implication is that "public opinion" itself may take on a different shape depending on the party inhabiting the White House. Because of their flimsier control over news frames, Democratic presidents may have less success manipulating the public's surveyed preferences against the opposing party than do the Republicans. Anticipated public reactions would thus pose less of a constraint on Republican than Democratic administrations. The comparison between coverage of Grenada and Panama under Reagan and George H. W. Bush, respectively, with Kosovo and Haiti under Clinton is revealing on this score. Somehow, the possibility of getting bogged down in a quagmire and enduring unacceptable costs for a murky set of benefits—while certainly not ignored—failed to bedevil Grenada or Panama policy, yet such critiques not only undermined but dominated coverage of Clinton's equally (or more) successful engagements. Still, testifying to post–Cold War changes, even George W. Bush had to contend with the media's quagmire worries in Iraq, as we will see.

A final explanation of party differences may be a change in standard operating procedure. The cognitive and operational habit of accepting the government's problem definition was still engrained in journalists at the end of the Cold War. Even during Vietnam, the media maintained allegiance to the government's core problem definitions—despite occasionally magnifying dissent on its policy choices and conveying critiques of official leadership.[23] But the demise of the Soviet Union shook this entrenched habit of deference. The habit was challenged in a major way during the 1990–91 debate about going to war against Iraq, though the White House won out then, as we saw in chapter 4, and after war began.[24] Yet elite confusion and ideological drift, the problematic end to the Gulf War, and the series of ambiguous difficulties that began with Somalia and Bosnia seemed after 1991 to weaken journalists' habit of deference, replacing it with the kind of skeptical questioning more common in domestic policy. It was Clinton's misfortune that this shift took root on his watch.

EXTENDING THE WAR ON TERRORISM
TO IRAQ AFTER SEPTEMBER 11TH

In the wake of September 11, 2001, the government propounded a line designed to revive habits of patriotic deference, to dampen elite dissent, dominate media texts, and reduce the threat of negative public reaction— to work just as the Cold War paradigm once did. In his 2002 State of the Union address, President George W. Bush defined terrorism as a global threat requiring a unified front of "civilized" nations against an adversarial "axis of evil" which sponsors and harbors terrorists. Like the communists of yore, the terrorists, driven by irrational ideology and opposed to freedom and capitalism, conspire in secret and brutalize their own people and therefore have no compunction about assaulting perceived enemies like the United States. If events seem to support this Manichean division of the world into enemy and friend, evil and good, U.S. elites might together once again sustain an anchoring paradigm comparable to the Cold War—particularly if the United States remains on high alert or "at war" against terrorism indefinitely.[25] In such circumstances media could revert to habitual subservience to the administration line. If opposing elites become as timid during the war on terrorism as they were bold during the Clinton administration, it would discourage successful counterframing.

The general cooperation—interrupted by spells of skepticism— that characterized the relationships between the media and the Bush administration after 9/11 are instructive in this regard, and worth considering at some length. In the aftermath of September 11th, Democrats took great care to publicly support the president's problem definitions and remedies in Afghanistan, and to praise his foreign policy leadership competence as well. That meant the media themselves had to take the initiative in challenging the administration, albeit in limited ways.[26] The relative weakness of news organizations' resistance to the Bush frame as compared with their defiance of Clinton reflected in part the unifying impact of September 11th, but it also illustrated the difference in potential media influence when a Republican rather than Democrat holds the White House. Two cases trace the arc of George W. Bush's effort to tame the media by building a new paradigm around terrorism. One case involved identifying Saudi Arabia rather than Iraq as the most important source of terrorist threat against America; the other focused on quagmire fears surrounding the Iraq war.

Even before the Afghanistan war, two well-known journalists, Seymour Hersh of the *New Yorker* magazine and Thomas Friedman, *New York Times* columnist, launched an independent effort to activate a different or at least supplementary problem definition. Contesting the government line was nothing new to investigative reporter Hersh, who began muckraking in the foreign policy arena in the mid-1960s. Indeed, his career stands as a challenge in itself to the strictest versions of the hegemony model. Hersh published an article in the *New Yorker* (22 October 2001; online version, 16 October) that described the extensive support—financial, cultural, and otherwise—that the Saudi leadership had given to Islamic extremism and terrorism. It suggested that it was no coincidence that both Osama bin Laden and fifteen of the nineteen hijackers of 9/11 were Saudis, and pointed toward the need to recognize that this putative ally was quite possibly a more critical target for American attention and, perhaps, wrath than Afghanistan. Thomas Friedman, on the other hand, is the quintessential *New York Times* insider, a respected mainstream voice with probably the most influential foreign affairs opinion column in American journalism. He published essays on October 5 and 30, 2001, that briefly raised serious questions about Saudi Arabia and included assertions that the Saudi royal family itself had links to terrorism.

Although at first the claims left little trace on the news or public discourse, the challenge to the dominant frame did not die entirely and, intriguingly, it picked up steam to become a part of mainstream discussion a few months after Hersh and Friedman first activated the terrorist–Saudi link.

Three things happened to magnify the Saudi issue. First, the *Washington Post* broke a story on August 7, 2002, that an expert who briefed the U.S. Defense Policy Board the previous month essentially made the Hersh–Friedman argument to this secretive and powerful advisory group. The membership consists of experts and former officials at the highest level, including former Secretary of State Henry Kissinger and former Defense

Secretaries Harold Brown and James Schlesinger.[27] This piece resulted in a flurry of news referring to allegations that Saudi Arabia supported terrorism.

Second, on August 15, 2002, families of 9/11 victims filed a lawsuit naming Saudi Arabian royals among the defendants, alleging their culpability in the terrorist attacks. The lawsuit generated some coverage, most briefly mentioning the Saudi–terrorism link, but some using the text of the lawsuit to provide far more detail on the connection than had previously appeared. Moreover, in a bit of cross-pollination, the lawsuit was cited in stories that mentioned the Defense Board briefing and vice versa.

Third, in part because of Saudi Arabia's adamant opposition to U.S. military action against Iraq (unlike its support for the first Gulf War in 1990–91), the Saudi problem became entangled with this increasingly controversial follow-up remedy for terrorism. This led to such pieces as "I'm With Dick! Let's Make War!"—a sarcastic *Times* column by Maureen Dowd, which began as follows:

> I was dubious at first. But now I think Dick Cheney has it right.
>
> Making the case for going to war in the Middle East to veterans on Monday, the vice president said that "our goal would be . . . a government that is democratic and pluralistic, a nation where the human rights of every ethnic and religious group are recognized and protected." O.K., I'm on board. Let's declare war on Saudi Arabia! Let's do "regime change" in a kingdom that gives medieval a bad name. (28 August 2002, A19)

At about this time, leading Republicans outside the administration, including former national security advisor Brent Scowcroft and former secretaries of state Lawrence Eagleburger and James Baker, launched what appeared to be a coordinated attack on the Iraq war option. In so doing they apparently echoed sentiments voiced within a divided administration by Secretary of State Colin Powell and others.[28] Even House Majority Leader Dick Armey and Senator Chuck Hagel, conservative Republicans, voiced skepticism. Republican stalwarts wrote opinion columns and appeared on talk shows urging that Bush reconsider the policy. Some of the news and editorial reaction used this as an opportunity to bring up not only the damaging Saudi failure to support the Iraq option, but also the perhaps more direct peril to America posed by Saudi support of terrorist groups and ideologies. All in all, for a couple of months during the summer of 2002, Republicans behaved like Democrats.[29]

A Nexis search of major U.S. newspapers came up with forty items during August 1–31, 2002, that explicitly linked Saudi Arabia and terrorism.

Of these, just twelve appeared on editorial pages, compared with twenty-eight news stories. This contrasts with the twenty-five items published during two full months (October and November 2001) after Hersh and Friedman's lonely campaigns to raise the Saudi connection's salience, most (nineteen) editorial opinion rather than news. It seemed that the Saudi–terrorism link had finally become newsworthy and had the potential to spread down to the public, which could have helped push it back up through elite levels where it might have affected administration policy. However, television news did not respond much to any of these developments.[30] Of the three major broadcast networks, only NBC (on the *Today Show* and *Dateline*) mentioned the Saudi–terrorism link during August 2002, and none of the nightly news shows even referred to the trillion-dollar lawsuit by the 9/11 families.[31] Nonetheless, a poll taken by a Republican firm found the unfavorable rating for Saudi Arabia increased from 49 percent in May to 63 percent in August 2002, suggesting the later negative publicity was attracting more public attention.[32]

How does all this support the cascade model? As noted in chapter 1, for the media to originate and spread ideas down to the public and all the way back up to elites and the administration is extremely difficult. An idea must usually have energetic sponsors among at least a few powerful leaders to receive sympathetic attention. Although the identification of the Saudi problem had no such sponsors during the first phase of coverage (October–November 2001), the idea did spread to elite circles later. For instance, the *Christian Science Monitor* (15 August 2002, 2) reported that "in May [2002] William Kristol, chairman of New American Century and a leading neoconservative voice, called at congressional hearings for the US to 'find an alternative . . . to a Saudi regime that funds and foments terror.'" Senators from both parties, including most prominently the Democratic candidate for vice president in 2000, Joseph Lieberman, publicly attacked Saudi Arabia for funding terrorism. The belief that Saudi Arabia contributed to the problem of terrorism attained enough energy to spread across the news only after some leaders began echoing that linkage back to the media.[33]

When in the summer of 2002 the extraordinary public debate pitting Republican leaders against each other erupted over Iraq, Saudi refusal to provide vital access to military bases for use as staging areas, and their general uncooperativeness, brought into relief the frame challenge that Hersh and Friedman had started back in October 2001. It was the Iraq War debate, though, that occupied center stage in the coverage. Elites, especially Congress members, lacked motivation to pursue the Saudi connection. In terms of the cascade model, the Saudi matter was perilously close to the tipping point between ambiguity and dissonant incongruity, for (as many of the editorials noted) identifying Saudi Arabia as an enemy would threaten oil supplies and raise the cost to Americans of their beloved gas-guzzling cars and SUVs. The Saudi problem was probably never destined to be more than a sidelight, albeit a nagging one from the Bush administration's perspective, but the intense opposition to Iraq did for a time gain significant media attention. The media's journey from accenting skepticism over Bush's plans in summer 2002 to celebrating the war itself in spring 2003 exemplifies the forces highlighted in the cascade model.

According to the Center for Media and Public Affairs (CMPA), a conservative media research organization, during the period July 1–August 25, 2002, 73 percent of sources quoted on ABC, CBS, and NBC news programs criticized the administration's "Iraq strategy," as did 71 percent of the sources quoted in the *New York Times*. Tellingly, 53 percent of Republican sources quoted were critical. Judging by the CMPA findings, far from serving as an administration mouthpiece, the leading media promoted opposition by conveying, even exaggerating, the scope of elite unrest over Bush's plans. But by the latter part of the prewar period, evidence suggests a reversal. A liberal media research organization, Fairness and Accuracy in Reporting (FAIR), found that in the week before and week after Colin Powell's February 5 U.N. speech, the ABC, CBS, NBC, and PBS evening news shows quoted 393 sources on camera. Of these, just 17 percent were critical of administration policy, the bulk of them non-Americans. Only 6 percent of U.S. sources opposed Bush's imminent war. Another FAIR study, of on-camera sources during the early war, found that 71 percent of the Americans appearing were war supporters and just 3 percent were opponents.[34]

None of these studies takes into account magnitude or resonance, so the data here are frustratingly incomplete. But assuming the CMPA and FAIR counts do roughly reflect media emphases, what accounts for the shift from slanting against the administration's "war soon" plan to slanting for it and underplaying the alternative of relying on the U.N.? The cascade model points to some explanations. First, as already noted, the elite source networks were buzzing with dissent in the summer of 2002. They featured the novel spectacle of Republicans attacking each other, thus satisfying the media's motivations to emphasize dramatic conflict. Scowcroft, ghostwriter to the senior George Bush, for instance, published a column in the *Wall Street Journal* directly contesting the younger Bush's attempt to connect 9/11 and Iraq: "There is scant evidence to tie Saddam to terrorist organizations, and even less to the September 11 attacks. Indeed Saddam's goals have little in common with the terrorists."[35] Some journalists used the opportunity to launch stinging analyses of Bush's foreign policy stewardship.[36]

By the fall, Republican dissenters had fallen silent, followed by most Democrats. Republicans resurrected the Cold War era charge that Democrats were "soft on defense," and most Democratic congressional leaders voiced support for presidential authority to wage war against Iraq.[37] Once Congress voted (by significantly larger margins than it had in 1991) to authorize war, opponents lost much hope of stopping Bush. In accordance with journalists' habit of calibrating attention to likelihood of influencing policy, the capitulation of Congress to Bush's war plans made remaining domestic opposition all but irrelevant. In this respect, at least, the war on terrorism apparently served the Republican president as a rhetorically effective replacement for the Cold War. Foreigners became the primary elite sources regularly attacking Bush's "war soon" frame, and the media relied largely on them, and on their own analyses, to convey the case against administration policy—the case for working through the allies and the U.N. For instance, *Time* presented two articles totaling seven pages in its issue of February 3, 2003, one detailing the objections of European allies, the other analyzing the potential for "catastrophic" chemical/biological counterattacks from Iraq and al-Qaeda.[38]

Meanwhile, the Bush administration relentlessly pursued its framing strategy, frequently linking Saddam Hussein with al-Qaeda, 9/11, weapons of mass destruction, and a direct terrorist threat on the United States. Polls suggest this campaign met considerable success. For example, a survey taken as late as July 24–25, 2003, found fully 72 percent of respondents saying, "Iraq was harboring al Qaeda terrorists and helping them to develop chemical weapons," a dubious claim that even the administration never pressed very hard.[39] By connecting Saddam to Osama bin Laden's al-Qaeda, the administration elevated the threat. This in turn cemented a sense of congruence between dominant cultural schemas and the president's frame, dampening (though not eliminating) the public's quagmire fears and isolationist impulses and further discouraging journalists from highlighting opposition.

Although much evidence suggested the public preferred U.N. reliance to unilateral invasion, the polls were, as is often the case, ambiguous. Consider an innovative survey on what to do about Iraq, conducted in February 2003, by the Program on International Policy Attitudes at the University of Maryland. It presented arguments supporting both sides of the basic dispute, war soon vs. waiting for U.N. inspections. Large majorities found both sides persuasive. For example, 69 percent thought this pro-administration argument convincing: "The longer we wait, the more advanced Iraq's weapons program will become. Saddam Hussein will be more able to the threaten the U.S. and his neighbors than he is now, and the harder it will be to stop him. So an invasion of Iraq should be launched as soon as possible." Seventy-one percent of the same sample found this antiwar argument convincing, too: "The disarmament process is a better method than invasion, because if Iraq is invaded, Saddam Hussein would have nothing left to lose and would likely use weapons of mass destruction against U.S. forces and U.S. cities, and distribute these weapons to terrorist groups." Notice that both arguments accept central and debatable premises of Bush's prowar frame, including the notion that Saddam might directly attack the United States with weapons of mass destruction, but relevant here is that majorities found arguments on both sides persuasive.

After presenting respondents with these arguments, the survey asked them to state their own preferences. By a 60–38 percent margin, respondents favored "urg[ing] the U.N. to act" over immediate, unilateral American invasion. But responses to a further question complicate the picture. Asked how they would react if the United States did go ahead and invade "on its own," 37 percent said they would agree with the decision, 36 percent that they would not agree, and 25 percent that they "would not agree with this decision" but "would still support the president." So, what does this poll tell us about majority opinion before the war? By one count, the figures depict a 62–36 percent majority supporting Bush's decision; by another, a 61–37 percent majority opposing it.[40] Even a sophisticated survey cannot pin down a clear majority opinion. As chapter 6 discusses in detail, the openness of public opinion to varying interpretations allows media frames to play a central role in shaping elites' perceptions of the public's views. In this case, supportive news frames and confusing polls reinforced elites' tendencies to soft-peddle attacks on the president, further diminishing the media's interest in questioning Bush's plans.

Moreover, as suggested earlier in this chapter, many in the media have themselves favored a muscular, interventionist American foreign policy, and they seemed genuinely persuaded by the Bush administration's arguments. Thus even the reputedly liberal *Washington Post* took a hawkish stand on Iraq. It ran nine prowar (and no antiwar) unsigned editorials between December 1, 2002, and February 21, 2003, along with 39 prowar and just 12 antiwar op-ed columns.[41]

Finally, Bush and top officials in the administration brought intense pressure to bear on media personnel and organizations to toe the White House line. After 9/11, with exceptions discussed below, media bosses seemed wary indeed about appearing to tolerate employees with anti-administration sentiments. MSNBC, for example, canceled the *Phil Donahue Show* before the war because he was, according to an internal memo, "a tired, leftwing liberal out of touch with the current marketplace," who would be "a difficult public face for NBC in a time of war" and would offer "a home for the liberal antiwar agenda at the same time that our competitors are waving the flag at every opportunity."[42] Separately, Erik Sorenson, MSNBC's president, said he was trying to differentiate his network's approach: "After September 11th the country wants more optimism and benefit of the doubt. . . . It's about being positive as opposed to being negative. If it ends up negative, so be it. But a big criticism of the mainstream press is that the beginning point is negative: 'On Day 2,we're in a quagmire.'"[43] As war approached, a member of the Dixie Chicks country music band criticized President Bush, unleashing a wave of condemnation that spread across the talk radio world and gained amplification by other rightwing media voices. Clear Channel, the country's largest radio station owner, boycotted the band's music,[44] and also used some of its stations to organize prowar rallies. CBS pressed for the firing of a documentary producer for obliquely critical remarks on the war in an interview published by *TV Guide.*[45]

This updated form of "red-baiting" (intimidating opponents by distorting their positions to connect them with a reviled enemy)[46] targeted congressional dissenters as well. For instance, the Republican Speaker of the House and the chairman of the Republican National Committee virtually charged Senate Democratic leader Tom Daschle (who voted for the war resolution in October 2002) with treason merely because he said he was saddened that Bush's diplomacy had "failed so miserably." Other congressional Republicans and the White House press secretary joined in what a report in the *Washington Post* labeled as "coordinated rebuttals."[47] Many of the same Republicans denouncing Daschle had roundly criticized President Clinton when he projected American power in Kosovo and elsewhere, without Democratic leaders accusing them of unpatriotic behavior. The contrast illustrates the difference between the two parties' aggressiveness in pressing dissent.[48]

That the Bush administration and its allies felt obliged to orchestrate such pressure shows that even a Republican president, even after 9/11, feared the potential of media unruliness and sought to quell it.[49] With instructive exceptions, when war came, the administration succeeded in containing the potential, particularly on television. This is important because Americans typically relied on television for Iraq war coverage, with majorities apparently feeling it to be the most reliable and complete source of information; even normally heavy newspaper readers tended to increase their reliance on television rather than on newspapers.[50] Although comprehensive studies of war news were not available at press time, informal observation and impressions gleaned from obtainable data suggest that television supported the administration line in most respects, from the studio to the battlefield—at least until Bush's declaration in a May 1 speech given on an aircraft carrier that "major combat operations" were over.

The coverage then and afterward illustrates again the vacillation between propaganda and critical distance characteristic of post–Cold War news. Networks verbally and visually hyped the president's dramatic landing on the deck and carried the speech itself live. While acknowledging the event's political goals, most reports did not clarify the full scope of manipulation: rather than sailing into port, the ship anchored a mere thirty miles offshore, just to allow the telegenic but unnecessary presidential touchdown. Contradicting theatrical images of America triumphant, however, Iraqi guerrilla actions continued thereafter to kill Americans, and the frame contest again shifted toward more parity. Mutually reinforcing elite opposition, media coverage, and deteriorating polls stoked quagmire anxieties. Representative of the new media tone, *Time* magazine's lead story on July 7, 2003, was headlined "THE WAR THAT **NEVER** ENDS," and on its cover for July 14 appeared "**UN**TRUTH & CONSEQUENCES" over a picture of Bush giving the 2003 State of the Union address. The head on *Newsweek*'s lead story for July 21 read "STILL FIGHTING SADDAM," and—in clear allusion to Vietnam quagmire—the issue pictured each soldier slain after May 1. These images capture a change from general support of the war frame between February and early May to frequently vivid counterframing that challenged Bush's problem definition, remedy, and even moral status.

Television's presentation of the war before May 1 contained a profusion of visual features such as crawling text, flashing symbols, dissolving montages, and scratchy videophone images, arguably discouraging analytical thought and quiet cogitation in favor of a more emotional experience akin to playing a video game or watching a movie. Cable and broadcast networks used American flag motifs and logos, and most of their on-camera experts were former military officers, reinforcing the emphasis on battlefield events at the expense of broader diplomatic and historical context. Newspapers offered more context and opportunity for contemplation, yet driven by competition and declining circulation, many also tended to magnify battlefield coverage by placing it on front pages and using splashy graphics.[51]

Perhaps the most politically volatile dimension of visual coverage was the depiction of civilian and military casualties. American television usually employed visual symbols (puffs of smoke, flames) and sounds (booming explosions) to stand in for the actual violence, the physical suffering and obliteration of humans on both sides. Much of the time, studio reports shared the screen with images of explosions from cameras stationed on rooftops in Baghdad and other cities. These pictures functioned as "wall-paper" behind news readers, providing little information but perhaps entertaining and diverting audience members reared on video games and explosion-filled movies. But those visuals might even have de-sensitized audiences to the real human lives being lost.

New technology permitted live reports from the battlefield, affording opportunities to show the nature and consequences of combat in unprece-dented detail. The Project for Excellence in Journalism at Columbia Univer-sity studied the reports of journalists "embedded" with combat units in a sample of 40.5 hours of major newscasts on the broadcast networks, CNN, and Fox News, from the first few days of the war. Sixty-one percent of the reports were live and unedited. The advantage of live reporting is immedi-acy, but for this war immediacy was watered down. According to the study, "Not a single story examined showed pictures of people being hit by fired weapons." This, of course, is the ultimate and immediate reality of war. In one perspective the emphasis on live but restricted reports wound up "sanitizing" the war, though Bush supporters might argue that zooming in on the inevitable, appalling but well-known physical reality of human suffering in combat inherently editorializes against a war. In truth, though, reactions to seeing the true horrors of war depend heavily on the words used to frame them; images of the 9/11 carnage certainly did not spawn a wave of pacifism in America.

Perhaps having the embedded reporters as close witnesses to some as-pects of the war was better than keeping them away from combat entirely, as was the general practice during the Gulf War of 1991. But the other prob-lems with live battlefield coverage are loss of context and the potential for confusion and mistake. Reporters traveling with an individual combat unit could only know, at best, what was happening to that one group, not the larger story. As for confusion, a study by *Editor and Publisher* found fifteen different matters during the first week of the war on which "the media got it 'wrong or misreported a sliver of fact into a major event,'" largely because impressions from the embedded journalists were misinterpreted by editors and others back at the newsroom.[52]

Aside from television, the more word-reliant print media also seemed largely to reinforce the administration's frame. For example, even in the

New York Times, generally America's most liberal and independent elite newspaper, this was the description of the war's official commencement:

BAGHDAD, Iraq, March 21—The American war on Saddam Hussein exploded tonight in a ferocious display of precision bombing and cruise missile strikes that blasted the heart of the Iraqi ruler's power with a spectacular opening bulls-eye on his most forbidding palace and continued with at least 100 more devastating volleys in the first two hours.

Most of the strikes appeared aimed at the few square miles of the capital that have been the monumental showcase for Mr. Hussein's brutal form of authoritarian rule.[53]

Although all of this is arguably factual, it is difficult to imagine the Pentagon's own public relations staff coming up with a more rousing and resonant note on which to launch its invasion. Still, this story did describe the war accurately as "American," in contrast to other journalists' habitual use of the term "coalition forces" for combat units that were in most cases 100 percent American. Aside from Britain and unlike in the 1991 Gulf War, none of the other "coalition" partners in 2003 took significant combat roles. Using that word played into the administration's hands by de-emphasizing the essentially unilateral nature of this intervention.

More important to the frame was the Bush administration's key problem definition: Iraq's threatening "weapons of mass destruction" (WMD). This term became a kind of symbolic mantra in the war discourse. Secretary of State Colin Powell's core argument in his dramatic plea for support at the U.N. (5 February 2003) was that Iraq had enough chemical weapons to fill sixteen thousand battlefield shells and was still trying to fabricate nuclear weapons. A Nexis search came up with 586 news or editorial page items that used the term during the first week of war coverage alone, in just the four newspapers of largest national circulation (the *Los Angeles Times, New York Times, USA Today,* and *Washington Post*).[54] Yet in its greatest hour of peril Saddam Hussein's regime failed to use any WMD, and neither U.N. inspectors nor American forces found any after weeks or months of searching.

There was considerable evidence that the administration knew all along that significant caches of these weapons were unlikely to turn up. After Saddam fell, officials began admitting (as critics before the war had said) that the administration's real objectives went far beyond disarming Iraq. The goal was to reshape the Middle East itself by projecting American power throughout the region, establishing stability and ameliorating the conditions that bred fundamentalist Islamic terrorism. These real goals of

the war were certainly defensible if not unassailable. Yet rather than announce them, according to an ABC report by John Cochran, the administration "emphasized the danger of Saddam's weapons . . . in order to gain
legal justification for war from the United Nations and to emphasize the
danger here at home to our own people. We were not lying, said one official, who added, 'it was just a matter of emphasis.'"[55] Despite this, during
"major combat," many news narratives accepted that the core purpose of
the war was to rid Iraq of WMD that directly endangered the United States.
As one measure of this stance, major polling organizations used wording
that presumed the existence and direct threat of the weapons as a fact (such
as the Maryland polls quoted above). As another, four months after the
war started, 71 percent of respondents to one survey said they still believed
Iraq had WMD.[56]

Beyond the media's early acceptance of the administration's central
WMD theme, there is the matter of how they treated the dissent that persisted. Although journalistic skepticism grew after the president's May 1
declaration of virtual victory, before the 2003 war began, media treatment
tended to accord with practices established for antiwar protests during Vietnam: framing protesters to accentuate their marginality and irrelevance to
policy, undercounting their numbers, underplaying their substantive arguments, and focusing on the antics of the most outlandishly attired participants.[57] CNN's prime-time news host, Aaron Brown, said that the justifiability of the war was "just not a relevant question" once it started.[58] A
reasonable position, perhaps, yet only a few months earlier (summer 2002)
Republicans, including at least three prominent retired generals (Scowcroft, Norman Schwarzkopf, and Powell), were labeling Iraq a distraction
from the war on terrorism. In other words they suggested that invading
Iraq was not in America's national interests. Brown was surely correct in
the sense that the probability of protesters actually forcing an end to this
war was nil. Yet, as we saw in the first Gulf War debate, calibrating media attention to an actor's predicted influence over policy can feed a self-
fulfilling prophecy of futility.

All this makes it more noteworthy that when the war briefly seemed to
bog down early on, fears of "quagmire" materialized, and journalists did
start raising critical questions. A Nexis search of the same four major national papers mentioned above revealed the word itself appearing in eight
items during the first four days of war (20–23 March), increasing to thirteen
in the next four-day period, and seventeen the following—only to plunge
to four mentions during 2–5 April. Still, even if they did not use *quagmire,*
plenty of other skeptical voices were heard for a few days. As one example

of the media's rapid mood change, a laudatory front-page news analysis in the Washington Post on March 22, 2003, was headed "A Daring Race to Baghdad; Military Leaves Reputation for Caution in Dust." Just two days later, the same author wrote another front-page analysis headed "U.S. Casualties Expose Risks, Raise Doubts about Strategy."[59] The following excerpt from another story gives a sense of the tone that prevailed in much reporting for those few days:[60]

After 10 days of watching smart bombs, sandstorms and stiff resistance from the Iraqi regime, a capital that usually embraces the president and his strategy in wartime is beginning to show fissures. . . .

There are the Central Intelligence Agency analysts, quietly complaining that their warnings that Saddam Hussein's government might not crack like peanut brittle were dismissed. There are ex-generals on nightly television, expressing unease about a plan that relied more on speed than on numbers, and that seemed overly dependent on welcoming cheers from the Iraqis. There are field commanders like Lt. Gen. William Wallace, whose public complaints of an enemy that was "different from the one we'd war-gamed against" set off alarm bells and denials at Central Command. . . .[61]

Retired military officers and a few active in the field fed reporters' insistent questioning of defense secretary Donald Rumsfeld by attacking the secretary's war plan. The critique reflected internal debates between proponents of the "massive force" doctrine initiated by Colin Powell when he was chief of staff, and those of a new doctrine championed by Rumsfeld which called for lighter, more mobile forces protected by high-tech weaponry and air power. Rumsfeld quite reasonably complained about reporters' seeming demand for instant success.

But for our purposes, the key point is that even in the midst of the generally passive and supportive journalism of the pre–May 1 Iraq war, reporters remained exquisitely sensitive to signs of policy failure and unacceptable costs. Only when they believed that military victory would in fact be won in short order and at comparatively low cost did quagmire fears abate and celebratory coverage resume center stage. While illustrating a post–Cold War expansion in the media's potential to offer more autonomous coverage and exert independent influence, the trajectory of Iraq war coverage also traces the limits to journalists' inclinations and capacity to distance themselves from the administration and other elites, especially with a Republican in the White House. Some of the normative issues raised by the 2003 war coverage will be discussed in the concluding chapter of the book.

Conclusion

The end of the Cold War loosened cognitive constraints, creating conditions for heightened media influence. However, the conventional caveats apply with more force than usual in this chapter: The hypothesized traits of the post–Cold War media–opinion–foreign policy system are just that. Methodical analysis of media content and other data is necessary to generate a more precise and comprehensive understanding of that system.

The hypotheses suggest we might expect increased media influence under some circumstances. However, we must also remember that President Clinton plunged ahead despite unsupportive media: in Haiti (where he dispatched American troops in 1994 to knock out a dictatorial regime and promote democracy) and in Bosnia and Kosovo. Officials have motivations that can override news frames and indicators of public opposition. Hidden diplomatic opportunities or espionage data, political courage, and rational calculation of national self-interest can trump domestic political calculations—which many would argue is just as it should be.[62] Furthermore, as the cascade model reminds us, given time and skill, presidents need not accept the media's and public's "no" for an answer. They can attempt to change news frames. And in line with the prediction that Republicans enjoy more success at this than Democrats, President George W. Bush's experience differed from Clinton's.

Suggesting that the media enjoyed increased opportunities to exert independent influence after the Cold War in no way implies that the media came to *determine* public opinion or public policy by themselves. As the cascade model makes clear, the media are enmeshed in a hierarchical system of interdependence, the White House remains at its apex, and the framing of foreign news is susceptible to multiple influences from above and below. But it does appear reasonable to suspect that the hierarchy flattened a bit, that power over news frames became less unequal than before. Put in terms of the model, the Cold War's end produced what we might call *network disruption*. Habitual associations among ideas no longer appeared so predictably. Elite source networks began to produce more variable ideas, and news texts to contain more contradiction of the White House line. Within Republican and Democratic administrations alike, uncertainty and dissent would erupt, occasionally in surprising places, opening space for— though certainly not guaranteeing—a less regimented media text.

The findings suggest the difficulty of reviving habits of thought previously tied to Soviet communism and connecting them consistently to a new paradigm of global war on terrorism. Linking all foreign problems together as part of the terrorist threat against the United States proved a tougher sell than was constructing similar associations to Cold War communism, as illustrated by the Republicans' arguments over taking action against Iraq in 2002. Terrorism's shifting locales and villains, and its transnational, global organizations provided a weaker basis than the Red Menace for a new dominant paradigm. Communism had a clear and unchanging headquarters in the Soviet Union, a superpower whose armed might posed a direct threat. A war on terrorism must encompass a kaleidoscopic mix of nations, most of which pose no plausible direct threat to America even if they give aid and comfort to groups that might. Osama bin Laden, al-Qaeda, and the Taliban, however demonic, were not trying to take over the United States (or Europe), as most believed the Soviet Union would have liked to do. Only by instilling the belief that Saddam Hussein's Iraq was part of the terrorist conspiracy to attack the United States itself could the 2003 war be sold to many Americans. Other nations do not provide such familiar, villainous leaders to connect with a terrorism paradigm. Consider that all but two of the 9/11 terrorists came from Egypt or Saudi Arabia, two previously friendly regimes whose leaders the White House could not suddenly frame as enemies. Yet the leader of al-Qaeda and much of its funding and ideological foundation also came from Saudi Arabia.

In a further mark of the confusing ambiguity arising even from September 11th, the country that turned out to be the most important ally in defeating the Taliban was Pakistan, which until *that very day* had been the Taliban's strongest diplomatic supporter. Pakistan also gave critical assistance in North Korea's development of nuclear weapons—the same North Korea that George W. Bush cited in the 2002 State of the Union speech as part of the "axis of evil" (along with Iraq and Iran). This revitalized nuclear program precipitated a severe heightening of tensions between North Korea and the United States even as America continued to rely on Pakistan's aid in the war on terrorism. The kinds of convoluted relationships exhibited among Pakistan, Afghanistan, North Korea, and the United States in the wake of September 11th resist simple enemy/friend classifications, and most importantly for our purposes, they might enhance opportunities for increased media distance from the White House line.

Despite the Bush administration's general strategic skill and success in turning media toward applying its "war on terrorism" frame to Iraq rather than Saudi Arabia, something like frame parity over going to war unilaterally against Iraq did arise during summer 2002. The unusual spectacle of open internecine warfare within Republican ranks made it happen, but journalists' professional motivations contributed independently to the framing. The media's apparent tilt did *not* reflect forceful dissent from Democratic elites, or open revolt by hoards of Republican lawmakers. Most of them cooperated or remained mum. Journalists have career incentives to exploit internal administration discord and to balance White House frame dominance—when cultural ambiguity permits, as it did that summer. For during that time, the link between the policy of making war on Iraq and the unifying war-on-terrorism frame remained murky. The White House did not stand still for this situation. During the autumn of 2002 it deployed not just public relations skills but power over the government apparatus to reassert frame control and legitimize the urgency of war. For instance, the Pentagon created a new unit to produce intelligence finding more supportive of Iraq's link to terrorism than CIA reports had been.[63]

Nonetheless, pressure from media and foreign (and internal) dissent imposed real diplomatic and economic costs on the United States and political costs on the administration. The latter became especially acute when Saddam Hussein's fall was followed not by peace but by mounting American casualties and financial costs. Although the media celebrated the deaths of Saddam's two villainous sons in late July 2003, questions about Bush's main justifications for going to war (and Saudi complicity in 9/11) kept percolating, and by then Bush's approval ratings were down significantly in various polls from their April peak. (For instance, *Newsweek*'s survey of 24–25 July showed overall approval deteriorating from 71 to 57 percent.) The media alone certainly did not cause these difficulties for the Bush administration, but they did contribute to the cascade of thoughts and events, constraints and choices, with which the White House had to contend.

Beyond empirical matters, this chapter suggests a pressing obligation to think through the normative issues. What do we want the media and the public to do, now that the Cold War is over and we have a radically reconfigured international system? What is a legitimate role for public opinion? How do we judge media performance: do we want pictures of horror in Somalia, Kosovo, or Liberia, or of precision bombs in Afghanistan and Iraq surgically hitting their unseen or inanimate targets, to frame public thinking and elites' rhetoric and policy options? If not, what do we want? These questions receive further attention in the final two chapters.

6. REPRESENTING THE PUBLIC'S OPINIONS IN FOREIGN POLICY

My focus thus far has been on the downward cascading of framed interpretations moving from the administration and other leaders to journalists and their reports, and on to the public. But we have already seen that influence flows the other way as well: leaders calculate the political costs and benefits of attacking the administration by assessing the apparent state of public opinion, and sometimes the White House finds itself constrained by public sentiments as well. This chapter looks in greater detail at the role of media frames in forming impressions of public opinion, with specific reference to public sentiments on the U.S. defense budget and on nuclear arms control. The ultimate goal is to clarify democratic representation in foreign policy: can and does the public exert much independent influence over officials' thinking and actions? The answer: it is difficult to say. This chapter shows that public opinion, officials' behavior, and news frames are so thoroughly *inter*dependent that definitive conclusions about the citizenry's power and representation remain elusive.[1]

Prior research into the impact of public opinion on public policy offers surprisingly little insight into exactly how elites figure out what the public is thinking. Most treatments simply assume that political motivations lead officials more or less accurately to detect and respond to public opinion. This chapter opens up this critical path of political communication to reveal the complex interplay of news frames with the thinking of elites and citizens. Three insights from the cascade model are especially pertinent here:

1. The public's actual opinions arise from framed information, from selected highlights of events, issues, and problems rather than from direct contact with the realities of foreign affairs.
2. Elites for their part cannot know the full reality of public thinking and feeling, but must rely on selective interpretations that draw heavily on news frames.
3. Policymakers relentlessly contend to influence the very news frames that influence them.

In this process, officials must take account of several facets of public opinion, not just the standard measure of majority preferences. Despite their importance to leaders, these distinct faces of public opinion are rarely teased apart in empirical research. Elucidating and suggesting how news frames influence them is the first task of this chapter. Next I illustrate the usefulness of the distinctions through exploring and expanding on previous research into the impact of public opinion on defense spending, with particular attention to the role not just of public opinion but also of media in spurring the military buildup under President Reagan. The discussion concludes with an analysis of public opinion expressed via a social movement, the nuclear freeze campaign, rather than through the crude channel of survey responses (as with defense spending). The freeze movement was undermined by media frames despite its mainstream orientation, and despite surveys that consistently showed overwhelming public approval of its proposal.

Framing Is Inescapable

Although the schemas and interpretations within individuals' minds arise from prior beliefs and interpersonal communication as well as from the media's words and images, there is no escape from framing. For foreign affairs, few people have direct data, and most information originates in media reports even if it is passed along selectively (or framed) in conversation with informants who themselves saw the news. Answers to questions on how much the United States should spend on defense, for instance (the case discussed below), respond to media threat signals—few citizens have anywhere else to get their information on enemies' military intentions and capabilities.[2] At least for foreign policy, there are few if any cases where a pure, unmediated public opinion emerges directly from reality. That does not mean everyone responds to the media's frames identically, but it does mean that most people's opinions will be influenced by their reactions to the frames.

This holds even for events as overwhelmingly blunt as the September 11, 2001, attacks. Americans would have responded with revulsion and outrage no matter what the media said. But this reaction in itself does not convey enough information about public opinion to be useful for policymakers or meaningful to representation. The real issue, and the important role for media and public opinion in the political process, is determining which problem definition, cause, and policy response gain widespread adherence. These interpretations are rarely automatically deduced from the event itself, even one as thoroughly evil as 9/11. As we saw in the previous chapter, the events of September 11 could have been framed differently, with Saudi Arabia portrayed as an enemy, a corrupt dictatorship operating as the chief financial and cultural sponsor of Islamic extremism and terrorism. The decision to go to war against the Taliban government of Afghanistan rather than the House of Saud was not an inescapable response to unmediated reality that every American would somehow naturally support no matter how the media depicted the terrorists.

Another example was President George W. Bush's framing of Iraq as a greater immediate problem for the United States than North Korea in early 2003, despite intelligence reports that the latter might be capable of launching nuclear missiles that could reach mainland America. At minimum Bush's decision to place the latter issue on the back burner while the nation prepared for war with Iraq was debatable, and the media's decisions to allocate far more magnitude and resonance to the Iraq crisis at that time, politically consequential.

So much should be clear from the preceding chapters. But the second point is that framing is just as inevitable going in the other direction, upward from the public's actual sentiments to officials' interpretations of public opinion. When we are considering frames of public opinion transmitted from the grassroots to the nation's leaders, a slightly simplified definition of "framing" probably applies best: selecting and highlighting aspects of a perceived reality—in this case, of public sentiments—to communicate a particular interpretation. Any description of public opinion is such a selective interpretation, an abstraction from the blooming, buzzing maelstrom of individual Americans' actual political thinking and emotions. Throughout the book, the term "indicators" of public opinion has been used because indicators are what both officials and researchers rely on: selected data that highlight some aspects of, or frame, the public's views.

Perceived public opinion, which may or may not closely match the views recorded in surveys,[3] is a valued resource very much worth arguing over and controlling, because leaders in a democracy need to associate their activities with public approval. Even in a traditionally elite-dominated process like the making of foreign policy,[4] the post-Vietnam conventional wisdom among officials holds that leaders should avoid perceptions that the public opposes their policy.[5] Selective interpretations of the public's views therefore enter the political fray just like arguments over policy itself, becoming objects of strategic, manipulative communications.

Research has shown that elites often misread public opinion, sometimes willfully, sometimes not.[6] One reason is that, except for presidents, who have the resources to support continuous, sophisticated polling operations,[7] leaders do not have good survey data. Powlick and Katz observe that "[p]olicy deliberations do not involve empirical indications of current public attitudes on a specific issue. . . . [T]he vast majority of officials have no institutionally generated information on public opinion upon which to rely."[8] Instead, "Congress and the news media represent important proxies or 'operationalizations' of public opinion for foreign policy officials."[9] Rather than attending carefully to polls, most leaders find their interpretations of public opinion by consulting *other leaders* and *news coverage*. Thus a 1998 survey of eighty-one members of Congress, ninety-eight presidential appointees, and 151 members of the Senior Executive Service[10] found evidence that media reports are the most important source of executive branch officials' perceptions of public sentiments, more important than polls (with the exception of the closely monitored survey tapping presidential job approval):

> [L]eaders rely heavily on the media. Three-in-four presidential appointees and fully 84% of senior executives list the media as their main source of information about public opinion. Members of Congress are more likely to cite personal contacts and communication from constituents, although those on the Hill also say the media is a major source of information. Few government leaders say they rely on public opinion polls, but as many as 80% could recall Clinton's approval ratings with reasonable accuracy at the time of the interview.

As we have seen throughout the book, leaders work proactively to shape media frames, promoting news that will stimulate public support, dampen opposition, and, most important, promote the *perception* that public opinion is in their corner.[11] From the KAL and Iran Air incidents to Grenada and Libya, Panama, Haiti, the Balkans, and Afghanistan, polls have shown public responsiveness to the dominant frames in the news. And irrespective of any impact on the public's responses to surveys, news frames influence elites' understanding of the political stakes in policy decisions, their substantive thinking about policy, and their perceptions of how other elites are assessing the policy substance and politics. Precisely because news frames influence their fellow elites in all these ways, even as they are themselves experiencing these effects, leaders try to shape the frames. The constant jousting to win frame contests and thus control "news spin" are designed as much to *influence their fellow leaders* as public opinion.

Information about public opinion only imperfectly reflects a rather complicated underlying reality. In fact, public opinion can be framed to highlight many different dimensions of public sentiments and promote a variety of interpretations. Among the most important of these facets of public opinion to elites' assessments of the political situation are the following:

(1) *Polling opinion* consists of the policy (or candidate) preferences that

are tapped by polls. Despite the well-known shortcomings of surveys,[12] the measures do matter to democratic politics and to foreign policy decisions. Although especially in the aggregate (that is, multiple poll results accumulated over significant periods of time) surveys may provide meaningful indicators of majority preferences,[13] polling opinion at any single point in time is particularly susceptible to framing and thus to media influence in several senses. Both media and pollsters frame issues for respondents, selecting cues that affect individual responses to survey questions. The framing effects come from the survey wording and interview experience, from recently publicized "top of the head" considerations that are most accessible as people briefly consider the question and give a quick answer without taking much time to think it over,[14] and from interactions of ignorance and knowledge with interpretation of the questions.[15] The media affect all of these framing operations (including pollsters' choices of questions and wording) through what they have been reporting around the time of the survey, and what they have *not* been reporting with sufficient magnitude and resonance to penetrate awareness.[16]

(2) *Perceived majorities* consist of the perceptions held by most journalists, political elites, and members of the public themselves[17] of just where the majority of the public stands. As already suggested, perceived majorities often do not match polling opinion. A good example is foreign aid. Most foreign policy leaders interviewed by Kull and Ramsay said Americans would prefer to eliminate foreign aid entirely. Repeated surveys actually show large majorities supporting substantial increases in foreign aid.[18] The same holds true for U.S. participation in U.N. peacekeeping missions: most policymakers felt majorities opposed this when polls have shown hefty majorities in support.[19] But polls often send conflicting signals and ignoring unfavorable surveys can be politically advantageous.[20] Perhaps in part for that reason, elites develop their perceptions of majority views less from surveys than from the dominant frames of the issues and events in the news, which are assumed to move public opinion in certain directions, from the way media reports invoke "public opinion" and frame Americans' views, and from the strategic talk and actions of other leaders who try to convince everyone that the "American people" favor their position.

(3) *Anticipated majorities* are the predictions of how majority opinion will respond to future outcomes. Politicians and other leaders anticipate public reactions when thinking through alternative courses of action.[21] The anticipation that an action will arouse strong opposition among majorities or key constituents can (and in many versions of democratic theory, should) exert a potent influence on policymaking. After all, officials seldom know

the political payoff of anything they do in advance. The unknown and risky future course of public opinion certainly concerns and constrains policymakers. Anticipating that majorities would oppose continued involvement and losses in Somalia, for example, President Clinton in 1993 withdrew U.S. forces soon after the battle of Mogadishu.[22] But that does not mean leaders always passively shy away from policies that might arouse the public's wrath. Instead, as we have seen throughout this book, they often mount campaigns to generate positive (or at least neutral) publicity.[23] Another name for this might be leadership.

(4) *Priorities* embody the trade-offs that people would prefer among different, incompatible preferences when making two key summary political choices: (i) voting and (ii) responding to surveys on "approval" of a president or other leader. By what they report and how they frame, the news media can help determine whether people heavily weigh personal character when rating a presidential candidate, whether they judge experience in foreign affairs rather than character as key, and so forth. The literature on framing and priming and other research[24] suggests that manipulating priorities may be easier than manipulating preferences themselves. For political purposes, that may be enough. Reducing a policy to low priority— that is, irrelevance to most Americans' voting decisions or to their responses in performance evaluation surveys ("How would you rate the job the president is doing?")—can be as politically consequential as generating actual support of the policy.[25] If politicians, who may infer these things largely from the magnitude and resonance of news frames, sense that public opinion about an event or issue is likely to hold a low priority when election time rolls around, they can heavily discount it.[26]

Consider Ronald Reagan's first term as president. His administration's political success arose more from its ability to manage priorities and perceived majorities than from inducing a majority of Americans to agree with his policies. If we believe the polls on issue preferences, majorities persistently disagreed with many of the foreign (and domestic) policies Reagan pursued,[27] including the two discussed in this chapter. Based on his 1984 reelection, however, we have to conclude that the majority of the voting public did not weigh such issues as arms control and defense spending heavily at the ballot box, poll results notwithstanding.

Perceived and anticipated majorities and priorities are more important than polling opinion. Leaders can be ignorant of, or misread, survey results. If they weigh public opinion in their decisions at all, it will be the public opinion and priorities they perceive and anticipate (perhaps along with the public opinion they think other leaders perceive and anticipate).

Representation in the National Defense

Like political leaders, scholars who endeavor to represent "public opinion" (through their research data and analyses) must also engage in framing. Since they cannot easily capture public thinking in all its dimensions, researchers also employ selected aspects highlighted by polls—normally, they treat *polling opinion* as equivalent to public opinion, and this creates complexities for empirical theory and normative judgment.[28] That observation brings us to the first case study in this chapter, on defense spending. An important article by Hartley and Russett[29] on the impact of public opinion on defense policy connects normative democratic theory with empirical data to ask "Who governs military spending in the United States?" It serves as a good basis for anchoring the analysis of the inescapability of framing in studying public opinion, and helps to clarify the often-neglected influences of news media on representation. Reflecting a view common in recent political science, the article concludes that "public opinion" significantly helps "govern." However, if much of the public opinion this study identifies is actually polling opinion, and thus has been influenced by media frames, that conclusion demands further scrutiny.

The study finds that between 1965 and 1990, "changes in public opinion consistently exert an effect on changes in military spending."[30] It measures public opinion by responses to a standard survey question: whether government is spending too little, too much, or about the right amount on defense. Employing pooled estimates from six different polling organizations to generate unusually reliable estimates, Hartley and Russett find that changes in the levels of "too little" (or "too much") responses significantly predict alteration in the total defense obligations Congress approved (spending figures in constant 1982 dollars).[31] On this basis the authors argue that, judging by the case of defense spending, Congress responded to public opinion, fulfilling its representative duties according to at least one reasonable version of democracy.

Of particular interest for our purposes here is the period encompassing the Carter and Reagan administrations (1977–89), which saw the widest swings in public sentiment and provided the best opportunity for congressional responsiveness, although similar arguments could be made for the Johnson and Nixon years. Surveys showed a large shift toward favoring more spending during the years 1978–81, and Congress did approve sharp increases in defense spending thereafter.

Yet Congress failed to respond to several other strains of what polls suggest were majority sentiments during the period. Congress did not mandate that Reagan approach nuclear negotiations seriously in his first term,[32] nor did it approve a nuclear freeze, though surveys showed majorities favoring such action, often by upwards of 75 percent. If one used the survey data only on the nuclear freeze while ignoring the data on defense spending, one could well conclude Congress was entirely unresponsive to the public on defense policy. Of course it may be that the public was conflicted on the nuclear freeze or that survey questions on it gave misleading impressions of the actual underlying individual preferences and priorities of citizens. But this only reinforces the point that public opinion is usually a product of selective interpretation or framing.

Add the fact that, as Bartels notes, the same polls recording increases in public desires for higher spending on defense simultaneously recorded demands for "social programs, tax reduction, and fiscal responsibility," which "manifestly limited the ability of Congress to respond to each of them separately."[33] In this sense it would appear nearly arbitrary to pick one dimension where opinion and congressional action seemed to coincide while neglecting others where they did not, and then drawing general conclusions on government responsiveness.

Looking more carefully at defense spending data raises additional questions about representation. As figure 6.1 suggests,[34] there was a noticeable lack of representation from 1982 to 1985, when Congress continued to raise defense spending despite the sharp dovish turn in polling opinion. Those favoring an increase rose from 40 percent in 1979 to 58 percent in 1980 and 60 percent in 1981. But the next year saw this proportion plummet to 35 percent, then to 22 percent in 1983, and even lower after that. Surveyed sentiment shifted even more sharply *away* from defense spending during this time than it had turned *toward* support between 1977 and 1981, so if Congress was responding to altered public sentiment it should have cut defense—or at least slowed the rate of increase—by 1983 or 1984. Yet defense spending began declining in real terms only in *fiscal 1990*. Defense allocations kept growing as public support declined. The *rate* of growth in spending began slowing notably in fiscal 1987, which might signify a response to public opinion.[35] But here we had decisions to raise defense budgets that persisted for eight years (1982–89) against a sharp and persistent dovish trend in opinion, a trend that soon reduced the proportion of citizens favoring those increases to a small minority. Classifying such policies as responsive would seem to mark a striking redefinition of democratic representation.[36]

Now it might be that officials interpreted the 1983 surge in negative media symbols spurred by the KAL incident (see chapter 2 and below) as sig-

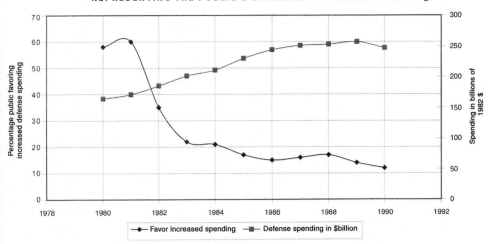

FIGURE 6.1 *Increased Defense Spending Despite Drop in Public Support, 1980–90*

naling that public opinion favored even more spending hikes, despite polls showing it did not. Such a possibility would be consistent with the research cited earlier, indicating that officials infer elements of public opinion—perceived and anticipated majorities, and priorities—from media content. Perhaps elites anticipated that majorities would prefer more defense spending once they digested the heightened threat, and would weigh defense as a high enough priority to punish softness come election time. In addition, public opinion was frequently depicted in the media as highly supportive of the unabashedly hawkish Reagan. Even though Reagan's average approval ratings were actually quite low in his first term, news reports tended to laud his popularity.[37] And indeed, by his second term Reagan's average approval was relatively high. From the perceived majority support in his first term and actual polling opinion in his second, officials might well have inferred a low priority for the public's apparent desires to cut defense spending—and maybe they were correct. This could explain, in part, the lack of congressional responsiveness to the clear turn of surveyed majorities against higher defense budgets starting in 1982.

But another major reason for continued budget growth during this period was that long-term commitments to weapons systems had been made at the outset. Once weapons programs begin they are difficult to stop. Spending momentum is reinforced by electoral incentives in specific congressional districts where military spending is vital to the economy; their representatives often exert disproportionate influence over defense budgets. And an enormous military-industrial complex—very much including the Pentagon itself—has compelling incentives and vast resources to lobby Congress and engage in public relations initiatives to keep the defense contracts coming. These points further underscore the complexity of generalizing about government responsiveness to public opinion.

Further, although surveys did not ask, surely few Americans preferred defense money to be spent carelessly, corruptly, or without real congressional oversight. Nor would Americans have favored giving free rein to a Pentagon bureaucracy ill prepared to handle rapid budgetary growth, to an agency where intense rivalries between the armed services guaranteed that protecting turf and prestige would often weigh more heavily in decisions than the goal of securing the most effective national defense. Yet Congress (and the White House) did allow bureaucratic mismanagement to flourish, as the costly "Pentagon procurement scandal"[38] of the 1980s confirmed.[39] Unless we classify only positive acts, not failures to act, or failures to act responsibly, as part of the legislative "response," Congress's neglect of careful policy analysis and oversight suggests a lack of responsiveness to public desires.

Beyond this, the survey data on raising or cutting defense spending cannot tell us whether the public ever wanted the *magnitude* of increase approved by Congress during the 1980s. A much smaller increase might have been enough to satisfy most Americans even at their most hawkish. This seems especially likely in view of many other poll findings, some from the very surveys on "more" or "less" government spending that the authors use, of large majorities desiring higher budgets for crime fighting, education, health care, or other domestic priorities.[40] For example, the net polling opinion in 1982 (the percentage saying "cut back" spending subtracted from that saying "expand" it) was +52 percent for education, +43 percent for Social Security, but −10 percent for defense. Apparently, more people wanted to cut than expand defense, while by substantial margins they favored increased domestic spending.[41] In fact, asked specifically in 1982 whether they favored the 18 percent increase in defense spending proposed by President Reagan for fiscal 1983, only a small minority of respondents (19 percent) said yes. Favoring a lesser increase were 20 percent, and supporting no increase or a cut, 59 percent.[42]

Furthermore, probing defense spending attitudes during the 1990s, after military budgets were reduced, Kull and Ramsay still found substantial willingness to support further cuts, so long as opinions were probed in detail and in larger context rather than simply asking the one question on spending more or less. Their data also showed elites tending to overestimate public support for high defense spending:

> [P]olls that probe more deeply show support for substantial cuts, including polls that ask respondents to (1) specify their preferred spending level; (2) consider defense spending in a budgetary context when respondents are informed about the actual amount of defense spending; (3) propose defense spending levels relative to potential enemies; (4) make tradeoffs between defense spending and nonmilitary international spending; and (5) evaluate the requirement for the United States to be prepared to fight two major regional wars. If the president and Congress were to agree to cut defense spending 10–20%, strong majorities say they would be supportive. If these funds were to be explicitly redirected into popular domestic programs, overwhelming majorities say they would approve.[43]

Of course, public opinion could and did change in response to new circumstances, such as the terrorist attacks of September 11, 2001.

But going back to the 1980s, to conclude from some poll evidence that the public then really preferred to raise defense spending as much as Congress did over alternative uses of the money, scholars and Congress members themselves had to select some polling data and disregard the kinds of polls just cited. Include all the information at once and guidance from public opinion (or the "popular will")[44] becomes, at the least, murky. This brings up the cyclical majority problem,[45] the common situation in which a majority might prefer option a to b and c (say defense spending increases to education increases and tax cuts), but a majority composed of different people might prefer b to a and c (education over the other two) and a still differently composed majority might most prefer c (tax cuts). The cycle goes around with no "correct" resolution. The decision among the three is determined by the structure of political rules and strategic communication among decisionmakers, most importantly the framing of the choices so that a particular dimension of the trade-off is highlighted and others suppressed.[46]

Acknowledging this process suggests limited expectations for democratic responsiveness. Public opinion includes a variety of individual preferences and intensities, contradictions and harmonies, which are imperfectly susceptible to measurement and aggregation whether by public officials or by scholars.[47] As for measuring government response, aside from whatever Congress as a whole decided, the degree to which individual legislators were responding to mass opinion also varied from member to member.

Many voting for increased spending had long propagated pessimistic readings of Soviet intentions and thus "responded" to perceived or anticipated majorities they helped engender[48] (although no doubt others more genuinely responded by voting for more spending than they seemed to prefer personally).[49]

The Hartley and Russett study does consider more broadly this possibility that public opinion is a dependent variable, that public support followed rather than preceded military spending increases. But it concludes that changes in defense spending do not cause parallel changes in opinion, and thus that public opinion contributes independently to defense policy. However, the absence of a statistical relationship between actual level of defense spending and the public's surveyed preferences raises an important puzzle. It would be difficult to understand, let alone represent, a citizenry that remained indifferent to *current* levels of defense spending when asked about spending more or less. A "spend more" or "spend less" response would appear meaningless if we assume respondents in the aggregate do not assess current spending levels. Yet just such a disengaged public and problematic survey response are implied if we accept the finding that spending levels have no influence on polling opinion.[50] It seems more likely, for example, that the well-publicized sharp increases in defense expenditures, along with messages in the (news and entertainment) media about the horrors of nuclear war[51] stimulated an anti–defense spending reaction in 1982–85.[52] Many more people had "top of the head" concerns about nuclear war, and perceptions that spending had already increased substantially, so their opinion statements changed.[53] And indeed such change suggests a "pretty prudent" public reacting reasonably to news reports of altered conditions.[54]

In fact, the degree of Soviet threat represented in the mass media corresponds closely to the movement of polling opinion on defense spending. The data in table 6.1 were compiled by searching for all *Washington Post* stories since 1977 (the first year the *Post*'s archives were computerized) in which the words "Russia" or "Soviet" occurred within twenty-five words of "aggression," "buildup," or "threat." Each story was checked to ensure the passages containing the terms did refer to the USSR's actions or intentions.[55]

The relationship graphs nicely; figure 6.2 shows how the two moved in tandem. The number of threat references peaked in 1980, and public backing of higher defense budgets peaked the following year. (The sharp upward movement in mediated threats during 1983 resulted from Reagan's "evil empire" speech in March of that year and, especially, the autumn crisis over the Soviets' destruction of Korean Airlines Flight 007, after which the

TABLE 6.1 *Public Support of Increased Defense Spending and Stories of Soviet Threat*

	Percent Favor More Spending	No. of USSR Threat Stories
1977	33	149
1978	37	176
1979	40	232
1980	58	527
1981	60	385
1982	35	305
1983	22	432
1984	21	212
1985	17	186
1986	15	170
1987	16	211
1988	17	154
1989	14	103
1990	12	139

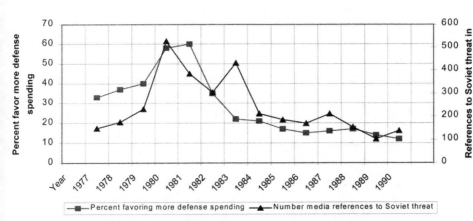

FIGURE 6.2 *Support for More Defense Spending and Media References to Soviet Threat*

trend continued downward.) The correlation is quite high for this kind of research (Pearson's $r = .69$, $p < .01$), and the measure is not even very refined. With enough searching and fine-tuning one could probably match up media content with the movement of public opinion even more precisely.[56]

Indeed, if the media measure were entered into the Hartley–Russett calculations while omitting the survey data, one might conclude that Congress responds attentively to *media* rather than to public opinion. That is *not* the argument here. These data do not allow us to infer that alterations in the news caused policy changes; for one thing, again, defense spending did not drop significantly until 1990 despite the decline in mediated threats. Nor can the data prove that the changes in these symbols of threat were significant causes of the shifts in polling opinion. The point is quite different: namely, that it is difficult even conceptually to disentangle these relationships. Entering both the polling and media data together into an equation to explain variation in defense spending would not be appropriate to the complexity of the underlying relationships. Perceived and actual public sentiments influence and are influenced by elites and policy; all of these influence and are influenced by media; and obtainable measures of elite and mass opinion, of policy itself[57] and of media content, are all deeply problematic.

Let us illustrate this point more concretely by sketching a scenario of how the perception of increased Soviet threat might have arisen in the first place, a scenario supported by Rojecki's historical analysis.[58] The setting begins with the earliest murmurings of heightened threat originating from presidential candidate Ronald Reagan and other hawks in 1976. These views were not responses to a clear leap forward in Soviet capability, nor did they reflect a marked deterioration in America's military superiority; rather they represented a combination of sincere conviction with a calculation that the public would respond favorably to another round of bashing communists. They stimulated a snowballing trend of increasingly negative framing of the Soviet Union in the news. Although Ronald Reagan failed to secure the GOP nomination in 1976, the primary fight gave President Gerald Ford a big scare, and Ford toughened his rhetoric and policy stands in response, even going to the extent of having the CIA commission an outside review of Soviet intentions by a "Team B" of hard-line alarmists. Their report predictably found America in dire peril. Reacting to this document and to continual pressure from Ford and other leaders during the campaign and after his narrow victory in November, President Jimmy Carter also backed off from initial proposals to cut the defense budget and promised to maintain American superiority while vigilantly confronting the Soviets. When they invaded Afghanistan the last week of 1979, less than two months after Americans were taken hostage in Iran, Carter's rhetoric and actions became about as strident as Reagan's and filled the media with more intensely negative images.

Notice that although these certainly appeared to be troubling developments at the time, it was not inevitable that they be framed to heighten a sense of threat. The media were full of assertions that the Soviet invasion was just a first step on the way to wider aggression that would threaten the Middle East and its oil supplies. And President Carter framed the hostage situation as a world-historical crisis. The Afghanistan invasion turned out to be a colossal blunder, one that accelerated the collapse of Soviet communism. The last gasp of a dying empire, the invasion never portended Soviet willingness to risk World War III by invading Iran or Saudi Arabia. And the hostage situation, painful as it was to the individuals involved, was not inherently a crisis for the entire nation. Carter may have hyped the incident in part out of his anticipation that public opinion would rally around his presidency, which it did for a while. But failing to resolve this crisis arguably cost Carter reelection in 1980.[59] So Carter was responsive to public opinion, and public opinion responsive to him, but neither side was very happy in the end.

President Reagan learned from Carter's mistakes and played down the hostage situation that he faced in Lebanon, even though it could well have been considered a virtually identical crisis, one similarly humiliating of the United States. (Although it involved only a handful of hostages compared with the fifty-two in Tehran, those in Lebanon remained captives far longer, and at least one was murdered, whereas no American hostages died in Iran.)[60] But together the dominant framings of the Afghanistan invasion and Iran hostage incident propelled a sharp increase in mediated symbols of threat against America, and public support for defense spending in the standard survey question shot up in 1980, only to fall back to near normal levels by 1982.

Now, looking at all these forces at play, it appears the media played a role in shaping outcomes, along with leaders' talk, actions, and perceptions of public opinion, and the public's actual sentiments. In this jumbled spiral, this double helix, of reciprocal influences, movements, and resistances among elites and the public, evidence for the independent influence of public opinion on policy, or for genuinely democratic control of government by the public, is likely to remain incomplete.[61]

The dramatic divergence between surveyed opinion and defense spending during most of the 1980s suggests the need to develop more inclusive models that can explain the many spells of clear unresponsiveness as well as periods that seem to indicate responsiveness, that can distinguish the episodes where polling opinion changes independent of elite information blitzes from those where any shift arises from the White House's management of the news. Public opinion—whether framed as polling opinion, perceived and anticipated majorities, or priorities—appears to be a sporadic constraint,[62] not a controlling force on which government depends to guide its choices. Although media frames do serve as a kind of transmission belt, communicating the public's thinking up to elites as well as moving information in the reverse direction, so many complexities and imperfections mark this process that optimistic conclusions about public control[63] appear unfounded. The appendix to this chapter considers another, far more complex model of responsiveness to public opinion (on domestic policy); it argues that the model would be more accurate (although perhaps less elegant) if it took news frames into account.

The Frozen Out Public

When we turn to public opinion articulated in a more active and precise form than merely answering survey questions, evidence suggests that far from being eager to respond, journalists and elites may in some instances not even favor much public input into foreign policy. Scholars have long recognized that, however accounted and described, public opinion surveys send imprecise signals.[64] Perhaps a more efficient vehicle for the expression of public opinion than surveys are social movements. A paper written jointly with Andrew Rojecki[65] explored the media's unfavorable framing of the "nuclear freeze" movement. This section summarizes its findings and draws lessons for the questions raised in this chapter.

Two factors make the freeze particularly noteworthy as a test of media frames' ability to influence perceptions of public opinion and, through cascading activation, perhaps affect government responses. First, poll after poll revealed a stable and large majority in favor of the movement's basic proposal: freezing the nuclear arsenals of the United States and its prime adversary, the Soviet Union, at the levels of overkill prevailing in the early 1980s, and then negotiating strategic arms limitations. If Congress were consistently responsive to public opinion (or in the terms of this chapter, to polling opinion), we would expect to see passage of legislation supporting this stable majority. Second, the freeze was a policy option actively pressed on government by a large, organized, and determinedly mainstream political movement in the best tradition of grassroots activism. Unlike many prior movements, most notably the groups protesting the Vietnam War, freeze advocates and leaders were at pains to portray the movement in ways that would reassure rather than alienate the average, moderate American.[66]

For a movement with national ambitions, grassroots networks can help spread activation, but the media will be crucial for getting the word out to the mass of potential supporters. Given the "logic of collective action," incentives for any individual to participate actively in a movement are inherently fragile;[67] thus, unfavorable media assessments can seriously weaken a group's recruitment efforts. Apart from this, the news helps determine whether elites feel pressure to support the movement's policy goals. Since elites use news treatment as surrogates for public opinion, positive coverage can convey to them that citizens favor the policy and that the issue merits a high and favorable place on the agenda.[68]

Unfavorable media framing of the movement discouraged involvement by those ordinary citizens who supported the remedy but remained outside the group's activities; these potential recruits may not have been able to tell that they were actually part of a vast majority. The power of the media's framing was to inhibit ordinary Americans—and their leaders—from making mental associations between the freeze and such legitimizing concepts as "democracy" and "public opinion." Instead news frames tended to make delegitimizing associations, at least within media texts, and perhaps influenced audiences' minds. For example, stories frequently alluded to the frivolous hippies or the even more unpopular antiwar dissidents of the 1960s. The dearth of favorable publicity diminished any sense among the movement's inactive supporters that the freeze idea might legitimately demand a place on the agenda and a positive, concrete government response—or that perhaps they should vote against officials who failed to respond. In this way negative media treatment might have lowered the pressure elites felt to act favorably on the proposal—in the terms of the earlier discussion, reducing the *priority* of this particular policy preference—thereby providing political cover for an unresponsive government.

The way framing works to reduce priority weights can be understood in terms of cascading activation as attenuating (for example, by distracting) or blocking associations between thoughts about whom to vote for and thoughts about, in this case, nuclear arms control. And, indeed, Russett[69] notes that Reagan "diverted public concern away from concluding agreements on strategic arms control to being satisfied with the process of negotiation and the prospect of a perfect defense [the Strategic Defense Initiative]. . . . (Previously the administration had succeeded in making the nuclear freeze movement fade away without conceding any discernible shift in policy.)"[70] Moreover, Russett observes, "Reagan's leadership ratings were higher for his handling of defense and Soviet-American relations than were his general ratings. . . ."[71] This suggests most Americans attached low priority to Reagan's active fight against the profreeze majority and his consistent raising of the military budget after 1982.

Of course it might also be argued that the failure of many profreeze Americans to punish the GOP with a disapproving response to the presidential rating question or with a vote for Walter Mondale in 1984 or Michael Dukakis in 1988 involved quite rational and independent weighing of more important priorities, such as the economy. But if many Americans' priorities were based on distraction, as Russett says, or on false premises[72] or patterned ignorance,[73] as other scholars suggest in other contexts, then we might conclude that the media's emphases and silences played a significant role.

How exactly could news of the freeze movement lower the priority of its policy proposal for many Americans, inhibiting mental associations between it and the considerations that went into voting? Analysis of news about the antinuclear movement suggests that journalists evaluated it on seven traits. Following tendencies documented in chapters 4 and 5, all of these evaluations have to do with *political process* rather than with the substance of the movement's (or the administration's) thoughts about nuclear weapons policy. The coverage assessed the movement's technique, success, and representativeness in various ways:

1. Rationality/emotionality: whether the movement was driven by intellectually sound reasoning as opposed to emotion.
2. Expertise: whether the movement had the technical capacity to analyze and recommend valid policy.
3. Public support: how many Americans agreed with movement goals?
4. Partisanship: whether movement participants sought to influence policy through the use of political strategy and power.
5. Unity: the degree of agreement among those pursuing the movement goal.
6. Extremism: whether participants deviated from the mainstream.
7. Effectiveness: whether the movement was likely to influence government policy.

However, other actors were not held to the same standards. Although supportive of grassroots democracy in the abstract, journalists appear to harbor suspicions of mass movements once they organize to exert political power.[74] Whereas journalists consistently assessed the movement and public opinion, they were far less judgmental in their evaluative critiques of the Reagan administration officials and Congress members who made decisions about the movement's proposed frame. The media in general belittled the public and its involvement, whereas their critiques of elites' technique or representativeness were rare, muted, and inconsistent.[75]

Summarizing more extensive studies published elsewhere,[76] we can consider the *New York Times*'s coverage of what was then the largest single demonstration in modern American history, the June 12, 1982, freeze rally. Over 750,000 people marched. In its key article on the event, nearly seventeen hundred words long, the *Times* made only two brief references to the speeches given at the rally in Central Park. The greater part of the article—replete with references to the frivolous and radical 1960s—focused on the logistics of moving the crowd and descriptions of the participants. By highlighting logistics (that is, process) and "color," the coverage disembodied the march from its political purpose, undermining the group's ability to achieve the key aim of the event: conveying information to activate new ideas and spread political involvement and connection among the tens of millions of freeze supporters outside the movement.

Editorial commentary placed the movement in a double bind. As it gained widespread support, it was charged with a variety of political sins accompanying popularity; yet had it not gained such support it would have been politically impotent and unworthy of coverage. In its editorial on the day of the march, the *Times* acknowledged the widespread support of the American public for the freeze, but stated that "the very size and fervor of this movement make it inarticulate" (13 June 1982, 22). It cautioned the public to come to terms with the intellectual issues surrounding arms control: "The nuclear nations still have much to learn from citizens who march and mobilize—if those citizens now master the arcane vocabulary and logic of stable deterrence. Anxiety is not enough" (ibid.).

This quotation illustrates two procedural framing judgments frequently invoked in the news. One asserted that the movement's analysis emerged from emotion not rationality. The other questioned the movement's expertise. The media focused on the fears exhibited by freeze participants rather than on the rationally defensible policy proposed by the movement's leaders, whose substantive expertise equaled that of Reagan's advisors.

The highest levels of the Reagan administration were heavily populated with members of the Committee on the Present Danger (CPD), a sort of elite-level social movement. The committee had been established in the mid-1970s by Norman Podhoretz, Paul Nitze, and Eugene Rostow; its members dominated "Team B," which issued the frightening report about the increasing Soviet menace. The CPD gathered a corps of conservative intellectuals to develop a counterweight to détente with the Soviet Union, which they considered dangerous to American interests. CPD publications and statements made alarming assertions about nuclear war and American vulnerability; the very name "Present Danger" seemed designed to provoke anxiety, as it reflected anxiety on the part of its founders. The CPD asserted that the Soviets aimed to achieve nuclear superiority over the United States and warned that the communists could vanquish the United States in a nuclear war. A CPD member himself, Ronald Reagan appointed over fifty committee colleagues to key government positions.[77] The CPD's empirical claims on Soviet strength and intentions and U.S. weakness were seriously challenged by a myriad of defense analysts,[78] but media coverage of the freeze overlooked the anxiety-ridden tone and the problematic quality of evidence animating CPD analyses, perhaps because of its elite status. President Reagan's (occasionally reported) ignorance of specific weapons systems and other policy details was not used in freeze movement stories to question whether *he* possessed sufficient expertise to serve as final arbiter of American policy. As one among many examples, Reagan publicly asserted that the vessel's commander could recall submarine-based ballistic missiles after launch. This notion was false.

This is not to argue that critiques of Reagan's hawkish defense posture were absent from the news; news stories and editorial commentary regularly took issue with the administration's bellicosity. Such coverage might have reinforced public tendencies to back nuclear arms limitation. However, the criticism rarely occurred in stories about the freeze movement—illustrating the way the frame helped to impede the uninvolved from making mental connections from their policy preference to political action. The freeze case supports the notion that priorities may be a particularly manipulable facet of public opinion. The media on balance diminished the likelihood of active public participation in the movement and dampened pressure on congressional elites to support the freeze—despite stable and large polling majorities.[79]

Conclusion

Public opinion cannot be divorced from the political discourse and media frames that surround it. The apparent impact of the public on government policy often arises from a circular process in which government officials respond to the polling opinions, anticipated or perceived majorities, and priorities that many of them helped create.[80] Arguably that was the case with defense spending. And when it came to the nuclear freeze proposal, government disregarded and journalists on balance derogated an immense and stable majority of poll respondents. Just as Destler and others have suggested, there is some evidence in this that, rhetorical endorsements of democracy notwithstanding, foreign policy elites (and journalists) would just as soon keep the public out of the loop.[81] In any case, governing elites at best respond to selected interpretations of public opinion, and that almost certainly gives media frames a central role in the process of representation. For these and other reasons discussed above, any match between the majority positions registered by surveys and government decisions supplies imperfect evidence for the extent of democracy in the foreign policymaking process. The final chapter assesses the democracy–media–foreign policy nexus from a normative perspective and in light of the cascade model and the findings presented in previous chapters.

APPENDIX TO CHAPTER 6

. . . .

The approach of those who see significant government responsiveness to public opinion for domestic policy is exemplified in Erikson, MacKuen, and Stimson's *The Macro Polity* and receives narrower treatment for defense policy in articles and book chapters by Hartley and Russett, Wlezien, Bryan Jones, and Shapiro and Jacobs.[1] The purpose of this brief appendix is to address the models of representation used by these scholars more directly than was necessary to the chapter's main arguments. The appendix shows that the cascade model is compatible with these models, which see the relationship between public opinion and public policy as one of covariance. The cascade model fills in some blanks and points out some lacunae.

Covariance models can be summarized in briefest compass as follows (adapting the summary chart from *The Macro Polity*):

- Elites' policy activity, plus
- the balance of power between the political parties, yields
- policy decisions and effects and conditions such as unemployment and inflation, (and in the case of foreign affairs, war and peace), and
- these outcomes shape public opinion,
- to which elites respond by further policy activity,
- while public opinion also shapes citizens' voting, which determines the partisan balance of power.[2]

As Jones suggests, however, "[r]epresentation implies not a mechanistic response to citizen preferences, which in any case may well be contradictory. Rather, some preferences are more important than others."[3] Furthermore, he writes, "the exact nature of the linkage" between public preferences and policy "is not really known."[4] The cascade model helps illuminate the process by which some preferences become "more important" to policymaking. It does this by adding the intervening influence of the media and, in particular, news frames. This influence runs in both directions, affecting not just what the public thinks but also what leaders believe. Blending the cascade model into the *Macro Polity* model as just summarized would yield the following alterations (in boldface):

- Elites' policy activity, plus
- the balance of power between the political parties, **plus**
- **elites communicating strategically through, among other things, framing contests in the media, influence**
- **officials' policy preferences, and their interpretations of public opinion and other political calculations. These yield**
- policy decisions and effects and conditions such as unemployment and inflation, (and in the case of foreign affairs, war and peace). Then,
- **news selectively frames these decisions, effects, and conditions, and the framing of**
- these outcomes shape public opinion,
- **which elites interpret based in substantial measure on news frames,**
- to which elites respond by further policy activity,
- while public opinion **(as influenced by news frames during and between election campaigns)** also shapes citizens' voting, which determines the partisan balance of power.

This portrait is more cumbersome than the one detailed by Erikson, Mac-Kuen, and Stimson, but it does seem a more complete if still oversimplified portrait of what Jones calls the "exact nature of the linkage" — of how communication between those who govern and the citizenry actually flows.

Unfortunately, as suggested in chapter 6, any effort to empirically validate causal relationships in this cascading chain would encounter enormous obstacles. Suppose at the extreme it could be shown empirically that variation in public opinion is completely determined by media frames, and that those frames in turn are 100 percent determined by elites' strategic communication activities. One interpretation would be that public opinion is manipulated and the opinion–policy correlation is a sham. But we also know that in shaping their rhetoric, elites anticipate how media, other elites, and the public will respond (and those other elites themselves behave partly in response to their anticipation of media and public reactions). This means that elites' activities are to some degree constrained by and responsive to their images of the public's views (images partially rooted in news media frames). So even if we could explain all the variance in public opinion by reference to elites and media, we could not conclude the public is irrelevant to policy or that representation is empty. But to find out more about exactly how much the public inspired the leadership behavior, we would have to peer into the hearts and minds of leaders in ways requiring a level of cooperation, introspection, and honesty on the part of elite informants that political scientists are unlikely to receive. That leaves us finally little alternative but to make debatable normative judgments about whether the process is sufficiently representative or responsive.

7. DIVERSIFYING THE CASCADE OF IDEAS

Democratic politics is all about convincing others to see things as you do, so that they will support your goals. That means conveying ideas and framing choices in ways that make your side of the story seem the most persuasive.[1] In order to succeed in foreign policy, presidents now more than ever engage in this process of selling their perspectives and choices to diverse audiences in the United States and around the world. The mass media's frames of foreign policy are major channels for these marketing efforts—for moving information between government and the public, and for political communication among leaders. The central goal of this book has been to explain the relationship between the White House's preferred versions of foreign issues and events, and the way the media actually frame them. This chapter first summarizes the cascade model, its propositions, and findings from the case studies. It then explores the implications for democratic theory.

The case studies suggest that news of foreign affairs does not fall into the iron grip of hegemonic elite control, nor does it always provide a straightforward index of elite discussion. Ever since the Cold War began to fade, the news has become messier than either of these approaches lead us to expect—less predictable, less easily categorized and regulated. The cascade model attempts to illuminate the increasingly complicated process of framing foreign affairs, explaining how and why some views activate and spread from the president to other elites, to the media, and to the public. It reveals both the hierarchies in the cascading flow of influence and the feedback paths and interactions that make foreign news something more than a mere reflection of official Washington's views and maneuvers. Cascading network activation provides a framework for more complex analyses of the (verbal *and* visual) media content that shapes audiences' political sentiments and, just as important, officials' *perceptions* of public opinion. The model thus provides a theoretical basis for grappling with the long-standing disputes throughout the fields of cultural and media studies on audience reception and effects. The model's explanations are developed by reference to the interactions of cultural congruence, motivations, power, and strategy.

Cultural congruence is the starting point. Some schemas, defined for our purposes as networks of linked ideas and feelings that provide people their major templates for interpreting foreign policy, readily come to mind for most Americans in response to foreign events. When events appear congruent with these habitual mental associations, all participants in the system, from the president through the administration, other elites, journalists, and members of the public will tend to respond similarly. When an event or issue is clearly congruent in this way, it becomes relatively easy for presidents to frame it so that most participants think alike. By the same token, some foreign events have the potential to induce serious cognitive and emotional dissonance with habitual schemas. Again with little prompting, Americans usually react to these culturally incongruent stimuli similarly, by channeling their thoughts away from the troubling implications and responding in ways that are more comfortable both cognitively and emotionally. For the clearly congruent or incongruent matters, motivations, power, and strategy have less impact on which frame dominates Americans' thinking than for culturally ambiguous matters. Power and strategy will still come into play for congruent and incongruent situations, however, since little about the public's thinking is automatic, especially in the post–Cold War era. As we saw, even the terrorist attacks of September 11, 2001, required some strategic framing on the part of the Bush administration, which itself faced a frame contest when shifting the problem focus from Afghanistan to Iraq.

Culturally ambiguous developments in foreign affairs are in some ways the most interesting, and most of the cases in the book fall into that category. These arise when dominant schemas suggest conflicting interpretations, or when they seem to offer no guidance at all. In these cases, the interactions of power, strategy, and motivations determine the outcomes of frame contests and thus help to shape foreign policy and public opinion.

A number of propositions derived from the cascade model guided the analysis of the case studies in chapters 2–6. The first is that presidential control over the framing of foreign affairs can indeed look a lot like hegemonic domination—but only when there is clear congruence or obvious incongruence between the foreign event or issue and prominent cultural schemas. Ambiguous guidance from the political culture is the key to opening space for dissent from the White House's framing. The second proposition holds that under ambiguity—a situation that became commonplace after the Cold War ended—journalists' motivations push them toward including opposition to the White House in their coverage, even when Washington leaders are not voicing much criticism. But the third proposition is that leaders outside the administration have countervailing motivations of their own. When their soundings of public opinion suggest the public is leaning heavily toward the White House, opposition along the elite source network will dry up. Because the media rely heavily on these other elite sources to keep dissent percolating in news reports, leaders' responsiveness to perceived public opinion can undermine the spread of opposition. On the other hand, when public opinion appears split, these leaders may actively challenge the administration, and then the framing battle is truly joined. The outcomes of these frame contests will be decided by who applies power and strategy most skillfully. A fourth idea suggested by the cascade model is that the dominant political culture is *not* a totally reliable tool for presidents. In the absence of the familiar Cold War paradigm, and the patriotic deference this worldview encouraged, journalists and other elites who oppose the president can use shared cultural schemas not merely to contest the White House frame but actually to dominate it. So much for hegemony. The model's final proposition is that the more chaotic, less predictable, and poorly understood international system heightens leaders' political anxieties and sensitivity to indicators of public opinion. But rather than promoting democratic accountability, this situation may enhance the *media's* influence because the very news frames that leaders are trying to manipulate to advance their objectives also serve as surrogate indicators of public opinion. This lends the frames added influence over officials and politicians.

Briefly, here is a recap of the fit between the case studies and these five propositions. Chapter 2 dissected the KAL and Iran Air tragedies. As framed by the Reagan administration, KAL was about as congruent with the dominant Cold War paradigm as an event could be, and the news was full of revived words and images excoriating the communist menace. Quite the opposite situation arose for President Reagan when U.S. forces shot down the Iran Air jetliner. This was quintessentially incongruent material. In principle, the news could have suggested that the United States was as morally culpable as the Soviet Union had been five years earlier in the KAL shootdown, that only a callous nation could put hundreds of innocent civilians to death without having taken all precautions to ensure against such preventable horrors. These notions would of course have aroused dissonance for most Americans. The administration responded by channeling news coverage to normally arcane matters of military technology, human–computer interaction, and other exculpatory minutiae. Comparing the two incidents reveals how frames work in news texts, reflecting and reinforcing habitual schemas and blind spots that together help to establish a nation's political culture. The Reagan administration's success in dominating the frames of these two events yielded reactions that served the White House's political and policy goals.

Having demonstrated the usefulness of the framing concept and cascade model, I turned to explaining the media's responses to events and issues that are neither clearly congruent nor threateningly incongruent with culture. When schemas give uncertain or conflicting guidance, space opens for frame contests. Whether contests occur decisively depends on the motivations, strategy, and power exerted by the White House, its opponents, and journalists themselves. The model predicts that ambiguous stimuli, such as those arising from events in Third World countries that cannot mount a plausible threat to the United States, will call forth strong journalistic motivations to contest the president's line. In the absence of a Cold (or hot) War, the dispersion of institutional powers in the U.S. system heightens the probability of such dissent arising and spreading. Elites outside the administration (and sometimes renegades inside as well) may say more challenging things in these situations, and driven by their own incentives, journalists will construct texts disputing some elements of the president's line. These motivations include career interests in "good" stories (those featuring conflict, drama, heroes, and villains) and in following professional norms that legitimize and even compel assessments of politicians' competence.[2]

Chapters 3 and 4 explored ambiguous events and issues, with one major difference between them: the projections of power in Grenada, Libya, and Panama did not arouse much opposition from elites outside the administration, leaving journalists alone to carry the burden of contesting the White House line, whereas going to war with Iraq in 1990–91 stirred up lively dissent throughout the Washington establishment. For the issues discussed in chapter 3, which occurred during the waning years of the Cold War, findings ran somewhat contrary to the drift of the hegemony and indexing models. More media dissent appeared than might have been expected given that barely any American leaders raised much objection, at least in public. The ambiguity surrounding these issues set journalists to work trying to construct a degree of balance in the news even though Congress members timorously shrank from disputing the White House. Elites' passivity did prevent journalists from constructing a useable counterframe, however, ensuring instead that much of the critical discussion focused on process rather than substance. Although substantive dissent appeared, much of it originated with low-credibility and low-power foreign sources. Journalists, understanding that foreign criticism was unlikely to alter either the politics or the policy outcomes, tended to give the foreigners' assertions less prominent treatment, further diminishing their potential to activate new under-standings.

Yet on the editorial pages many journalists' true, and truly negative, opinions about projecting American power in Grenada, Libya, and Panama found expression. What is striking about this separation of "news" from "opinion" is how *thorough* was the partition. It meant that the White House obtained the highest-magnitude coverage, on page one, for the crucial framing function of problem definition—the very White House the editorial pages were sometimes denouncing for misleading and even immoral poli-cymaking. And that domination of high-visibility coverage, not the editorial polemics, shaped the political environment by producing an apparently supportive public opinion. Thus going beyond indexing elite dissent, the news featured more criticism than did the floors of Congress. But the find-ings do support a basic insight of indexing: if (in this book's terms) open dissent does not spread along the American elite network, challenges to the White House's frame will probably not affect policy very much.

Chapter 4 asked what happens when elites outside the administration *are* actively pushing against the president's frame. At least judging by the case of the debate on what to do about Iraq's invasion of Kuwait in 1990, the answer appears to be that it depends on how much power opponents can wield over policy decisions. The playing field among the substantive ideas themselves was fairly level, so to speak. Habitual schemas pointed in conflicting directions (protect American interests and dominance versus stay out of quagmires). The power of the White House to make the final policy determination, and to create newsworthy events and actions, subtly influenced the framing. A simple count of claims and counterclaims would show rough equality between the administration and opponents. But the administration's clout allowed it to time new events to push criticism off the front pages, and helped it guide much of the critical thrust toward proce-dural conflict rather than policy substance. As was true in chapter 3, the media conveyed opposition frequently and sometimes vividly, but much of it was relegated to the back pages, diminishing its political impact. Despite a strong strategic push from powerful Democrats in Congress, such as Sena-tor Sam Nunn, to spread support for sanctions instead of going to war imme-diately as the Bush administration wanted, the inability of Congress mem-bers and other nonadministration elites (for example, *former* chiefs of staff of the U.S. military) to exert much power over outcomes relegated their ideas to secondary status. Journalists themselves again were the primary sources for the most vivid and convincing arguments against the White House's policy choice that appeared in the media, but mostly on the editorial pages. News organizations' insistence on the separation of editorial and news staffs and content undermined the effectiveness of the dissent.

On the other hand, when a president acts against habitual schemas, especially one who cannot pull off unified media strategies (most often, a Democrat), his authority and that of the "state" over news framing can dissolve quite thoroughly. Jimmy Carter found this out when he questioned America's status as the dominant power in the world, a seriously dissonant self-portrayal for most Americans.[3] Ambiguity can also increase the efficacy of frame challenges originating in the media, and that was the main topic of chapter 5. Bill Clinton's experiences belie the belief that presidents hegemonically control foreign policy discourse. Ambiguous events and issues kept coming up. Moreover, his first days in office he blundered by taking on the defense establishment's policy concerning gays in the military, and even before that, his efforts to evade the draft during Vietnam had become central to the public's schemas of "Slick Willie."[4] He failed the tests of presidential technique early on, and that first impression was never quite dislodged despite Clinton's later foreign policy successes. To make matters worse, Clinton never enjoyed strong and disciplined support from his party, and he had tenacious, skilled, and all but unanimous opponents in the GOP. Leading Democrats were sincerely divided over intervention, and their career motivations impelled many to separate themselves from Clinton. In consequence, judging from the admittedly incomplete evidence presented in chapter 5, even Clinton's substantive successes in foreign policy yielded little political benefit. Indeed, during execution of Clinton's policies, far from dominating news frames, the White House was often reduced to competing for frame control on virtually even terms with journalists and other elites.

My argument in chapter 5 was that the end of the Cold War disrupted familiar networks of association among ideas and participants. So did the Internet and the rise of infotainment.[5] New developments overseas could be framed in a wider variety of ways. This loosening of thought patterns once tightly constrained enhanced the potential power of media as against the White House and made journalists more independent of the elites outside the administration too. The chapter illustrated the relatively greater power of the media—a partial but significant flattening of hierarchy in control over framing since the 1991 collapse of the Soviet Union—by briefly considering the cases of Somalia, Haiti, Bosnia, and Kosovo. In each instance, the White House had trouble controlling the frame. Democrats' chronic disunity and strategic ineptitude, the ambiguous implications of events, the contradiction between deeply held American values (for example, national self-determination versus human rights), and Clinton's inability to dominate problem definition by evoking a patriotic duty to support the White House all further weakened the administration's hand. At least during the 1990s, the media moved in to fill part of the framing vacuum. The Clinton presidency illustrates the applicability of the cascading network activation model to a post–Cold War environment where the administration, Congress, other elites, journalists, and even indicators of public opinion all jostle for space on the same discursive stage.

That brings us to the war on terrorism launched in the aftermath of September 11th. Whether terrorism can supplant the Cold War as an enduring dominant paradigm that guides most interpretations of international affairs cannot be predicted with much confidence. However, the cascade model would lead us to expect that when events, issues, or actors arise that do not clearly relate to threats of terrorism against America, the media will continue to enjoy opportunities to exert more influence over framing than they typically did during the Cold War. In fact, as discussed in chapter 5, the ability of terrorism to trump fears about excessively costly projections of power varied with specific conditions. Although opposition to the Afghanistan war was muted, at least initially that was not true for Iraq. Perhaps following the schema planted first by the Gulf War, those within and outside the U.S. who opposed that plan demanded the equivalent of what the senior Bush had provided in 1990–91: U.N. blessing, and American intervention as part of a large multilateral coalition. Though congressional dissent on Iraq never was very energetic—the Democratic leadership mostly sided with George W. Bush—the media used foreign critiques to provide some balance in covering the debate over the president's "war soon" posture and helped build pressure on Bush to obtain U.N. approval. Even if foreign sources themselves enjoy scant credibility with most Americans, overseas opposition—more accessible than ever because of the Internet—may stimulate more independent counterframing by journalists, and that can reinforce dissent among U.S. citizens.[6] Not only does this situation suggest limits on the White House's ability to connect every foreign issue to a unifying war on terrorism, but it also indicates that the significance of foreign dissent to U.S. policy decisions may be greater in the twenty-first century than in the past. To reduce the cost and enhance the effectiveness of global leadership, America's leaders can ill afford to ignore the views of allies and the United Nations. Foreign leaders might belong at the nonadministration elite (second) level of the cascade in figure 1.2.

Of course, although the opposition delayed the invasion, George W. Bush went ahead without the U.N.'s consent, so we should not exaggerate the importance either of foreign opinion or of news organizations. Although the media's leeway to break free from the bounds of American elites' discourse may be greater than previously recognized, the limits must be underscored. The dominant media, those studied in this book, operate within what Hallin calls the sphere of legitimate conflict, as of course do political elites; they usually ignore or denounce views that penetrate the sphere of deviance, or in my terms, that are culturally incongruent. For elites or journalists to voice such notions would mean trying to convince colleagues and citizens of what is basically unthinkable to them. Shared motivations work against the spread of such ideas—expressing them can endanger political and journalistic careers.

To continue using the Iraq war of 2003 as an example, in conveying dissent from the George W. Bush position, the mainstream media gave little attention to America's central role in sponsoring Saddam Hussein in the first place. The Reagan and the earlier Bush administrations not only tolerated but aided Iraq's leader in his use of chemical weapons and development of biological and nuclear capabilities during the Iran–Iraq war (1980–88). These were the very weapons of mass destruction that the later Bush administration cited as the central justification for attacking Iraq. The international relations theorists John Mearsheimer (University of Chicago) and Stephen Walt (Harvard) described this seeming incongruity in the following way:

Unfortunately for those who now favor war, [the Bush administration's] argument is difficult to reconcile with the United States' past support for Iraq, support that coincided with some of the behavior now being invoked to portray him as an irrational madman. The United States backed Iraq during the 1980s—when Saddam was gassing Kurds and Iranians—and helped Iraq use chemical weapons more effectively by providing it with satellite imagery of Iranian troop positions. The Reagan administration also facilitated Iraq's efforts to develop biological weapons by allowing Baghdad to import disease-producing biological materials such as anthrax, West Nile virus, and botulinal toxin. A central figure in the effort to court Iraq was none other than current U.S. Defense Secretary Donald Rumsfeld, who was then President Ronald Reagan's special envoy to the Middle East. He visited Baghdad and met with Saddam in 1983, with the explicit aim of fostering better relations between the United States and Iraq. In October 1989, about a year after Saddam gassed the Kurds, President George H. W. Bush signed a formal national security directive declaring, "Normal relations between the United States and Iraq would serve our longer-term interests and promote stability in both the Gulf and the Middle East."[7]

Since Iraq's chemical attacks on civilians fit the definition of terrorism, this arguably put the United States in the awkward position of itself being a nation with a record of supporting terrorism—and of finding Saddam Hussein's possession of weapons of mass destruction perfectly acceptable. The history of American coziness with Saddam Hussein during the 1980s did not necessarily point to a particular policy choice fifteen years later, and as the senior Bush asserted, there was an argument based on rational self-interest for what the United States did back then. Still, knowing this context could have altered the political environment—injecting realism (in several senses of that word) into mainstream discourse about George W. Bush's frame. Yet the sway of dominant cultural schemas at every level of the cascading system makes it virtually impossible for the major media to emphasize this kind of dissonant information.

Even within the normal sphere of dissent, as we have seen throughout the book, the media's independence comes up against boundaries. In Grenada, Libya, Panama, and during the Gulf War debate as well, dissent focused largely on just one of the four aspects of framing: the remedy. Only during the Clinton administration did the media construct more complete counterframes to the White House line, and that can be traced to vigorous dissent from Republicans and many Democratic elites energizing, deepening, and legitimizing critiques from journalists themselves. The pendulum appeared largely and, based on this book's analysis, predictably to have swung back for the Republican administration when it came to Iraq in 2002–3. The White House's determination to define the chief foreign policy problem as Iraq rather than, say, Saudi Arabia or North Korea, did receive sporadic critiques, but attention to Saddam Hussein dwarfed that given these other issues. The framing contest was restricted mostly to arguing over "war soon" or "work through the U.N.," not over the problem definition and causal analysis that pointed to disarming Iraq, or over moral condemnation of the Iraqi leader. Arguments about these matters usually occurred in academic or intellectual journals such as the one just quoted above. As happened during the Gulf War of 1991, limits on the counterframe would leave American audiences scant cognitive or emotional basis for anything but a rally around the president once hostilities commenced. When American troops are actively engaged in a large-scale military action, we

should continue to expect the kind of one-sided treatment that characterized Iraq war coverage in 1991 and early 2003. The president's control over
military deployments and other key newsworthy action is unchallenged,
the cultural power of the "support our troops" schema remains high, and
elites and journalists have strong incentives to side with the inevitable patriotic groundswell. These forces make it unlikely that American media will
offer balanced depictions—*unless* an operation does turn into a costly quagmire. Journalists remained vigilant for signs of quagmire even during the
massively popular post-9/11 wars in Afghanistan and Iraq, and questioned
administration officials aggressively when they thought such signs were
present, as in the months after Saddam fell. Guerilla attacks and instability
persisted, and news highlighted the mounting costs. The media's potential
to exert more autonomous influence has grown since the Cold War;
whether and how far they will distance themselves from the White House
depends on the interaction of the forces identified by the cascade model.

In chapter 6, the book turned from a focus on interactions between elites
and journalists that produce news frames to the role of framing in conveying perceptions of public opinion to leaders. I suggested that research
on public opinion and foreign policy must acknowledge the different facets
of "public opinion" and the difficulty of measuring their effects on government officials. Elites and news organizations alike have devoted increasing
resources to monitoring public opinion, and citizens' reactions, less anchored by a reliable paradigm, have become less stable and predictable.
The chapter's main argument is that this situation has given news frames
a central role in representation. Public officials seeking to ascertain Americans' desires must rely on those facets of public sentiment that are selected
and highlighted by pollsters, media, and other informants. Poll results come
from questions framed by survey organizations, and those queries are usually rooted in desires to gauge Americans' reaction to news frames. Research also suggests that many politicians and officials use media frames
as surrogates for public opinion, inferring citizens' reactions directly from
the way the news covers an event or issue.

The specific case of defense spending reveals that what might at first
appear to be evidence of public influence on policy could be read as media
influence on policy, or elite manipulation of media to generate a frame of
public opinion, a perceived majority, that ratified what elites wanted to do
in the first place.[8] In the final analysis, chapter 6 argued, correlations between public opinion and government policy incorporate so many simultaneous interactions among leaders, media, and citizens that determining
who influences whom remains a large intellectual challenge. The nuclear

freeze movement of the early 1980s illustrated another way that media frames distribute power and shape the impacts of public opinion. By disdaining the movement and denigrating the public's qualifications to even press its views on government, media frames discouraged citizens from granting higher priority to their own profreeze sentiments. The Reagan administration and the Congress were thus able to ignore public opinion or respond to it symbolically until the KAL incident, framed to confirm the Soviet Union's continued evil intentions, sealed the movement's demise as a political force.

Media Autonomy and Democracy in Foreign Policymaking

Has the media's increasing ability to stake out critical distance from the White House served to make foreign policymaking more democratic? If so, is that a good thing? It may not be axiomatic that having the media aggressively stir up public opposition to government policy is always desirable. International relations theorists sometimes argue that, because informed public opinion constrains government, democracies do not fight each other. But they also acknowledge that democracies, very much including the United States, can take aggressive stands because of, not despite, the influence of public opinion calculations by leaders. The issue quickly becomes complicated; Gaubatz, for example, suggests that democratic elections tend to reduce incentives to go to war in the short run but may increase the likelihood or severity of war in the longer run.[9] Moreover, realist theories of international relations tend to see public opinion as a troublesome impediment to rational foreign policymaking rather than a desirable participant. Thus, the democracy–war linkage is unsettled both empirically and normatively.

Consider the cases explored in this book. During the military operations against Grenada, Libya, and Panama, Congress responded to public opinion, or more precisely to polling opinion, that seemed to support administration policy each time. After voicing some tentative criticism around the start of each operation, opponents fell silent in the face of the polls, and the impression of public support fed positive news coverage. The Congress's accommodation to these indications of public approval meant the media had to rely on sources outside government, including foreign elites, for oppositional information. Few Washington elites criticized administration policies in Grenada, Libya, and Panama because the media and polls claimed they were very popular. Yet perhaps they were so popular because the public knew so little about them—and their knowledge was so limited because their representatives, slavishly attentive to constituents' presumed sentiments, apparently feared to engage in critical discussion of the poli-cies. Thus the normative irony: government responsiveness may not be de-sirable when it is responding to an underinformed public—underinformed in large part because Washington politicians are so exquisitely sensitive to the imagined public, to their perceptions of public opinion.[10] In these cases, rather than promoting government accountability to a deliberating or even rational citizenry, political leaders' responsiveness to indicators of public opinion short-circuited the media's ability to publicize more balanced views of the policies.

It seems problematic to consider all instances where polling opinion matches government policy as examples of democracy in action. For one thing, polls frequently contradict one another, and it is improper to select only the matching results. Even leaving that point aside, for the notion of responsiveness to have meaning, it is not enough that survey results merely correlate with policy decisions. Such congruence could be the product of governing elites' manipulation, misinformation, and, perhaps as in Gre-nada, Libya, and Panama, failures to engage in public debate. Implementa-tion of the policies was essentially over, as was high-visibility news cover-age, before issues raised by opponents could be aired thoroughly—if they ever were. For example, the number of civilian casualties during the Pan-ama operation remains a mystery.[11] The shaky status of the Libya bombing in light of international law received some attention, but little concerted follow-up. The distance between the patriotic celebration of the U.S. victory over the lightly armed Cuban construction engineers who constituted the major opposition force in Grenada and the serious and numerous military snafus the operation actually experienced were only reported much later. More than two years after the events, the *Washington Post* ran a story that cited the following as just one of the mix-ups:

> Incompatible radio equipment resulted in Army officers not being able to call in supporting fire from Navy ships. They resorted to ham radios, sent couriers to vessels by helicopter and in one case, according to a Senate Armed Services Committee report, used an AT&T credit card to place a call on a civilian telephone to Fort Bragg, N.C., in the hope of having a request relayed.[12]

Another telling example of delay rendering counterframing facts politi-cally irrelevant was the reported success of the Patriot antimissile weapon during the 1991 Gulf War. Initially depicted as nearly perfect (96 percent success) in destroying incoming offensive weapons, later investigation showed a success rate of 9 percent at best and likely much lower—perhaps even 0 percent.[13]

Such untimely exposure of problems is inevitable; one cannot expect comprehensive assessments of policy implementation to appear until evaluation data have been collected and analyzed. Yet one might expect somewhat less credulous treatment of government claims in real time than journalists actually provided. After all, the lessons not just of Vietnam but going back through history show that government deliberately or inadvertently misleads the press time and again, as much to protect their own political security as national security.[14] Better late than never, perhaps, but the key point is that neither the justifications nor the costs of many military operations were ever fully accounted for in a manner likely to be noticed by most of the public. Audiences never had a practical chance to learn—to store mental associations, to build new event and issue schemas for activation in response to future problems—or to hold officials retrospectively accountable.

As a second democratic conundrum, consider the story told by Neil Sheehan,[15] describing the hesitancy of the Bush and early Clinton administrations to establish full diplomatic and economic ties with Vietnam. That policy would have promoted important U.S. foreign policy and economic objectives in the region *and* advanced the humane treatment of the Vietnamese (not to mention honoring America's peace treaty commitments from 1972). The reason was fear of a public opinion backlash. A large number of Americans continued to believe that the Vietnamese were hiding information about still-living prisoners of war and Americans missing in action. This belief was orchestrated by a combination of a real grassroots movement (presumably something we welcome in a democracy) and deeply cynical elites starting with President Richard Nixon. Knowing that the chance of finding a live American POW was infinitesimal—none ever was discovered[16]—Nixon and his minions nonetheless created and nurtured the myth for political gain. Because the Vietnamese did cooperate with the United States in hunting for these chimerical survivors (a search that cost the taxpayers $100 million in 1992), the Clinton administration took incremental steps in the direction of rational policy in 1993. It ended American opposition to the granting of credit to Vietnam by international lending institutions and opened a small diplomatic office.[17] But, Bill Clinton—experiencing record-low public approval ratings for much of his first year—was in 1993 loath to take on an intense citizen movement with powerful allies in the government and outside, a movement possessing ready access to patriotic heartstrings. It and previous administrations responded to anticipated and perceived public opinion. Vietnamese and American interests alike suffered as full normalization of relations was postponed for decades.

Government's compliance with public sentiment was traceable in part to the daily news media's inability to convey the complexity and historical context that could have belied the POW/MIA myth. Leaders who might have supported a move toward full normalization (and the saving of $100 million annually, which might have been used instead to compensate families of missing American vets) were cowed—in part because of their anticipation that journalists would be unable to convey the complex truth that support of normalization was in the best national interests of the United States. Ideally too, independent news coverage would have revealed the political opportunism that kept the myth alive, providing a disincentive to such manipulation by future politicians. Of course the Sheehan report was just such a piece; but it appeared in a low-circulation magazine of opinion, not daily news, and could not and did not stimulate a government investigation or a wide perception that this was a scandal. (Deliberately stoking for two decades the possibility that U.S. military personnel might still be alive, in the process cruelly tantalizing loved ones just for political gain, surely qualifies as a scandal if anything does.) Absent a scandal counterframe and repeated reporting, the political landmines surrounding the issue persisted.

A third example of the problematic nature of democracy in this arena concerns the tragic conflicts in the former territories of Yugoslavia. As discussed in chapter 5, the debate over U.S. intervention in Bosnia in 1993 involved much pressure for decisive involvement from elite media, including resonant language and visual images and high-magnitude story play, decided by editors and producers who treated the issue as one of great moment. By assigning correspondents and running their dispatches on the front page or including them on the evening news, media organizations in early 1993 reinforced pressures on President Clinton's agenda. This was against his seeming preference—and an electoral mandate—to focus on the domestic economy, and it persisted despite the decided coolness toward military involvement detected in surveys.

In part the aggressive insistence of the elite press on reporting Bosnia was due to the administration's early ineptitude in managing foreign news coverage, something at which the Reagan and both Bush administrations generally excelled. But the coverage was certainly *not* a result of administration prodding to keep Bosnia a high-visibility issue; nor did it appear to be an example of the media's reflecting or indexing debate among government elites. Few in Congress or the executive branch were actively urging decisive American involvement in this intractable conflict or pushing it as a matter for urgent administration attention. Instead Bosnia reveals a case of Washington policy experts and interest groups, and media personnel themselves, independently promoting a policy of American intervention against a reluctant administration (with an assist from a handful of dissenting members and staff on the Hill and in the bureaucracy).[18] Here then would seemingly be an example of just what critics of the media want and democratic theory calls for: independent media putting together issue frames via their own enterprise reporting and interpreting, in defiance of rather than deference to the White House. But the media were also acting in opposition to public opinion. One reason the administration feared involvement was precisely that poll majorities largely opposed intervention, despite media pressure, so here journalistic independence meant bolstering a policy opposed to the public's surveyed preferences (unlike the POW/MIA case). And here, responding to American polling opinion entailed following a dovish policy rather than a bellicose one (as in Grenada, Libya and Panama). Yet keeping U.S. troops out of Bosnia did not necessarily promote peace for Bosnia itself, and ethnic slaughter went on for at least two years when earlier intervention might have curtailed it. A very similar story could be told of Rwanda. These instances represent another side to the problematic operation of independent reporting and public opinion in U.S. foreign policymaking.

Finally, what are we to make of the 2003 Iraq war? Although no data can directly test the hypothesis, the behavior of news executives and opposing politicians alike suggests they calculated that proponents of war had stronger feelings than opponents—that prowar sentiments held higher priority for hawks than antiwar sentiments for doves. Many politicians seemed to feel they would lose more votes (and contributions) from hawks by opposing the war than they would gain from doves. From all accounts, news organizations feared complaints about war coverage from the belligerent right more than from the peacenik left. Surveys suggest this inference about public priorities was right, that many Americans felt supporting the president took precedence over supporting their own preferences. Whereas before the war started, about 60 percent said they preferred to continue working through the U.N. over going to war immediately, after the war began, 67 percent agreed that President Bush had given "international diplomacy enough time to work before taking military action against Iraq."[19] That finding suggests many people actually revised their preferences retrospectively! In a convoluted sense, by giving less salient attention to the antiwar arguments than to the prowar, especially after combat began, the media were reflecting majority sentiments, as were the antiwar elites from both parties who failed to speak out vigorously against Bush's decision.

The Media's Role in a Democratic Public Sphere

The distinguished political theorist Robert Dahl has identified the importance of nonmanipulated information to democracy. He writes of the need for "enlightened understanding" on the part of democratic citizens, by which he means that they have the ability to make political choices identical with "whatever they would choose with the fullest attainable understanding of the experience resulting from that choice and its most relevant alternatives."[20] Common in this and other discussions of democratic citizenship and participation is the central importance of reflexivity, of citizens' being able to discuss the rules shaping discussion, to notice the framing that underlies and limits the discourse, and to debate the substantive ends of policy, not just the procedural means. The cascade model in this light would identify the democratic goal as stimulating and enabling weakly motivated citizens to follow foreign policy more actively and critically. They would have easy access to diverse information possessing sufficient magnitude and resonance to allow them to engage in "central processing,"[21] or in this book's terms, to make their own mental connections even when habit might lead down a different path.

But such ideals must be operationalized in terms of actual political practice. When we turn to the real world of politics, problems develop. Jurgen Habermas, at one time perhaps the most optimistic of democratic theorists (some say naively so), more recently offered some implicit guidance:

> Of course, these [public] opinions must be given shape in the form of decisions by democratically constituted decision-making bodies. The responsibility for practically consequential decisions must be based in an institution. Discourses do not govern. They generate a communicative power that cannot take the place of administration but can only influence it. This influence is limited to the procurement and withdrawal of legitimation.[22]

The legitimation point suggests that the critical and perhaps only realistically attainable goal is for the public to influence deliberation by those government administrators—not to participate themselves. Interestingly enough, the godfather of public choice theory, William Riker, makes a similar point in his discussion of the limits of liberal democracy. As he shows, and as mentioned in chapter 6, for technical and practical reasons, public opinion or the public "will" is often indeterminate and public influence on government, therefore, indirect and sporadic.[23]

Research supports the view that the American public can engage in what Habermas calls "procurement and withdrawal of legitimation" for U.S. foreign policies basically in just two ways:[24]

- By registering high approval or disapproval of a policy or of the president in public opinion surveys.
- By actually voting against the president or his party during elections.

Both poll results and election returns are subject to multiple causes and hence multiple framings.[25] That means policy of shaky legitimacy can persist, often until negative polling opinion turns supportive in response to media frames and strategically crafted talk;[26] or the policy may persist because elites' and journalists' (and therefore the public's) attention has moved on to another topic.[27] But the provision or withdrawal of legitimacy from a president or policy, and the media's role in facilitating or undermining it, can significantly influence foreign policy.

The problem with democracy in foreign policy is that public opinion (leaving aside uncertainties about defining that term) may be poorly informed or driven by emotion and deference to authority. In recent years scholars have converged to refute the early conclusion[28] that public opinion tends to be unstable, easily manipulable, and rooted in superficial understanding and instead to write of the stability and considerable rationality of public opinion in this area. Citizens use "heuristics," schematic thinking and shortcuts, to minimize cognitive costs and still make some connections between their values and their political positions.[29] Yet most scholars agree that ordinary citizens possess underdeveloped ideologies, uncertain motivations to deliberate carefully on policy issues, and tenuous command of important facts.[30] Put into the terms used in this book, ideologies can be defined as meta-schemas that individuals use to (1) reduce cognitive costs entailed in thinking about new issues or events and (2) draw conscious associations between the novel information and their established core values or interests. This definition is compatible with Dahl's and Habermas's standards of democratic citizenship.[31]

The examples of public opinion's questionable rationality described earlier in this chapter suggest that—at least with respect to relatively short-term buildups and projections of military power—the public's cost-reducing heuristics are poor substitutes for the somewhat more sophisticated ideological thinking and citizenship envisioned by Habermas and Dahl, among others.[32] And because public officials do weigh indicators of the public's priorities and opinions (anticipated and perceived majorities, polling opinion) heavily, this shortcoming appears in some instances to have negative consequences. It has sometimes led the U.S. government to make or persist in foreign policies that do not rationally maximize U.S. interests. Moreover, the uneven quality of public reasoning bolsters elites' incentives to protect their legitimacy by manipulating news frames and public opinion indicators.[33]

The Elite Public Sphere in Washington

Given the deficiencies of public opinion, what might media realistically do to enhance democracy in foreign and national security policy? And what should they do? The interlaced and shifting power relationships among the media, government, and public may call for a new normative standard, one that recognizes structural limitations on the citizenry's ability and motivation to obtain the information they need to hold government to genuine account. Combining the early insights of Walter Lippmann on the failings of public opinion[34] with recent research on bounded citizen rationality[35] might yield a more realistic normative vision. Lacking faith in the media's ability to bring the bulk of Americans into anything resembling a deliberative public sphere, I propose that what is critical and practically achievable is for *elites,* what Habermas calls "public administration" or "the state," to generate a freer, more self-aware discourse.

As we have seen, along with the president and executive branch, the network of other elite sources shapes the news and thus the publicly available information on foreign policy. Some members are government employees (Congress members and their staffs) and others not (experts and former officials affiliated with think tanks, universities, interest groups). These people mingle with the administration, ironically, to form something very much akin to Habermas's ideal public sphere, albeit with a severely confined membership. Elites concerned with foreign policy in Washington interact regularly, creating a networked community of active discourse and deliberation among people having a range of informed views they can articulately debate. In this elite public sphere, individuals from different groups might have predictable policy positions, cognitive and emotional biases, rhetorical strategies, and rules for how they interact with others, but violations, anomalies, intragroup disputes—and ambiguous stimuli—will crop up frequently and keep things interesting.[36] The national opinion columnists, reporters, and editors are very much part of this elite public sphere.

Jacobs and Shapiro suggest one way to "liberate" (my word) elites from the negative spiral of fear induced by disapproving poll majorities—fear that itself blocks leaders' ability to promote alternative interpretations through the media and into public consciousness. Their idea is that the media should cover the faces of public opinion in far more detail, with sensitivity to context. Over time such coverage might educate the public and elites alike to treat claims about public opinion more critically.[37] It would also help if news organizations could, in their roles as major paying clients and consumers of polling organizations, start demanding more nuanced survey instruments. Publicizing poll data that control for public ignorance and knowledge and attempt to register trade-offs among preferences held at different intensities could significantly improve public discourse. The main problem with this suggestion is the same one bedeviling prior news critics: news organizations have rarely shown much appetite for making daily news stories more complicated and detailed, whether about public opinion, foreign policy, or domestic policy. Commercial incentives (that is, audience tastes) point in the other direction, all the more so with the rise of competition from newer media technologies and formats.[38] It is unlikely that many readers and viewers of the daily news beyond, at best, the most attentive 10 percent would digest such sophisticated reporting on public opinion. But it is a commendable ideal nonetheless, one that could at least stimulate new practices by the likes of the *New York Times*, because such reporting would indeed nourish the elite public sphere. As we have seen, elites, especially elected officials, do react in some degree to their perceptions of public opinion, and allowing them to draw more nuanced interpretations could improve policy.

Another means for improving the flow of ideas within the elite sphere, one more compatible with motivations at a somewhat broader range of media, would be the creation of a new position: *liaison editors*. Their assignment would be to help maintain more reliable connections between editorial and news staffs—to spread activation of ideas across the organizational gap between them—and likewise to encourage a more rationally considered linkage among ideas present in different stories on different days. As we have seen throughout this study, news coverage often contradicts facts or factual inferences that are convincingly argued on the editorial pages or in stories from other staff members. Reflect on four examples of the need for the liaison function in the newsroom. Recall the *subverted contradiction* in coverage of the KAL tragedy—the *Newsweek* issue with a propagandistic cover headline "Why Moscow Did It" that also featured a story providing a far more accurate analysis showing "Moscow" almost certainly did not do it. Think about the striking chasm between editorials denouncing the Reagan White House's rationales and motivations for military action against Grenada and Libya, and news coverage that promoted the administration line while marginalizing the positions of opponents—the very positions being voiced on the editorial pages. Remember the contradiction between the editorials urging a vigorous public dialogue on the Gulf War and the daily news coverage in the *Washington Post* and *New York Times* that made it hard even for educated readers of the two leading newspapers to participate knowledgeably in such a discussion. And consider the double binds that coverage imposed on the Clinton administration by demanding U.S. intervention to solve humanitarian crises in the Balkans, Somalia, and elsewhere, while at the same time denouncing the administration for risking costly quagmires. These examples and others argue for creating this kind of position, not just on newspapers but in television news organizations and newsmagazines as well.

Liaison editors would not be enforcers, ensuring that the news coverage slants in favor of the organization's editorial positions. Rather their charge would be to illuminate connections and contradictions that might otherwise be overlooked. Liaison editors would understand that news coverage tends to fall into patterns that create frames, and would pursue the goal of enriching discourse by constructing explicit counterframes. They would monitor their own outlet's coverage, looking for subverted contradiction and other logical gaps, urging reporters and editors to take their colleagues' findings into account. On newspapers, they would bring some internal organizational focus to consider whether the framing that emerges from the standard operating procedures and hurly-burly of daily news production actually reflects the insights generated by those working under less deadline pressure on the editorial page. At the television networks they might actually take the time to analyze each evening news program and compare its frames to what is featured on the morning news, *60 Minutes, Nightline,* and their ilk.

No doubt liaison editors would create organizational tensions. Reporters and editors might resent the second-guessing and might even feel the liaison editor's critiques and suggestions as impinging on their professional autonomy. But clearing up contradictions to reduce confusion and encourage understanding seems an unassailable objective for news organizations, one that serves their economic interests in maintaining circulation, ratings and prestige. Newsrooms always experience friction; ultimately, the liaison editor should bring a creative rather than destructive sort of tension. There is some precedent for this position in that of ombudsman, appointed by some organizations to monitor their output to ensure accuracy and fairness. But liaison editors would not publish their findings in regular columns, as do ombudsmen—surely to the dismay of reporters whose stories they publicly fault. Unlike ombudsmen, who serve a public relations function, liaison editors would be purely internal operators, supporting the loftiest principles of the profession, privately helping individual journalists fulfill their civic ideals.

A kind of analogous position to represent and prod elites would be *designated statesmen* and *designated stateswomen* (DS). In order to ensure that DS's would be considered politically relevant, and to protect the role of the parties, an equal number of DS's might be appointed from each party. Their job would be to speak their individual minds and consciences. The rules of this game would be made clear to all: DS's speak for themselves, not the party. They would plainly announce their positions and analyses as coming from their own best thinking, without regard for politics. But it is important that DS's see their role as articulating positions in line with what they personally take to be the core principles of their party. Otherwise, this institution would be just another in the assemblage of forces that have been diminishing party identification and loyalty. Given the critical role responsible parties can play in minimizing information costs and assisting citizenship, DS's should represent the best of their parties' basic ideologies. No doubt DS's would be vulnerable to pressure from the White House or from party leaders. To insulate them a bit, DS's could be appointed by a bipartisan commission rather than by the parties themselves, for fixed terms, along the lines of the independent regulatory agencies (e.g., the Federal Communications Commission). Being a DS should become an attractive post-Congress option for members tired of the reelection grind but still interested in public policy. Playing philosopher king as a DS could hold more allure than becoming just another K-Street lobbyist. Nor would the DS's necessarily have to come from the ranks of Congress. Retired military officers, defense policy intellectuals, maybe even university professors could fill the bill.

Their expertise and mandate to speak freely and honestly would make DS's highly newsworthy. The DS's goal would be spreading activation of novel ideas, relatively free of contamination by political motive. Receiving institutional support (staff, budget, and office space), they would be easily accessible to journalists. They could float trial balloons, actively seeking to challenge (or support) presidential frames. Regardless of whether their perspectives ultimately came close to parity in news reports with the White House's frame, at least there would be some pressure pushing novel ideas into the elite public sphere in Washington. If editorialists or news reports are supportive, this could encourage further notice and discussion among elites. In some cases that development could even stimulate polling organizations to ask reframed questions. Ultimately the new ideas could spread among the larger public, generating some extra motivation for leaders to make the right decision without fear of negative political consequences. But in light of the many constraints on responsiveness to public opinion, the more important goal might be to free up elites' own thinking.

These two proposals are not panaceas. Readers will no doubt find flaws. There may be more effective means of enriching the elite public sphere. Whatever they are, they should be encouraged and cherished—and funded.

As an initial presentation of a new model, this book could not offer comprehensive tests of every implication or definitive conclusions. Much research lies ahead: empirical analyses, refined theoretical and normative propositions, applications to domestic policy, and, ultimately, new models that can deepen understanding of the media's evolving role in shaping the play of power.

In the meantime, arguably the U.S. government *has* shown some democratic responsiveness and rationality in foreign and defense policy—and the news media occasionally encouraged these qualities. The United States long avoided another Vietnam-scale debacle. It helped prevent the collapse of the Soviet Union from setting off World War III and dramatically reduced the threat of nuclear annihilation. Prodded by the media, America sometimes deployed military force for humanitarian ends, saving lives and advancing democracy, sometimes in cooperation with global organizations that (sporadically) promote justice and peace. Perhaps that is about as much democracy and rationality as we can expect from the world's only superpower.

NOTES

. . . .

CHAPTER ONE

1. Text at http://multimedia.belointeractive.com/attack/news/0912bushstatement.
   html (12 September 2001); audio at http://www.whitehouse.gov/news/
   releases/2001/09/20010912-4.v.smil.
2. The aggression was undertaken not by a hostile state, but by a loosely organized
   network of terrorists expressing deep rage but no apparent territorial ambitions
   in North America. Indeed, at the time he first invoked "war," President Bush
   had not even confirmed that the attackers were affiliated with any larger organization. Unlike Japan after Pearl Harbor, al-Qaeda could not mount continuing
   military attacks in anything resembling what the United States had previously
   experienced as war. Al-Qaeda clearly represented a grave danger to America,
   but reasonable people might have chosen different frames for the atrocities of
   September 11. Cf. Lemann 2002. According to Woodward (2002, 15–16), Bush
   himself described the "act of war" frame as a "gut reaction," but also reported
   that he consciously waited to invoke the term publicly until the day after the
   attacks (30–31). Katharine Q. Seelye and Elizabeth Bumiller write that Bush's
   words on September 12 "were more pointed than those he used in his address
   to the nation on Tuesday night [September 11], when he called the attacks 'evil,
   despicable acts of terror' and 'acts of mass murder.' [On September 12] he said
   the attacks 'were more than acts of terror; they were acts of war,' a distinction
   intended to lay the military, political and psychological groundwork for military
   action." See "After the Attacks: The President," *New York Times,* 13 September
   2001, A1.
3. Let me say from the beginning that by stating the possibility for alternative framing of a given event, issue, or actor I do not mean to deny the validity of the
   administration's frame. In the case of George W. Bush's response to September
   11th, my personal view, for what it's worth, is that overthrowing the Taliban in
   Afghanistan and disrupting or destroying the al-Qaeda terrorist network there
   were worthy objectives. On other matters discussed in the book, my own view
   may be more or less supportive of an administration's perspective. I hope that
   readers will judge the book's arguments on their own merits.
4. A Gallup Poll taken October 11–14, 2001, found 88 percent of respondents supporting military action against Afghanistan, and an ABC poll the same month
   found 92 percent of the public approved of "the way Bush is handling the U.S.
   campaign against terrorism." These figures and others can be found at http://
   www.pollingreport.com/terror.htm.
5. Interview on *Late Show with David Letterman,* 18 September 2001; see Hart and
   Ackerman 2001.
6. Cf. MacArthur 1992, on the Gulf War.

7. See Howard Kurtz, "Times Takes Flak on Iraq: Conservatives Call Coverage of Bush Policy Slanted." *Washington Post,* 21 August 2002, C1.
8. Edelman 1988, 2001.
9. Examples include Augelli and Murphy 1988; Herman and Chromsky 1988; Parenti 1993; Rachlin 1988. The use of "hegemony" here, in the sense originated by Antonio Gramsci, should not be confused with its usage in international relations theory.
10. Althaus 2002; Bennett 1989, 1990; Bennett and Manheim 1993; Hallin 1993; Mermin 1999; Robinson 2002.
11. Mermin 1999, 7. The other book that relies heavily on indexing is Robinson 2002.
12. Mermin 1999, 143.
13. See, e.g., Jacobs and Shapiro 2000; Kernell 1992.
14. Among those discussing framing as a central conceptual tool are Entman 1993; Pan and Kosicki 1993, 2001; Reese, Gandy, and Grant 2001; Scheufele 1999.
15. Substantive frames in the news typically perform the four functions in reporting on three different political topics: *events, actors* (who may be individual leaders, groups, or nations), and *issues.* More detail on the functions and objects of framing can be found in the appendix to this chapter.
16. Patterson 1993; Cappella and Jamieson 1997; Jacobs and Shapiro 2000, chap. 2 and *passim.*
17. Cf. on resonance Miller and Riechert 2001; Snow and Benford 1988.
18. This is not to imply that all effective frames must stimulate emotion, only that words or images for which the culture's common schemas evoke strong emotional responses have a greater probability of influencing more people than other words or images, if only because emotional stimuli typically receive more attention from otherwise distracted, apolitical citizens (Marcus, Neuman, and MacKuen 2000). Scholars have now shown that the cognitive and affective realms, thinking and emotion, are thoroughly intertwined. (E.g., Cacioppo and Gardner 1999; Forgas 2001; Graber 2001; Kuklinski 2001; Lodge and Taber 2000, 212–13; Marcus, Neuman, and MacKuen 2000.) They often work together to enhance reasoning (assuming that the information they use, as Page and Shapiro (1992) note, is not wrong or misleading); in this view, emotion is not the opposite of rational thought but its frequent companion. In any case, however much based in cognition or emotion, people seem to have a motivation, rooted in evolution, to evaluate stimuli as positive or negative, to judge whether they pose threats or promise benefits. Cacioppo and Gardner 1999, 204 term these two dimensions aversion and appetition; cf. Marcus, Neuman, and MacKuen 2000.
19. Of course the meaning was not in the early minutes self-evident at all. The first jet could have represented a bizarre accident. Once a second flew into the tower, it became clearer that this was a hostile act. Moreover, hardly any images appear in the media without accompanying words that provide some verbal framing or explanation.
20. Cf. Kuklinski 2001; Iyengar 1991; experimental work by such scholars as Gilliam and Iyengar 2000; Mendelberg 2001; and Nelson, Clawson, and Oxley 1997 confirms the power potentially exerted by a single exposure to a racialized visual

stimulus, for instance. Yet research on media effects typically relates amount of exposure directly to opinions, neglecting that a single experience with the right kind of message can yield strong impacts (cf. Shrum 1996). By the same token, media content studies typically only measure magnitude by counting the repetitions of a particular message, often without even including prominence (for example, page 1 or page 22), let alone cultural resonance. Yet multiple exposures to bits of information that fail to engage the culture can be literally meaningless to most people, especially if they appear in more obscure corners of the news.

21. Fiske and Taylor 1991.

22. Sniderman, Brody, and Tetlock 1991.

23. Schank and Abelson 1977.

24. According to the "exposure rule," seeing culturally resonant words and images in news texts will tend to activate matching thoughts in audience members. See Taber, Lodge, and Glathar 2001, 202–3.

25. Ibid., 202. Fiske and Taylor (1991, 131) define schemas as "cognitive structures that represent knowledge about a concept or type of stimulus, including its attributes and the relations among the attributes."

26. Building on recent advances in the technology of brain imaging, Gabrieli (1998, 93) reports on extensive neurological research into how information processing works physiologically. He finds "remarkable specificity in the cortical representation of long-term memories." Gabrieli notes how young this science is—that it is just beginning to use neuro-imaging in healthy rather than diseased brains. He writes that there has to be "a great deal of psychological interpretation involved in understanding the meaning of an activation [of a neural network], i.e., in specifying what mental process is signified by an activation." The complexity "places a new premium upon the thoughtfulness" of the analyst (ibid. 89). So cognitive scientists have not reached consensus on how knowledge, memory, and information processing operate, whether we are speaking about those who study these phenomena at the physiological level like Gabrieli or the psychological like Kintsch (1998). In light of all this, readers should understand the discussion here as an adaptation of insights from a rapidly developing field rather than a definitive application of settled scientific knowledge.

27. Kintsch 1998, 412.

28. Lodge and Stroh 1993, 248 (emphasis added).

29. This portrayal represents my own synthesis of Lodge and Stroh 1993 with Taber, Lodge, and Glathar 2001 and with other related models described in Kintsch 1998; Kuklinski 2001; Lodge and Taber 2000; Iyengar and McGuire 1993 (especially Sears 1993; and Jervis 1993); and Fiske and Taylor 1991; cf. Sniderman, Brody, and Tetlock 1991. Lodge and Stroh's earlier explanation (1993) seems especially useful for those interested in impacts of news frames. To summarize their theory of long term memory (ibid., 247–48): "The basic characteristics of long-term memory are 1) node strength, the inherent strength or accessibility of a node that determines the ease with which it is brought to mind; 2) belief strength, the strength of association between connected nodes; 3) affective tags, the evaluative weight of each node; and 4) the implicational relation believed to exist between connected nodes."

30. As Lodge and Stroh (1993, 250) put it, "First impressions count most heavily in

an overall evaluation because they 1) generate the initial set of strong inferences, which then (2) occupy a place in working memory to the exclusion of weaker inferences drawn from subsequent stimuli."

31. On the other hand, recency and repetition of stimuli will become more important where the object of concern is already familiar, already enmeshed in a knowledge network.

32. Another term sometimes used interchangeably with frames is "prototype" (Lakoff 1987). And the discussion here does not exhaust all terminological issues surrounding the concept of framing, which are explored further in the appendix to this chapter. Other important works on framing include Gamson 1988, 1992; Gamson and Modigliani 1987, 1989; Gamson et al. 1992; Goffman 1974; Pan and Kosicki 2001, Reese 2001 and other chapters in Reese, Gandy, and Grant 2001; Schon and Rein 1995. On the connections between agenda setting and framing, see McCombs and Ghanem 2001; cf. McCombs and Shaw 1993.

33. The model of frame contestation advanced here can be compared with that suggested by Wolfsfeld 1997. His main concern (and dependent variable) is *change* in media frames in response to group competition (particularly pro- and anti-Palestinian news coverage). Although Wolfsfeld's model emphasizes different dependent and independent variables, it is not incompatible with much of the discussion here; cf. Wolfsfeld 2003.

34. Using the metaphor of spreading activation does not assume precisely analogous processes at every level of the cascading system. Spreading activation of interpretations within individuals' knowledge networks is a largely automatic and unconscious psychological process. On the other hand, the spread of interpretative schemas within and across other levels of the system is rarely automatic or unconscious. Indeed, the purpose of the cascade model is to explain how variations in strategy, motivation, power, and cultural congruence all affect the degree to which competing ideas spread. I am grateful to Scott Althaus (private communication) for highlighting this issue. What is analogous across the levels is the existence of *networks of association:* among ideas, among people, and among the communicating symbols (words and images). The usefulness of the metaphor thus rests in its highlighting of the similarities in the ways ideas activate and spread from one location on the network to others, often quickly and with little trouble, but other times with considerable conflict (internal/mental, interpersonal, interorganizational, or rhetorical).

35. Think tank and academic experts and perhaps others with cultural, political, or economic capital may have the most intellectual autonomy of all. They can activate their own cognitive and affective associations in response to the event, unmediated by calculations of personal political benefit or strategy. However, they also have the least influence on the news (cf. Mermin 1999).

36. To be a part of this "Washington" network it is no longer necessary (if it ever was) to actually live in D.C. Virtually free long distance telephone and fax, and free e-mail, make for easy and close communication between faculty at Harvard and Stanford and experts resident at Brookings or the American Enterprise Institute. I suspect, however, that to win acceptance as a full-fledged member of the

network, one does have to reside in Washington for a few years, working in the government or at a think tank, going to the cocktail parties and conferences that are the currency of "networking" in the popular sense of the term. For discussions of the unofficial source network's operations, see Manheim 1994 on the influence of strategic public relations on media coverage of foreign nations and events; Coleman and Perl 1999 on international policy networks; cf. Cook 1998.

37. Among many studies supporting this notion are Cook 1998; Entman and Rojecki 2000; Gans 2002; Iyengar 1991; Page and Shapiro 1992; Patterson 1993; Sobel 2001.

38. For the purposes of understanding the media's role in foreign policy debate and decision, it does not necessarily matter whether the individuals operating the media exercise free will. For that matter, the same doubts could be raised about whether members of Congress or the executive branch enjoy free will and ultimately determine their own actions, or rather are largely hamstrung by institutional roles, norms, and pressures. Research suggests that the growing relative independence of journalism in fact poses a variety of constraints and frustrations to leaders; see, e.g., Entman 1989; Patterson 1993.

39. A finding supported by the previous literature, e.g., Bennett 2001; Graber 2001.

40. Iyengar and McGuire 1993; Sniderman, Brody, and Tetlock 1991.

41. Fiske and Taylor 1991; Marcus, Neuman, and MacKuen 2000.

42. Simon 1997, 118–20.

43. The public consists of a diverse assortment of individuals, some of them quite interested in and well-informed about foreign policy, others attentive only in times of crisis, still others content to remain in blissful ignorance of international affairs. Estimates vary, but as Sobel (2001) and others suggest, perhaps 5–10 percent of the general public follows world politics with some care. This segment's opinions may exert more influence on government officials than the public as a whole, but discerning the actual state of informed opinion is no easy task, as survey organizations do not limit their polling to that group alone.

44. Robinson 2002 provides a model that falls somewhere between hegemony and indexing. It emphasizes "policy certainty"—or what might be termed "unity"—within the administration as the key variable that, interacting with levels of elite dissent, produces more or less media criticism, and media impact on policy. If an administration is still debating a policy, its uncertainty opens the way for mediated dissent to influence its actions, according to Robinson. But if the administration has come to a policy decision, media criticism or elite disputation rarely make much difference. Although it does not explicitly encompass the other variables in the cascade model, Robinson's study provides a useful synthesis of the two older models, one compatible with much of the discussion in this book.

45. Cf. Lodge and Taber 2000 and Taber, Lodge, and Glathar 2001, on motivations of average citizens to process political information and develop evaluations based on active or automatic thought and affect.

46. E.g., Bennett 2001; Cook 1998; Entman 1989; Gans 1979; Graber 2001; Patterson 1993; Tuchman 1978.

47. Also see Wolfsfeld 1997, 65 and *passim;* 2003.

48. These categories of congruent, ambiguous, and incongruent can be compared to Hallin's (1986) formulation of three spheres in public discourse: of consensus, legitimate controversy, and deviance.

49. E.g., Lodge and Taber 2000.

50. In fact, those few journalists with the temerity to challenge even mildly the framing of 9/11 were blocked from inculcating similar future mental associations—they were dismissed or thoroughly reprimanded. Bohlen 2001 describes how Bill Maher, the host of ABC's *Politically Incorrect,* suggested the terrorists of September 11 were not, as President Bush proclaimed, "cowards." Maher, echoing a word just used by his guest, conservative analyst D'nesh D'Souza, apparently meant this as oblique criticism of Bush's predecessor, President Clinton, who (Maher implied) tried to limit U.S. military engagements to "safe" bombing from high altitudes. This one misunderstood remark unleashed a storm of criticism that resulted in several advertisers pulling their commercials, and culminated in the network's canceling the program. Also see Carter and Barringer 2001, writing about journalists in Oregon and Texas and others who either lost their jobs or came under intense public pressure merely for criticizing Bush's behavior on September 11. Similar pressures on media arose during the 2003 war in Iraq, as discussed in chapter 5.

51. Cf. Marcus, Neuman, and MacKuen 2000.

52. For example, a *New York Times*/CBS News poll (10–12 February 2003) asked respondents "Which of the following do you think is the most important thing for Congress to concentrate on: the war on terror, the economy, Iraq or North Korea?" Fully 41 percent answered "the economy," 29 percent "war on terror," 16 percent "Iraq," and just 7 percent "North Korea." See Adam Clymer and Janet Elder "Threats and Responses; The Poll; Poll Finds Unease on Terror Fight and Concerns about War on Iraq," *New York Times,* 8 September 2002, sec. 1-1. A January 2003 Pew Research Center survey (2003, 2) found 55 percent of the public saying they followed Iraq news "very closely," compared with 34 percent for North Korea. On the administration's exertions to avoid framing the nuclear threat from North Korea as a crisis in early 2003, see James Dao, "Threats and Responses: Nuclear Standoff; Bush Administration Defends Its Approach on North Korea," *New York Times,* 7 February 2003, A13.

53. Cf. Page and Shapiro 1992; Zaller 1991; Zaller and Chiu 2000.

54. See Lane 1962 on the problems with morselization.

55. On Rwanda, see Power 2001.

56. On the heightened monitoring of public opinion, see Cook, Barabus, and Page 2002; Jacobs and Shapiro 2000.

APPENDIX TO CHAPTER ONE

1. The use here is analogous to Kuhn's (1962) notion of paradigms that guide information processing by scientists engaged in "normal science." As with dominant paradigms in scientific inquiry, so with the paradigms that guide social and political discussion: they channel perceptions and information processing but are subject to disruption by anomalous events that can force revision and even stimulate a new paradigm. The collapse of the Soviet Union permanently disrupted

the Cold War paradigm with major consequences for news and public discourse, as detailed in chapter 5 of this volume.

2. Terrorism was by September 2001 a familiar concept from many high-magnitude, high-resonance events; cf. Livingston 1994.

3. E.g., Neuman, Just, and Crigler 1992; Semetko and Valkenburg 2000.

4. Entman and Rojecki 2000, chap. 7.

5. E.g., Kahneman and Tversky 1984; Kinder and Sanders 1996; Sniderman, Brody, and Tetlock 1991; Zaller 1992.

6. Such as Iyengar 1991 and Kinder and Sanders 1996.

7. Kahneman and Tversky 1984.

8. Kinder and Sanders 1996.

9. Sniderman, Brody, and Tetlock 1991, 51.

10. Also see Sniderman, Tetlock, and Elms 2001; cf. Zaller 1992.

11. E.g., Murray and Cowden 1999; Hermann and Voss 1997.

CHAPTER TWO

1. The dates on the magazines are 12 and 19 September 1983, and 18 and 25 July 1988. The newsmagazines come out on a Monday but carry the dates of the following Monday, so that, for example, the 12 September issue actually was released on 5 September, four days after the shootdown.

2. See Gans 1979, 4.

3. See Entman 1989; cf. Bennett 2001; Gamson 1989, 23–24; Gans 1979; Graber 1988.

4. Corcoran 1986; Rachlin 1988; Young and Launer 1988, 38.

5. Hersh 1986.

6. Cf. Entman 1989.

7. The Iran Air incident came in the midst of a presidential campaign, which may help explain the lesser magnitude of coverage. But it stretches credulity to argue that this is the whole explanation for the difference in attention. The tragedy *could* have fueled controversy in the campaign, after all. In any case, the chief concern here is the contrast in the two event frames, whatever the reasons, and the competing news explanation does not apply to the content, only to the magnitude of the frame.

8. Young and Launer (1988, 11) observe: "The destruction of KAL 007 was handled as a crisis because Reagan's advisors made it into one. It was their premise that the behavior of the Soviet government had followed the 'rational actor' model. This assumption created a false reality that accorded with their preconceptions."

9. A word count is not available, so the average length of the stories cannot be compared. But, for example, the *Post*'s 169 KAL articles took up 1.02 megabytes of disk space, while the eighty-two Iran Air items occupied 536 kilobytes. This suggests that average story length was slightly greater for Iran Air, bolstering the argument in the text.

10. In fact, the *Vincennes* did possess a civilian air schedule, but crewmembers checked it only in the tangled rush of events after the unidentified plane was first discovered on radar screens. At that point, nobody spotted the listing of Flight 655, which was on time and on course.

11. Although Admiral Crowe here provides a mitigating circumstance, later investigations showed the *Vincennes* was not "engaged with threatening Iranian surface units" at the time of the incident.

12. Hersh 1986; U.S. House of Representatives 1988.

13. See Entman 1991 for illustrations of the newsmagazine graphics.

14. The cover did, however, imply agency on the part of the *Vincennes* and in this sense might have stimulated some audience members to make causal inferences (blaming the United States) that were discouraged by the rest of the coverage.

15. Johnson (1987, 36) asserts that the KAL plane probably did not explode or burn when first hit by the missile; none of the recovered wreckage showed fire damage, and at thirty-two thousand feet the air was too thin, he argues, to allow combustion. Also, radar showed that the plane was still in one piece as it fell to the ground. On the other hand, the Iran Air plane was at a relatively low altitude where it could explode and burn. Yet no graphics showed the impact of the missile on the Iran Air plane.

16. The Iran Air coverage did include some pictures of anonymous bodies floating in the water after the accident, and some illustrations of Iranians not identified by name who were angrily demonstrating against the United States and also presumably grieving the loss.

17. *Time,* 12 September 1983, 12.

18. Cf. Galtung and Ruge 1965.

19. As Smith (1985) documents, the words Ronald Reagan himself used most frequently to describe the KAL incident were "massacre," "tragedy," and "attack," all of which the present study reveals to be key components of the media text.

20. The *Post* and *Times* analyses count only the words "atrocity," "crime," "kill," "massacre," and "murder" as guilt attributions, and the words "accident," "blunder," and "mistake" as exculpatory.

21. Full-text databases for the *Post*'s and *Times*'s coverage during the sample periods were drawn from NEXIS by selecting all stories containing any form of the words "Korea" or "Iran" within fifty words of any word beginning "air." Stories were checked to ensure they did report on the incidents of interest.

22. In the *Post,* "barbaric/barbarous" appeared fourteen times, "deliberate/deliberately" ten times, and "murderous," "brutal/brutally," and "wanton/wantonly" eight times each; in the *Times,* "brutal/brutally" appeared eighteen times, "horrible/horrifying(ly)" fourteen, and "deliberate/deliberately" and "wanton/wantonly" eleven times each.

23. The *Post* used "mistaken/mistakenly" twenty-eight times, "tragic" fifteen times, and "justified" nine times. In the *Times,* the most common were "tragic/tragically" (twenty times), "mistaken/mistakenly" (fifteen times), and "understandable" (four times).

24. This sort of comparison might arguably call for percentages rather than absolute numbers, since there was twice as much text on KAL. However, the absolute number of words is more pertinent, in my view, because one important feature of framing that the comparison reveals is precisely the volume of coverage: Iran Air generated much less copy than KAL. In any case, those asserting U.S. guilt were mostly foreign sources with little credibility in the United States.

25. On this and other way media construct enemies, cf. Edelman 1988, 2001.

26. Cf. Corcoran 1986.
27. The two that can be interpreted positively came in a column by Meg Greenfield in which she quoted hypothetical defenders of the Soviet Union, but then said that whether the Soviet Union was evil was irrelevant.
28. *Newsweek,* 19 September 1983, 23–24.
29. *Time,* 12 September 1983, 11, 18.
30. Cf. Marcus, Neuman, and MacKuen 2000.
31. The Soviets' failure to apologize after the KAL downing was one theme of the coverage.
32. Cf. Condit 1989.
33. Cf. Budd, Entman, and Steinman 1990; Gitlin 1980; Hall 1973.
34. Petty and Cacioppo 1986.
35. Ibid.
36. Masters 2001.
37. See Russett 1990, 41.
38. Cf. Hersh 1986; Johnson 1987, 153–54; Rojecki 1999.
39. *Newsweek,* 19 September 1983, 21.
40. Dallin 1985, 94.
41. Johnson 1987, 171.
42. Cf. Young and Launer 1988.
43. Cannon 1988.
44. Hersh 1986, 36.
45. Cf. MacKuen 1983.
46. Forbes 1990.
47. Treating all bits of praise and criticism of the administration's preferred framing in coverage of foreign policy equivalently can for this reason yield misleading or incomplete results. What is politically important is the presence of a relatively complete counterframe, not merely fragments of information strewn incoherently throughout the news.
48. Wyer and Gordon 1984, 96.
49. Cf. Gitlin 1980, 49–52.

CHAPTER THREE

1. The *Times* index was employed because the sheer volume of text on each crisis would have made detailed analysis impossible. Confidence in this approach is based on Bennett's useful and widely cited employment of the index (1989 and 1990); by reading over the *Times* coverage proper; by the congruence of the *Times* data found here with the network news data; and by a more detailed analysis of Libya coverage in the *Times,* some of which is referred to here (see Althaus et al. 1996). Also see Bennett and Manheim 1993 on the reliability of the *Times* index, and Althaus, Edy, and Phalen 2001. As for the television analysis, ABC transcripts could not be obtained for the two earlier crises, and CBS transcripts were unavailable for the later one. The literature amply supports the proposition that the three major broadcast network evening news programs have been similar enough to treat as equivalent. (e.g., Cook 1998; Graber 2001). The *Times* analysis covered 17 October–15 November 1983 (Grenada); 8–27 April 1986 (Libya); and 19 December 1989–26 January 1990 (Panama).

2. A few (nonexhaustive) examples of each category in the case of Grenada follow. Positive problem framing includes assertions that the new government in Grenada is a violent dictatorship or that Cuba and Russia are supporting the new government. Examples of negative problem framing assertions are that the new government is not violent or that U.S. citizens are not in danger. Positive policy assertions: military action simply described; military action shown as effective and efficient; civilian casualties are understandable, excusable, or Grenada's fault. Negative policy assertions: military action ineffective/inefficient; U.S. interests damaged by invasion. Leadership positive: U.S. action in accord with treaties and international law; U.S. not violating War Powers Act; press restrictions are proper. Leadership negative: U.S. violating treaties, international law; administration violates War Powers Act; press restrictions are inappropriate.

In keeping with the qualitative analysis reported later, it is important to note how, for example, a statement that European allies do not support U.S. bombing of Libya functions as both a policy critique and an implicit questioning of the underlying problem diagnosis. Statements are polysemic themselves and quantitative content analysis finally has to make judgments about predominant thrust, judgments that might not reflect the way the bulk of the audience actually responded to a given assertion. This complexity could suggest not dividing the text too finely into separate categories for purposes of frame analysis, of course. No doubt this difficulty is one reason most content analytical studies simply report on pro- and anti-administration (or Republican or Democrat or whatever the object of the framing contest might be); only by subsuming content to the most general category of positive or negative can high intercoder reliability be achieved. This study sacrifices some intercoder reliability for more theoretical insight into the text and its relationship to the government and public; it also uses qualitative interpretation of the texts to enhance understanding.

For example, the television news verbal code reliabilities, using a graduate student to recode approximately half the coverage, were as follows: .88, .87, and .83 for Grenada, Libya, and Panama respectively. Disagreements in only 2 of some 336 coded assertions were serious (that is, one of us coded an assertion as anti-administration that the other coded as pro). The rest of the conflicts consisted of one of us coding a statement the other either regarded as too implicit to code, or simply missed. The similar findings of Nacos (1990) boost confidence in the results reported here; cf. Dickson 1994 on Panama and Althaus et al. (1996) on Libya. The conclusions reached by another study (Mermin 1999) differ somewhat; although it finds reporting on both Grenada and Panama overwhelmingly pro-administration, the data indicate Grenada coverage was far more negative than Panama (about 8.3 percent of coded assertions on Grenada were negative compared with 1.6 percent on Panama). The coding protocol of that study does not distinguish what I call problem definition and policy remedy or procedural criticism, and its methodological and analytical approaches differ substantially from the one used here. I believe this accounts for any differences in the findings.

3. For example, the questionable premises and results of the U.S. invasion of Panama in 1989–90 were the subject of an Academy Award–winning documentary, *The Panama Deception;* also see Physicians for Human Rights 1991.

4. It is possible that the finding of relatively more benign treatment of the Panama intervention resulted from use of ABC rather than CBS transcripts. However, Nacos's (1990, 164–75) study of Grenada coverage, employing a somewhat different approach, yielded convergent results. It found that news coverage in the *Times* and *Washington Post* was dominated by the administration, although criticism of the invasion was frequent, especially from foreign sources. The *Times*'s editorials were extremely critical, the *Post*'s generally supportive.

5. These represent the percentage of negative assertions coming from hostile foreign sources, foreign allies, or from a mix of foreign sources including adversary, neutral, and allied nations. Similar findings on heavy representation of foreign sources are reported in Althaus et al. 1996 and Althaus 2002; Dickson 1994; Mermin 1999.

6. Cf., e.g., Masters 2001, 94; Page and Shapiro 1992. In the context of the Gulf War, Brody 1994, 220–21, provides evidence that foreign criticism may boomerang, heightening support for the president rather than diminishing it.

7. Cf. Althaus et al. 1996.

8. See Bissell 2002; Brosius 1993; Graber 2001; Jamieson 1992; Crigler and Just 1994; Lang and Friestad 1993; Masters 2001; Masters and Sullivan 1993; Moriarty and Popovich 1991; Newhagen and Reeves 1992.

9. Though cf. Masters 2001; continuing controversies in the cognitive psychology of visual representation are discussed in Chang and Ya-Qin 1999; Crigler and Just 1994; Edelman 1998.

10. Newhagen and Reeves 1992, 38–39.

11. Visual criticism or support of the chief actor's (administration's) leadership technique was also coded, since such process-oriented framing was so common in the written coverage. This turned out to yield few results. Most pictures of leaders were neutral head shots—stills of talking heads. Only in the case of Grenada were there many codeable pictures of Reagan, ten of them judged to reinforce his leadership skill and two critical of it. The latter were both cartoons attacking his administration's restrictions on press coverage of the invasion. Surveys tend to show large majorities of the public supporting restrictions on the press (the major theme of the leadership critiques). For instance, a poll of Georgia residents taken around the start of the Gulf War in January 1991 by the Harris organizations asked: "Which of the following statements comes closest to the way you feel about media coverage of the war: 1. There are too many restrictions on where reporters can go and what they can report, or 2. There is too much reporting of information that might help the enemy?" Ten percent answered there were too many restrictions; 74.3 percent answered too much reporting; 6.5 percent found both equal; 5.30 percent answered neither; 3.8 percent responded don't know / not ascertained.

Pictures counted as supportive evaluations of leadership were coded where the president was shown in consultation with expert advisers or members of Congress (one full page picture of President Reagan at his desk in the Oval Office was also coded this way). In Libya just two codeable pictures of Reagan appeared, both judged supportive, and in Panama no picture of Bush (except a small inset to a one-page photo showing Panama City "ablaze" and featuring superimposed *Time*'s logo for the invasion, an arm with bicep flexed, with a stars and stripes design). Perhaps it is noteworthy that the faces of Reagan and Bush were so scarce in Libya and Panama coverage, respectively—both policies were only equivocally successful and their handlers might have preferred putting other administration spokespersons out front to deal with the media. Once the purportedly threatened medical students came home from Grenada, on the other hand, the media trumpeted the invasion as an enormous triumph and prominently featured Reagan's visage.

12. When casualties do begin to mount significantly, however, opinion polls indicate deterioration in support of the policy; see Page and Shapiro 1992.

13. Roger Fowler (1991, 112–19) explored coverage of the Libya bombing in three different, class-oriented British newspapers: a left-leaning tabloid, a right-leaning one, and an elite paper. He found that the rightist tabloid veered toward overtly racist images of Arabs, labeled "rats" and the like; it also used the "Mad Dog" expression from Reagan's public description of Qaddafi repeatedly in headlines and text; and in an exhibit of intertextuality it invoked the notion of "Rambo Ronnie." The *Guardian,* the elite paper, was clearly critical compared to both the rightist and leftist tabloids.

14. This point is developed in detail with respect to the Gulf War in chapter 4.

15. Two other propagandistic elements in the coverage of all three actions were portrayals of the enemy nations as populated by irrational fanatics and stories of gallant sacrifice by American service personnel reminiscent of World War II.

16. The White House admitted a year later that Syria, not Libya, controlled the disco bombing. Cf. Lee and Soloman 1990, 129; Peffley, Langley, and Goidel 1995, n. 7.

17. Knightley 1975 writes of the much longer history of wartime disinformation.

18. A representative story is Douglas Jehl and Bob Secter, "Noriega's Inner Sanctum: Lair of 'Debauched Thug,'" *Los Angeles Times,* 23 December 1989, A1.

19. Dorman and Farhang 1987.

20. Hallin 1986.

21. Cf. Herman and Chomsky 1988.

22. Tuchman 1978.

23. Brody 1991; Mermin 1999; cf. Russett 1990.

24. Kernell 1993, 162–63.

25. See Smith 1983, 11.

26. Cf. Mermin 1999, chap. 3; Nacos 1990, 177.

27. A few Democrats with little congressional influence did call for Reagan's impeachment over Grenada; they were briefly reported on the inside pages of the *Times,* and went unmentioned on CBS.

28. Had my own children been in Grenada, I too would have felt relief on their safe return to the United States. I understand the emotions of parents, students, and empathizing Americans at large. On the other hand, even if personally involved, one might have—as the *Times* suggested—judged the U.S. invasion as a potentially self-defeating way of protecting students' lives.

29. The contrast with the *Times*'s own news pages is striking (see Hallin 1986 on a similar contradiction during Vietnam, and cf. Nacos 1990 for similar findings). It should also be noted, in defense of Congress, that journalists underreported some aspects of the dissent that Congress members were voicing and

overrepresented other aspects, at least on the Libya bombing (Althaus et al. 1996).

30. For a critical discussion of this generalization, see Kull and Ramsay 2001.
31. Hinckley 1992, 96.
32. Ibid., 96–97.
33. See Livingston 1994.
34. Kernell 1993, 163.
35. See ibid., 184 n. 13.
36. Warner 1987.
37. Brace and Hinckley 1992, 110.
38. Ibid., 111.
39. Also, as I have shown elsewhere, problem definition and causal analysis in framing coverage of the Beirut bombing did not focus on Reagan's personal responsibility but rather on the terrorists and on essentially anonymous lower-level U.S. military officers, because the administration successfully managed the news. See Entman 1989, chap. 3.
40. Cf. Zaller 1992.
41. Cf. MacArthur 1992.
42. Cf. Kintsch 1998; Lodge and Stroh 1993.
43. Cf. Meyrowitz 1986.
44. Cf. Cappella and Jamieson 1997; Patterson 2002.
45. Noelle-Neumann 1993.
46. See Entman 1989; Groeling, forthcoming. The elite spiral of silence illustrated in this chapter comes from leaders' fear of public displeasure, and also perhaps from anxiety about personal disapproval among colleagues in the elite network. (Noelle-Neumann's spiral of silence theory (1993) emphasizes the motivating force of personal relationships.) Ironically, because Washington is more a community of frequent face-to-face political conversation than is the typical community in which most Americans reside, because something like a Habermasian (1989) public sphere actually operates for Washington elites, Noelle-Neumann's original spiral theory may be more valid for the leadership of a country than for the ordinary citizens she studied. And an elite spiral of silence can arise even in response to small shifts in public sentiment. Kernell (1993, 167) notes:

> Even if a representative suspects that no more than 4 or 5 percent of the electorate will base its vote . . . on support of the president's program . . . marginal shifts of preferences . . . often have major political consequences. . . . The president makes an appeal; most citizens do not respond, but some do. A few of this latter group express their support actively. Most of the politicians who oppose the president's position will resist constituency pressure. A few whose positions are less fixed or who are electorally vulnerable will be persuaded. . . . Frequently, this is all that is required for the president to appear to have worked his magic.

47. It is fair to note that some leaders may also sincerely believe it their duty to put aside their own personal views in the face of an apparently overwhelming public consensus.

48. Cf. Mermin 1999, 10–11.
49. Gans 1979; Tuchman 1978.
50. Entman 1989.
51. If attacks on leadership are sufficiently persistent they can undermine elites' and journalists' respect for the president, feeding a vicious downward spiral of negative news slant that ultimately diminishes a president's power (Entman 1989). In addition, the boundary between substantive and procedural evaluation becomes murky when it comes to the institutional interests of news organizations. Journalists may and often do bitterly criticize administrations for withholding information, limiting reporters' access to the battlefield, or trying to manage the news. However, these criticisms appear to have little effect on most of the reporting and are largely confined to the editorial pages. When the chips were especially down, in the case of the draconian restrictions placed on reporters during the Persian Gulf War (1991), editorials were *not* backed up by legal action. Thus not one major media organization participated in a lawsuit challenging the Pentagon's restrictions on First Amendment grounds; only limited-circulation, left-leaning outlets backed the case. Nor did the chief executive officers or powerful elite board members of such organizations as ABC, CBS, NBC (owned by General Electric), *Time,* the *New York Times,* or other elite national media engage in energetic personal lobbying of the administration to lift the curbs. Consequently, once war commenced, news became by almost universal judgments from within the journalism profession as well as outside little more than propaganda for the Bush administration (Bennett and Paletz 1994; MacArthur 1992; Sharkey 1992)—at least until the ground war came to its somewhat anticlimactic and inconclusive end in the spring of 1991.

CHAPTER FOUR

1. Much of this study originally appeared in a paper coauthored with Benjamin Page and published in Bennett and Paletz 1994. In rewriting for this book, I have substantially altered the framing and analyses of the findings. Many thanks to Ben Page for his collaboration on the original paper. I would also like to thank Northwestern University's Center for Urban Affairs and Policy Research for providing research funds, Bea Chestnut, Michael Hostetler, Limor Peer, and Hiram Sachs for research assistance, and participants in the SSRC Working Group on the Media and U.S. Foreign Policy chaired by W. Lance Bennett for their helpful comments.
2. Mueller 1994; Sobel 2001.
3. *New York Times,* 14 December 1990, A8; 9 January 1991, A6; 15 January 1991, A13. Other polling data, however, tapping other dimensions of public thinking, indicate that the public started lining up with the Bush administration by November (see Mueller 1994). Thus news organizations might have found the signals about mass opinion to be ambiguous, if not leaning toward the administration, as early as November.
4. Coding protocols were slightly different during the two periods, because the major issues of the policy debate altered somewhat. The coding procedure also differed in that, for Period 2, only one coder was used for most of the text, while for Period 1 two coders were used for the *Washington Post* and *New York Times.*

For Period 2, there was much discussion to ensure consistent coding decisions, and coders resolved uncertainties by consulting with each other or with me. For the Period 1 stories from the *Post* and *Times,* initial intercoder reliability as to codeable assertions was .80, with the final data used reflecting only those assertions whose coding could be reconciled by the coders. "Reliability" was relatively low, reflecting the considerable ambiguity of real-world news and policy discourse. The key area of ambiguity tended to be whether an assertion that on its face was simply declarative would be read in the context of the ongoing news text and policy debate as a potentially evaluative claim. Often we found news messages to be suffused with implicit though sometimes ambiguous evaluation, and rather than throw out the many implicit assertions—which could predispose the analysis toward finding more administration dominance of the news, since criticism was more likely to be implicit—we counted them when both coders agreed on their relevance.

   An example of explicit opposition is "The chairman of the Senate Armed Services Committee today criticized the Bush administration's decision to drop its plan to station troops in Saudi Arabia, saying that it puts the United States on too fast a track toward war." Implicit opposition: "Senator Nunn and Representative Aspin agreed that the administration should seek congressional approval if it decided to wage war against Iraq." Implicit support: "The reason is that every month Iraq goes unbombed brings it a step closer to producing nuclear weapons." Explicit support: "His [Bush's] purpose is surely justifiable; Saddam Hussein's aggression cannot be allowed to stand."

5. Less systematic review of the coverage suggests that the administration received heavy preference on the visual dimensions of the television message. For example, administration figures were shown much more frequently smiling, in settings they control, and in juxtaposition with flags or other authority-enhancing symbols.

6. An assertion counts as appearing on page one if it appeared on the first page of the first section of the paper or on page one of the "Outlook" or "News of the Week in Review" Sunday summary sections of the *Post* or *Times,* respectively. (An assertion that appeared on page 7 of the Sunday summary sections counts the same as a page-7 assertion in the first section, and so forth.)

7. News about policy frequently includes debate over the administration's support base, especially because public opinion provides a standard of legitimacy for any proposed remedy and for evaluations of the sides' competence (cf. Entman 1989). Assertions were coded as falling in one of the procedural categories when they generally characterized the state of public support, but when the same assertion included mention of public opinion and also a substantive evaluation of the policy, the code was for policy substance. Thus a sentence saying "Polls show most Americans back Bush's policy" was coded as favorable to the administration, in the public support (procedural) category. But a sentence "Most Americans support Bush's Jan. 15 deadline as a necessary response to Saddam's aggression" contains a substantively grounded evaluation of the policy and was coded as substantively favoring Bush in the war versus sanctions category. In any case, references to public opinion were often reported in the context of Bush's actions or strategies, and thus they concerned procedural matters. Also, in coding Pe-

riod 2 assertions, there was more difficulty fitting all critical or supportive comments into these categories and thus several assertions were omitted. Most omissions were of supportive assertions, for example, praise of Bush's diplomatic skill in garnering U.N. support. A few critical claims were omitted, largely those involving wrangles over the specific date when Congress should go into session to vote on commencement of military action (discarded as too peripheral to the frame contest to be relevant). If anything, then, the data may overestimate the amount of media criticism.

8. Woodward (1991, 335–36) argues that public relations concerns were a paramount cause of the U.N. initiative (cf. MacArthur 1992).

9. Cf. LaMay 1991, 63–64.

10. Hinckley 1992, 111, and Brody 1994 indicate, though the matter is highly complicated (cf. Mueller 1994), that much of the support for Bush's policy in Iraq dropped off before November 8, as the typical postcrisis rally around the president faded. Approval declined from 78 percent on September 9 to 64 percent on October 14 and 59 percent on November 15. Then it stabilized during the very period of most intense elite debate covered here, so that by December 9 it went up slightly, to 62 percent. Approval reached 69 percent by January 9, and 83 percent on January 20, after the war got off to a rousing, seemingly successful start—decisively reducing "quagmire" fears.

11. One other fact: Members of Congress were just recovering from the 1990 elections during Period 1, indeed most were back in their districts, so that opposition was less organized than in Period 2, which should offer the best case.

12. Hallin 1986 demonstrates similar media strategies employed by the Johnson and Nixon administrations to distract attention from their escalations of the Vietnam intervention.

13. Sifry and Cerf 1991, 234.

14. Ibid.

15. Woodward 1991.

16. These findings illustrate the usefulness of coding support, not just criticism, of the administration (only the latter is done in Mermin 1999). In addition, by distinguishing substantive from procedural criticism, the coding protocol here helps delineate the limits and boundaries of mediated dissent from the White House.

17. One might also speculate that editorials are read far more often and closely by D.C. insiders than by ordinary Americans, so that a column or editorial denouncing, say, a president or secretary of defense actually has more salience inside the elite community than would the very same views voiced by members of the opposition party and appearing in a news story. Thus leaders might have somewhat stronger motivations to ingratiate themselves with editorialists than with reporters.

18. The count assessed the administration officials listed in the text plus the names of all testifiers at the Senate Armed Services Committee hearings and all members of the committee.

19. Delli Carpini and Keeter 1996, chap. 3.

20. Cf. Bennett and Paletz 1994, chaps. 3 and 7; Mermin 1999.

21. Cf. Freedman and Karsh 1995; Jentleson 1994; Mearsheimer and Walt 2003.

22. Edwards 1990; Entman 1989.
23. Embodied in so-called operational codes (cf. Walker and Shafer 1999) or ideologies (Holsti and Rosenau 1984).
24. Cf. Pan and Kosicki 2001 and Wolfsfeld 1997 on strategic framing.
25. See especially Althaus et al. 1996; Althaus 2002.
26. Bennett (1989 and 1990) shows how editorial policy, though somewhat independent of the White House and Congress, nonetheless takes cues from the elite network. On the other hand, Page and Shapiro (1992) analyze data suggesting that back when editorial commentary was common on network television news, it exerted significant influence on the public's responses to opinion polls.
27. Cf. Edelman 1988 and 2001, and Sears 2001 on the unimportance of self-interest in the mass public's political thinking.
28. Gans 1979; Sigal 1973.
29. Cf. Entman 1989.
30. Cook 1994; cf. Powlick and Katz 1998.
31. Dorman and Livingston 1994.
32. Hallin 1986.

CHAPTER FIVE
1. See also Gilboa 2002; Rojecki 2002.
2. Kuhn 1962.
3. In assessing the impact of the Cold War's end, I do not mean to imply that during its forty-five years the United States enjoyed uninterrupted harmony and unity among elites, the media, and the public. How best to contain the USSR, whether and how to fight in Korea and Vietnam, what to do about the Middle East—these and many other policy choices provoked disputes. However, with few exceptions, the basic problem definitions did not occasion conflict in mainstream discourse: containing an expansionist Soviet Union and preventing nuclear war. Disagreements centered on solutions and tactics. To be sure, Vietnam disrupted the bipartisan elite consensus on foreign policy that had generally reigned between World War II and the Kennedy administration (cf. Holsti 1996; Sobel 2001). But it is mainly since the Cold War definitively ended with the collapse of the Soviet Union that we see even the problem definitions arousing heated controversy among elites.
4. It is worth noting that different generational cohorts experience paradigms to different degrees. For older Americans, the Cold War paradigm faded in salience. For those entering adolescence after 1991, that paradigm was never operational (except perhaps as historical curiosity). As time passes, more and more Americans will enter the electorate having never believed in the paradigm.
5. Cf. Lakoff 2002.
6. Sobel 2001; cf. Hinckley 1992, chap. 2; Kull and Destler 1999; Russett 1990. Also see Chicago Council on Foreign Affairs 2002.
7. Similar impatience characterizes domestic reporting; cf. Entman 1997.
8. That these perceptions are often inaccurate is detailed in Kull and Ramsay 2001.
9. Robinson 2002, chap. 3 argues that policymakers' decision to intervene was not "caused" by media coverage (which he dubs "The CNN effect") in Somalia, but rather that media served "as an enabler and then as a builder of support" (62).

Pressure had been building inside the Washington policy community to do something about the humanitarian disaster in Somalia well before media interest peaked, Robinson demonstrates. Interestingly, however, Robinson finds that many officials, including the secretary of state and President Bush himself cited media images as primary motivating forces in their decisions. And the Robinson study only looks at coverage for the three weeks prior to the Bush administration's decision on March 25, 1992, to intervene, whereas media attention, featuring vivid language and pictures, extends back for months prior to that, as evidenced by the *Time* cover of December 7. In any case, it would be misleading to talk about media coverage as *the* cause of any policy decision, and Robinson's subtle analysis demonstrates that mediated communication played a significant role in the tangle of forces that influenced the thinking and behavior of decisionmakers.

10. Elliott, Barry, and Breslau 1994.

11. Robinson 2002, chap. 4.

12. Ibid., 78–79.

13. Interview of Lake by Robinson and of Gore and Clinton by Bob Woodward; quoted in ibid., 82–83.

14. See, e.g., *Newsweek,* 19 June 1995. According to some reports, the highly publicized concerns for O'Grady's fate during the time he was missing stalled NATO air strikes for a week. See Art Pine, "Wishing for a War without Blood; Americans' Low Tolerance for Casualties Causes Some to Wonder Whether the U.S. Has the Fortitude to Undertake a Major Military Operation," *Los Angeles Times,* 13 December 1995, A1.

15. See, e.g., the *Los Angeles Times* editorial of 10 December 1995, M4: "Bosnia: Political Clock Is Ticking for Clinton; Airlift Marks a Time of Growing Pressure for Administration."

16. Entman 1989.

17. See Robinson 2002, 83.

18. The power of visuals is suggested in work by Brosius 1993; Brosius, Donsbach, and Birk 1996; Graber 2001; Newhagen and Reeves 1992; Masters 2001. It remains, however, one of the political communication phenomena most in need of thorough investigation.

19. Cf. Livingston 1996.

20. Cf. Althaus et al. 1996.

21. Cf. Groeling and Kernell 2000.

22. Going back to the Carter administration we can find several examples of Democrats' relative weakness. One is Carter's aborted decision to deploy the neutron bomb in Europe, abandoned in major part because of political opposition generated by hostile media coverage (Linsky et al. 1986, chap. 3). Another is coverage of the failed attempt in 1980 to rescue American hostages in Iran; although it could readily have been portrayed as a heroic attempt of brave American soldiers against long odds, in fact the news was devastatingly critical and politically damaging to President Carter (Entman 1989, chap. 3). The SALT II treaty agreement with the Soviet Union offers one more instance. It received a great deal of negative publicity, orchestrated by the Committee on the Present Danger and

other conservative opponents of rapprochement with the USSR from both parties. The opposition finally forced President Carter to withdraw it from Senate consideration (see Russett 1990, 49–50; Destler, Gelb, and Lake 1984). The most obvious examples of Republican (Reagan–Bush) policies that aroused controversy were U.S. intervention in Lebanon (1982–83), aid to the Nicaraguan Contras in the mid-1980s, and the deployment of the Navy to the Persian Gulf in the late 1980s to protect oil routes. However, these stories are quite complicated. In Lebanon, news depictions of a suicide bombing that killed nearly three hundred American troops were followed by an *increase* in public support for Reagan's Lebanon policy (Entman, 1989, chap. 3). The bombing did encourage the administration to pull the Americans out of Lebanon quietly a few weeks later. On Nicaragua, Bennett (1990) showed that media coverage actually lagged behind rather than fed the public's skepticism. Chestnut (1995) showed how the media generally cooperated with the Reagan and Bush efforts to contain the Iran–Contra scandal, which arose from Reagan's determination to circumvent public and elite opposition to aiding the counterrevolutionaries in Nicaragua. And as chapter 2 revealed, the tragic Iran Air incident failed to derail the Persian Gulf policy as media coverage tracked the administration's frame. Aside from these problematic exceptions, typical during those twelve years of GOP administrations was the media siding with the White House against sporadic elite opposition, even when the public was split (as in the prewar debate on Iraq) or shared the opponents' view (as in the nuclear freeze, discussed in chapter 6).

23. Hallin 1986.
24. Bennett and Paletz 1994. Also see Kellner 1992; Reese and Buckalew 1995.
25. The long-standing power of terrorism as a concept—and event—generating high-volume media attention is discussed in Livingston 1994.
26. See David Carr, "A Nation at War; Reporting Reflects Anxiety," *New York Times,* 25 March 2003, B1.
27. Thomas E. Ricks, "Briefing Depicted Saudis as Enemies; Ultimatum Urged to Pentagon Board," *Washington Post,* 6 August 2002, A1.
28. See James Dao, "Powell Charts Low Key Path in Iraq Debate," *New York Times,* 2 September 2002, A1.
29. For instance, Todd S. Purdum, "Bush Team Is Divided over Getting Tougher with Saudis," *New York Times,* 12 August 2002, A7.
30. On the other hand, *The West Wing* did feature a fictional subplot in which the United States had to deal with Qumar, a two-faced Middle Eastern country, putatively allied with America, that oppressed its citizens and supported anti-American activities. On the show, the United States stood up to Qumar. See David Johnston, "Classified Section of Sept. 11 Report Faults Saudi Rulers," *New York Times,* 26 July 2003, A1.
31. CNN's prime-time and breaking news reports do not appear to deviate markedly from those of the three broadcast networks. According to a Nexis search for "September 11" and "lawsuit," only twice did CNN's round-the-clock news mention the families' lawsuits and the Saudi defendants (as did Fox News on one broadcast) during July or August 2002.

188 NOTES TO PAGES 110–115

32. Christopher Marquis, "Worried Saudis Pay Millions To Improve Image in the U.S.," *New York Times,* 29 August 2002, A1. Polls at http://www.fabmac.com/FMA%20-%202002-08-19%20-%20Saudi%20Ad%20Campaign.pdf.

33. See Greenberg, Wechsler, and Wolosky 2002 for an elite think tank report.

34. CMPA, "Media Knock Iraq Attack Plans." (9 September 2002). http://www.cmpa.com/pressrel/Iraq2002PR.htm. FAIR, "ACTION ALERT: In Iraq Crisis Networks Are Megaphones for Officials' Views," 18 March 2003; "Amplifying Officials, Squelching Dissent," *EXTRA* (May/June 2003).

35. Brent Scowcroft, "Don't Attack Saddam," *Wall Street Journal,* 15 August 2002.

36. For example, Robert G. Kaiser, "The Long and Short of It; The War on Terrorism Began So Well. Then the Focus Changed. What Is the Bush Administration Aiming to Do Now?" *Washington Post,* 8 September 2002, B1.

37. See David E. Rosenbaum, "Threats and Responses: The Democrats; United Voice on Iraq Eludes Majority Leader," *New York Times,* 4 October 2002, A-14. A Nexis search showed the term "soft on defense" turning up in coverage of House and Senate campaigns in state after state, for example, as a theme of GOP attacks on Democratic Senate candidates Max Cleland in Georgia, Frank Lautenberg in New Jersey, and Tim Johnson in South Dakota.

38. Johanna McGeary, "6 Reasons Why So Many Allies Want Bush to Slow Down," and Romesh Ratnesar, "Can They Strike Back?" *Time,* 3 February 2003, 34–39 and 42–44.

39. *Newsweek* poll (24–25 July 2003) at http://www.pollingreport.com/iraq.htm.

40. *The PIPA/Knowledge Network Polls: Americans on Iraq and the UN Inspections II.* http://www.pipa.org/OnlineReports/IraqUNinspec2/IraqUNInspII.pdf.

41. Reported by Todd Gitlin, "The Pro-War Post," *American Prospect,* April 2003, 43.

42. See Jim Naureckas, "MSNBC's Racism Is OK, Peace Activism Is Not," *EXTRA! Update,* April 2003, 3.

43. Quoted in Jim Rutenberg, "Cable's War Coverage Suggests a New 'Fox Effect' on Television," *New York Times,* 16 April 2003, B9.

44. Ellis Henican, "Entertaining McCarthyism," *Newsday,* 25 April 2003, A8.

45. See Howard Rosenberg, "He Fought Our Fear and the Fear Won," *Los Angeles Times,* 14 April 2003, part 5, 1. Other evidence of systematic pro-Bush pressure on news organizations, this time with respect to Afghanistan, can be found in Michael Sherer, "Framing the Flag," *Columbia Journalism Review,* March/April 2002, 10.

46. Cf. Bennett 1990.

47. Anne E. Kornblut and Wayne Washington, "Confronting Iraq / Capitol Hill Rancor; GOP Rebukes Daschle for War Plan Criticism; Parties Do Not Shy from Taking Shots," *Washington Post,* 19 March 2003, A1.

48. E. J. Dionne, "A Double Standard on Dissent," *Washington Post,* 21 March 2003, A37.

49. Also see Entman, forthcoming, on GOP fears of domestic scandal eruptions.

50. Readership Institute, *Report from the NAA National Convention* (27–30 April 2003). At http://www.readership.org.

51. *Report from the NAA National Convention.*

52. Project for Excellence in Journalism, *Embedded Reporters: What Are Americans Getting?* http://www.journalism.org/resources/research/reports/war/embed/default.asp.

53. John Burns, "A Staggering Blow to the Heart of the Iraqi Capital," *New York Times,* 22 March 2003, A1.

54. Excluding the *Wall Street Journal,* which ranks second in national circulation but specializes in finance.

55. Quotation from "Pulling the Trigger," *ABC Nightline,* 22 April 2003, which offered a sophisticated and quite independent analysis of the real reasons for the war. Also see Paul Krugman, "Matters of Emphasis," *New York Times,* 29 April 2003, A29.

56. *Newsweek* poll cited in note 39.

57. As Todd Gitlin shows in "From Put Down to Catch Up: The News and the Antiwar Movement," *American Prospect,* March 2003, 33, for the most part, it was business as usual in depicting antiwar groups. An exception arose in coverage of one major protest around the time the U.N. was debating the war, in January 2003. More generally, protest drew little interest even from the editorially antiwar *New York Times.* For instance, when the New York City Council voted by a large majority to oppose the war, the *Times* story appeared on page B4 and another on an antiwar protest after the war began (22 March) on page B11.

58. David Shaw, "A Skeptical Journalist Isn't an Unpatriotic One," *Los Angeles Times,* 20 April 2003, part 5, 16.

59. David Carr, "A Nation at War; Reporting Reflects Anxiety," *New York Times,* 25 March 2003, B1.

60. Billeaudeaux (forthcoming) offers copious data showing a sharp negative shift in war coverage during this time.

61. David Sanger, "A Nation at War: The Mood; As a Quick Victory Grows Less Likely, Doubts Are Quietly Voiced in Washington," *New York Times,* 29 March 2003, B10.

62. Some realist theories of international relations tend to treat the political process as largely irrelevant, since nations will do what they are compelled to do by the anarchic international system, no matter the pressures of domestic politics. Acknowledging the role of politics and of the media reminds us that conflicted, imperfect human beings control the government's military and diplomatic apparatus. They can make mistakes despite good intentions, or can follow a wise course despite bad intentions. It could at least be argued that increasing media independence can at times encourage decisions that accord with national self-interest. On the applicability of realist theories to Iraq, see Lemann 2002 and Mearsheimer and Walt 2003; on the importance of "soft power," see Nye 2002.

63. Hersh 2003.

CHAPTER SIX

1. A few passages from this chapter appeared in Entman and Herbst 2001. Coauthor Susan Herbst, whose contribution is gratefully acknowledged, should not

be held accountable for the significantly revised arguments that appear here. In addition, the case study on the nuclear freeze comes from an article jointly written with Andrew Rojecki (1993). Although he provided extremely useful comments on a draft of this chapter, he too should be absolved from responsibility for the arguments as presented here. His own book (1999) provides a far more extensive analysis of antinuclear movements and the media throughout the Cold War.

2. This is not to deny that personal ideology plays a major role too. Many Americans, elites and citizens alike, regularly see imminent threats from the communists, terrorists, or other enemies no matter what the media are reporting.

3. See Entman and Paletz 1980; cf. Mutz 1998.

4. See, e.g., Cohen 1973.

5. Powlick and Katz 1998, 44; cf. Manza and Cook 2002; Sobel 2001, 23–25.

6. See especially Kull and Ramsey 2000, 2002, and Kull and Destler 1999 on foreign policy; Cook, Barabas; and Page 2002 on domestic (Social Security).

7. Jacobs and Shapiro 2000.

8. Powlick and Katz 1998, 45; cf. Kull and Ramsay 2002, 213.

9. Powlick and Katz 1998, 45; cf. Kull and Ramsay 2002, 214–15; Herbst 1998.

10. Pew Research Center 1998, 3; cf. Herbst 1998; Jacobs and Shapiro 2000; Mutz 1998.

11. See Jacobs and Shapiro 2000; Lewis 2001.

12. Entman and Herbst 2001; Herbst 1993; Lewis 2001; Warren 2001 provides a defense of polling.

13. Page and Shapiro 1992 make this case most persuasively.

14. Zaller 1992.

15. Cf. Althaus 2003.

16. Cf. Lewis 2001, 166 and *passim*.

17. Cf. Mutz 1998.

18. Kull and Ramsay 2002, 208–9. The matter is more complex than this, as usual, for the surveys also show a greatly misinformed public. Respondents during the 1990s estimated that foreign aid takes up about 20 percent of the U.S. budget, and said they supported cuts to about half that perceived rate, or 10 percent of the budget. Yet the real answer is 1 percent; though they thought they were calling for major cuts, polling majorities were actually supporting a 1000 percent increase! Exactly where majorities stood is thus difficult to say, but the figures certainly contradict leaders' perceptions that Americans preferred to eliminate foreign aid completely.

19. Ibid., 206.

20. Lewis 2001, 200–201 and *passim*. Cf. Cook, Barabas, and Page 2002; Entman and Paletz 1980.

21. This point is developed for foreign policy in Powlick and Katz 1998 and Sobel 2001; and for policy generally in Erikson, MacKuen, and Stimson 2002; cf. Manza, Cook, and Page 2002.

22. Once again actual survey data on Somalia are complicated. See Kull and Ramsay 2002, 208.

23. Cf. Jacobs and Shapiro 2000. Sometimes the goal is no publicity at all, in order

to head off anticipated opposition; if the public is in the dark no majorities (actual or perceived) may even form (cf. Manheim 1997; Powlick and Katz 1998).

24. Such as Tetlock 2000.

25. Cf. Manza and Cook 2002, 26: "The power to increase the salience of an issue can alter the impact of opinion, even if policy preferences per se do not change." Page (2002, 335–37) summarizes evidence that government exhibits more apparent responsiveness to higher than lower salience issues. He also points out that the closer opinion–policy congruence might be traceable to elites engaging in more energetic efforts to manipulate and bring the public's opinions into line for the higher-salience issues, rather than to genuine responsiveness. Jones (1994, 125; cf. 128) even argues that "it may be that democratic governments are more responsive to changes in attentiveness to problems than they are to the particular distribution of opinion on a problem."

26. Cf. Destler 2001 on officials who consider public opinion an illegitimate intrusion on policymaking and thus have little motivation to worry about the actual preferences citizens possess.

27. Lewis 2001; Page and Shapiro 1992.

28. Cf. Jones 1994.

29. Hartley and Russett 1992; also see Wlezien 1996.

30. Hartley and Russett 1992, 905.

31. Ibid., 907.

32. See Talbott 1984, on Reagan's negotiating approach.

33. Bartels 1991, 466.

34. The public opinion figures are the same as those used by Hartley and Russett. The spending figures are actual defense expenditures (not as in Hartley and Russett, defense authorizations), in constant 1982 dollars, taken from the *Budget of the United States Government, Fiscal 1992*, 69–70. Figures on actual expenses reflect what government actually spent, so appear more appropriate to the theoretical issue here. The basic argument holds even if we use congressionally approved spending rather than actual expenditures.

35. Cf. Wlezien 1996, 87.

36. According to Erikson, MacKuen, and Stimson 2002, 359, it takes about eight years for policy (measured as major domestic policy laws passed by Congress) to catch up with and match opinion changes, which they view as appropriate to the Madisonian structure (checks and balances) of the U.S. government. So the findings here do accord with Erikson et al.'s model, since defense spending was finally cut in 1990, about eight years after polls indicated the public wanted reductions. However, if it takes eight years for government to respond to shifts in public opinion, a significant portion of the aggregation being represented has died by the time government grants its wishes, and with the passing years another significant portion has no doubt changed its mind. Certainly conditions in the world would have changed. If we accept the analysis of Erikson et al., we are left with a democracy that at any given moment is eight years out of phase with public opinion. Although no democratic theorists expect instant alignment of government budgets with every minute shift in public sentiments, presumably at some point—ten years? fifteen?—the lag would become large

enough to raise questions about whether the government is sufficiently responsive to merit classification as democratic. What the finding in this chapter and the findings of the far more complicated and exhaustive study by Erikson et al. reveal, of course, is that there is no objective basis for concluding a system is doing a good enough job of responding to public desires. This is a normative judgment, based on how one interprets, or frames, the data. For Hartley and Russett and for Erikson et al., the glass of democratic responsiveness tends to be half full.

37. This provides another example of the frequent disjunctions between perceived majorities as depicted in the news and actual polling opinion as measured by surveys. See King and Schudson 1991.

38. Pasztor 1995. The book describes how over ninety individuals and corporations (including eight of the fifteen largest defense contractors, among them GE and Boeing) were convicted of felonies in this matter.

39. Not all the mismanagement was traceable to corruption; much was simply standard bureaucratic behavior. See Stubbing 1986.

40. Page and Shapiro 1992, chaps. 2 and 4.

41. Rielly 1991, 11.

42. Harris Poll, national adult sample of 1,254, taken February 12–17, 1982. Stored in Roper Center P.O.L.L. database.

43. Kull and Ramsay 2002, 210.

44. Riker's (1986) term.

45. See ibid. for a clear explanation of the problem. Gaubatz 1995 shows how this "intransitivity" of public preferences makes it difficult for officials to respond to public opinion on foreign policy—and for scholars to detect its impacts on policymakers. Cf., for a somewhat more optimistic view, Zaller 1994; Zaller and Chiu 2000.

46. Riker 1986 provides clear illustrations of the importance of framing for coming to decision in the presence of intransitive preferences.

47. Cf. Herbst 1993, 1998; see Page and Shapiro 1992, 263–74 on the twists and turns in public and elite opinion about foreign policy, and Page 2002 on the many complexities of measuring public opinion and its impacts on policy.

48. Cf. Jacobs and Shapiro 2000.

49. Bartels 1991; also cf. Zaller and Chiu 2000.

50. Erikson, MacKuen, and Stimson 2002, on the other hand, do find that domestic policy decisions have significant impacts on changing public survey responses (or polling opinion), as does Wlezien 1996 in considering defense spending.

51. Feldman and Sigelman 1985.

52. This point is compatible with Jones's (1994) findings in reanalyzing the Hartley–Russett defense spending data; in his interpretation, public preferences by themselves did not have a statistically significant impact on defense spending, but the interaction of preferences with level of attention to foreign affairs did.

53. Zaller 1992.

54. Jentleson 1992; Jentleson and Britton 1998; Page and Shapiro 1992. For discussion of how empirical researchers have yet to establish definitively the degree to which majorities are rational (or "prudent"), see Knopf 1998; cf. Gaubatz 1995.

55. Spending opinion data from Hartley and Russett 1992, 909.

56. With the final four months of 1983 removed, threat references average twenty-eight per month, so the "normalized" annual total would be 336. Entering 336 negative references for 1983 brings the correlation up to $r = .77$ ($p < .001$). Negative references dropped to a near-average twenty-five in December 1983, there were twenty-seven in January 1984, and so forth, so the use of a normal average of twenty-eight seems right. A second measure was employed that counted *net* references to Soviet aggression, buildup, and threat. The measure reported in the text is the total of assertions that Soviets were aggressive, building up, and threatening. The net measure subtracts from this the total assertions saying the Soviets were not aggressive, building up, or threatening. These counterframe assertions remained fairly low, averaging twenty-five per year from 1977 through 1988. In 1989 they jumped to 137 and in 1990 to 254. The correlation of the net measure with the defense spending opinion is $r = .68$ ($p < .01$), compared with .69 for negative images only as reported in the text. The correlation using the correction for 1983 is .74 ($p < .001$), compared with the .77 mentioned above. Hence the relationship seems quite robust.

57. As we saw, for example, defense spending policy required not just decisions about how much to spend, but about exactly what to buy and how to oversee spending.

58. Rojecki 1999, chap. 6.

59. See Entman 1989, chap. 3.

60. As one more example of framing's power, news of Carter's failed attempt to rescue the hostages in Iran, which killed nine American servicemen, can be compared with Reagan's failed insertion of American troops to gain leverage in Lebanon, which led to the deaths of nearly three hundred servicemen in a terrorist bombing. Carter's political standing suffered grievously from negative coverage; Reagan's, if anything, benefited from benign coverage. See ibid.

61. Page 2002 provides a detailed analysis of these matters. Manza and Cook (2002, 21) write: "Quantitative studies have established a case for . . . policy responsiveness to public opinion. But because these studies tend to include few other covariates they may miss factors that mediate or precede the relationship between opinion and policy." They also note: "[B]ecause foreign and defense policies are often event- and crisis-driven, there are sharp problems of causal inference. When a foreign crisis changes the context within which the public views a question, rapid changes in public attitudes are possible, which may, in turn, appear to be associated with later changes in policy. But in such cases, it appears likely that the same factors that move public opinion also move elites and the overall direction of policy making" (30 n. 7).

62. Cf. Sobel 2001; Jacobs and Shapiro 2000; Powlick and Katz 1998.

63. Such as those of Hartley and Russett 1992, and Erikson, MacKuen, and Stimson 2002; Page 2002 offers a critique.

64. E.g., cf. Herbst 1993; Verba and Nie 1987.

65. Entman and Rojecki 1993; cf. Rojecki 1999. Also see Meyer 1995.

66. Cf. Gitlin 1980; Rojecki 1999.

67. Olson 1965; collective movements suffer from a "free rider" problem. Logic suggests to people that they can benefit from (free ride on) the movement's achieve-

ments without doing anything, because any one individual's failure to join will have no appreciable effect on its probability of success. In the light of such strong counterincentives for individuals to join, it seems reasonable to conclude that negative media coverage can significantly compound the inherent difficulties of movement recruitment.

68. Cf. Bennett 1993; Lipsky 1968.

69. Russett 1990, 18.

70. On the other hand, if we accept Erikson, MacKuen, and Stimson's (2002) Madisonian standard of an eight-year lag between opinion shifts and congruent policy moves, then the fact that the U.S. government did not get around to seriously negotiating arms control with the Soviet Union until the late 1980s does evidence responsiveness.

71. Russett 1990, 73.

72. Cf. Hochschild 2001.

73. Cf. Althaus 2002; Delli Carpini and Keeter 1996.

74. Cf. Gitlin 1980; Rojecki 1999.

75. In part this stance likely reflects the participation of foreign affairs reporters and editors from the important national media in Washington's social and policy networks, alongside official and unofficial foreign policy elites. Within that social milieu, Jacobs and Shapiro (2000, 301) write, there is "strong and consistent disdain for the public's competence to understand policy and offer reasoned input into policymaking."

76. Entman and Rojecki 1993; Rojecki 1999.

77. Scheer 1982, 39.

78. As one example, Holzman 1989, 102, suggests that CIA estimates of Soviet defense spending as a proportion of gross domestic product were exaggerated by 50–100 percent. Also see Stubbing 1986.

79. See McCleod and Detenber 1999 for empirical evidence that derogatory framing of protests dampens public support. Cf. Gamson (1992, 33) on the need for "hot cognitions" and emotional involvement to sustain political movements. Gamson also finds that media frames tend to discourage movement participation, but based on focus group analysis he believes the media's negative stance toward movements is less effective at stifling their political influence than is argued here.

80. Cf. Jacobs and Shapiro 2000 and Page 2002. Gaubatz (1995, 553) makes a related argument in the larger context of long-standing debates among international relations specialists about the representation of public opinion in foreign policy decisions:

> [T]he source of foreign policy stability is going to be found in the *institutions* that aggregate public opinion and translate it into policy effects, rather than in some underlying stability in either individual or aggregate public preferences. Particularly important in this regard will be institutions that allow the elite to shape the agenda in ways that overcome or even exploit public intransitivities. In the presence of intransitivities, the degree to which public opinion will either constrain or force action is a function of the ability of

elites to develop and maintain observable majorities. When pollsters and pundits can order the debate, there is an impression of a stable public-opinion majority, even where structurally no such majority exists. . . . A president will need to take the initiative to set the terms of the public debate. Failing this, the president must be aware that what looks like a majority today may prove to be vulnerable to other actors who can effectively change the agenda tomorrow.

81. Destler 2001; Powlick and Katz 1998. Adherents of the realist school (Keohane 1986; cf. Foyle 1999) would defend this elitist position of trying to maintain public quiescence (cf. Edelman 1988; Jacobs and Shapiro 2000) to allow officials maximum freedom of action so they can best pursue the national interest in the anarchic international system.

APPENDIX TO CHAPTER SIX

1. Hartley and Russett 1992; Jones 1994, chap. 5; Shapiro and Jacobs 2002; Wlezien 1996.
2. Erikson, MacKuen, and Stimson 2002, 391.
3. Jones 1994, 128.
4. Ibid., 125. See also Page 2002.

CHAPTER SEVEN

1. Riker 1986 offers the best succinct analysis of the centrality of strategic framing, which he dubs "heresthetics."
2. Entman 1989.
3. Ibid., chap. 3.
4. See Entman, forthcoming, for a detailed study of Clinton, former vice president Quayle, George W. Bush, and the draft.
5. Baum 2003 argues that many foreign crises and military actions now receive attention from "soft news" or "infotainment" shows that actually generate larger audiences than network news and newspapers. Many citizens get news, then, from sources that do not follow traditional journalistic routines or rely on standard source networks. Baum asserts that the rise of infotainment marks another path of influence for the media over foreign policy discourse. The Internet is another force that may help flatten traditional hierarchies. Global citizens can read one another's news and can use the Web to distribute petitions and organize protest marches; cf. Rojecki 2002.
6. Describing the impact of international public opinion on George W. Bush's Iraq policy, Patrick Tyler reported ("A New Power in the Streets; A Message to Bush Not to Rush to War," *New York Times*, 17 February 2003, A1), with perhaps some exaggeration, that "there may still be two superpowers on the planet: the United States and world public opinion." On the importance of international respect and legitimacy to global power, see Nye 2002; Schell 2003.
7. Mearsheimer and Walt 2003, 56; see, e.g., Jentleson 1994 for more historical background on American complicity with Iraq's chemical and nuclear weapons programs; and see Hallin 1986 on the spheres of deviance and legitimate dissent.

8. Cf. Jacobs and Shapiro 2000.

9. See, e.g., Waltz 1991 for the hypothesis on democracies and war. For complexities, see Gaubatz 1991; Huth and Allee 2002; Morgan and Campbell 1991; Schultz 1998.

10. The Haiti, Bosnia, and Kosovo experiences could have also betokened misfirings of democracy. Were it not for President Clinton's decision against perceived public opinion to intervene, apparent humanitarian successes might not have been achieved.

11. See for critiques of the official U.S. government claims, Independent Commission of Inquiry 1991; Physicians for Human Rights 1991. These issues were also covered in the Academy Award–winning documentary film *The Panama Deception*. However, this controversy generated virtually no coverage in the national media researched for this book, remaining at the left-leaning margin of public discourse.

12. Wilson and Weisskopf 1986.

13. Chandler 1994.

14. Knightley 1975.

15. Sheehan 1993, 44–51.

16. Keating 1994. In this study, a conservative commentator thoroughly investigates and debunks the myth of living ex-POWs, aside from a handful of Americans who collaborated with the North Vietnamese and remained in the country voluntarily after the war.

17. Friedman 1993.

18. See Robinson 2002.

19. See the *Los Angeles Times* survey (2–3 April 2003), and a *Newsweek* poll (10–11 April) showing similar results, at http://www.pollingreport.com/iraq.htm. Recall the University of Maryland poll mentioned in chapter 5, which showed about two-fifths of the 61 percent majority favoring U.N. reliance were ready to switch to support the moment the president decided to invade.

20. Dahl 1989; cf. Jacobs and Shapiro 2000, pt. 4; Page and Shapiro 1992; Zaller 1992, 313–14.

21. Petty and Cacioppo 1986.

22. Habermas 1992, 452.

23. Riker 1986, 241; cf. Gaubatz 1995; Jacobs and Shapiro 2000.

24. See for various views on this Brace and Hinckley 1992; Erikson, MacKuen, and Stimson 2002; Gaubatz 1995; Jacobs and Shapiro 2000; Kernell 1993; Page and Shapiro 1992.

25. Cf. on polls Zaller 1992; on interpreting elections Conley 2001 and Kelley 1983; also Verba and Nie 1987; Riker 1986.

26. See, e.g., Jacobs and Shapiro 2000 on the public's reversal toward the Clinton health reform initiative of 1993–94. On the other hand, Erikson, MacKuen, and Stimson 2002 suggest that public policy will lag behind public opinion by almost eight years, but that this is a legitimate degree of responsiveness.

27. A third path of legitimation or delegitimation arises from *procedural* framing. If the president is framed as inept or unresponsive, polls asking for approval of his leadership may undermine his legitimacy and thus his ability to command support for his policies. By the same token, a president whose leadership is posi-

tively framed gains legitimacy that may help him to pursue policies that might otherwise stimulate more substantive and effective opposition (cf. Entman 1989).

28. Almond 1950.
29. Jentleson 1992; Jentleson and Britton 1998; Page and Shapiro 1992; Peffley and Hurwitz 1992; Wittkopf 1990, 15.
30. See Delli Carpini and Keeter 1996; Kuklinski and Quirk 2000; Hochschild 2001.
31. Lodge and Taber 2000, 211, suggests the downside of ideological sophistication: that those with the strongest attitudes best anchored with factual knowledge are also least open to new, disconfirming information. If true, ideological style would of course lead to its own sort of irrationality. However, whether the costs and risks of ideological thinking outweigh its benefits to citizens' ability and inclination to deliberate remains to be more fully theorized and empirically investigated.
32. Destler 2001 and Kull and Ramsay 2001 are representative examples of scholars who defend public rationality or at least reasonability against those raising doubts; cf. Peffley and Hurwitz 1992, who argue that the heuristics people use in judging foreign affairs are adequate. (A general defense of heuristics in mass reasoning is Sniderman 2000.) This argument has considerable merit but its empirical support is limited to the stable general thrust of polling opinion on what might be called the standing issues of U.S. foreign policy. Destler, for instance, points out that stable majorities have long favored international engagement over isolationism, while supporting the United Nations and multilateralism. Yet in this same essay Destler acknowledges that polls show majorities favoring a reduction in foreign aid—because they overestimate the actual amount spent by 1,500–3,000 percent. If given the correct information, respondents support foreign aid, but that is small reassurance to real-world politicians who confront this sort of interaction of ignorance and bounded rationality in public opinion data all the time. As Destler and Kull and Ramsay both suggest (cf. Kull and Destler 1999), in fact, elites consistently misread public opinion on foreign policy, basing their assumptions less on the problematic indicators of polling opinion than on even *more* problematic media reports and self-reinforcing assumptions common along what the present study calls elite source networks. Destler (2001, 79) goes so far as to argue that the executive and legislative branches routinely and consciously ignore stable polling opinions on the standing foreign policy issues.

In any case, the optimists have little to say in defense of public knowledge or rationality when it comes to short-term policy events and issues of the sort involved in most projections of military power—the sort studied in this book, and the sort where anticipated and perceived majorities and polling opinion strongly influence elites' willingness to mount counterframing attacks against the White House. (Chapter 6, which did deal with longer-term policy responses on defense spending and nuclear arms control, presented evidence that government can ignore or distract the public sufficiently to avoid any significant political damage; cf. Gaubatz 1995.) As a specific example, although Destler emphasizes consistent polling majorities in favor of the principle of multilateralism, we have seen that practice is something else. Short-term polls on specific American interventions from Grenada through both Gulf Wars and the war on the Taliban in Afghanistan show large majorities favoring (low-cost, apparently successful) U.S. actions that were for all intents and purposes unilateral. Although the United States frequently bowed to multilateralism by orchestrating symbolic shows of support from allies or international organizations, in every instance save perhaps Bosnia and Kosovo, the United States thoroughly dominated policy analyses and decisions.

33. Cf. Jacobs and Shapiro 2000; Kuklinski and Quirk 2000, 181–82; Tetlock 2000, 263.
34. Lippmann 1922, 1925; cf. Gaubatz 1995.
35. E.g., Kuklinski and Quirk 2000.
36. It is worth noting that scholars of international politics have often observed that even elite officials exhibit seriously bounded rationality in their reasoning and decisions. See, e.g., Vertzberger 1990, 343, 347, and *passim;* cf. Jervis 1993.
37. Jacobs and Shapiro 2000, 334–35.
38. See Entman 1989; Bennett and Entman 2001; Baum 2003.

REFERENCES

Almond, Gabriel. 1950. *The American People and Foreign Policy.* New York: Harcourt Brace.

Althaus, Scott L. 2002. For Whom the Ball Rolls: The Impact of Spin Strategies, News Events, and Journalistic Norms on Nightly News about the Persian Gulf. Paper presented at the Annual Meeting of the American Political Science Association, Boston.

———. 2003. *Collective Preferences in Democratic Politics.* New York: Cambridge University Press.

Althaus, Scott L., Jill A. Edy, and Patricia Phalen. 2001. Using Substitutes for Full-Text News Stories in Content Analysis: Which Text Is Best? *American Journal of Political Science* 45, no. 3: 707–23.

Althaus, Scott L., Jill A. Edy, Robert M. Entman, and Patricia Phalen. 1996. Revising the Indexing Hypothesis: Officials, Media, and the Libya Crisis. *Political Communication* 13, no. 4: 407–21.

Augelli, Enrico, and Craig Murphy. 1988. *America's Quest for Supremacy in the Third World: A Gramscian Analysis.* London: Pinter Publishers.

Bartels, Larry M. 1991. Constituency Opinion and Congressional Policymaking: The Reagan Defense Buildup. *American Political Science Review* 85: 457–75.

Baum, Matthew. 2003. *Infotainment Wars: Public Opinion and Foreign Policy in the New Media Age.* Princeton: Princeton University Press.

Bennett, W. Lance. 1989. Marginalizing the Majority: Conditional Public Opinion to Accept Managerial Democracy. In *Manipulating Public Opinion: Essays on Public Opinion as a Dependent Variable,* ed. Michael Margolis and Gary A. Mauser, 321–61. Pacific Grove, Calif.: Brooks/Cole.

———. 1990. Toward a Theory of Press–State Relations in the United States. *Journal of Communication* 40, no. 2: 103–25.

———. 1993. Constructing Publics and Their Opinions. *Political Communication* 10, no. 2: 101–20.

———. 2002. *News: The Politics of Illusion.* 5th ed. New York: Longman.

Bennett, W. Lance, and David L. Paletz, eds. 1994. *Taken by Storm: The Media, Public Opinion, and U.S. Foreign Policy in the Gulf War.* Chicago: University of Chicago Press.

Bennett, W. Lance, and Jarol B. Manheim. 1993. Taking the Public by Storm: Information, Cuing, and the Democratic Process in the Gulf Conflict. *Political Communication* 10, no. 4: 331–52.

Bennett, W. Lance, and Robert M. Entman, eds. 2001. *Mediated Politics: Communication in the Future of Democracy.* Cambridge, UK: Cambridge University Press.

Billeaudeaux, Andre. Forthcoming. "Selling Two Wars." Master's thesis, University of Washington, Department of Communication.

Bissell, Kimberly L. 2002. The Crisis in Kosovo: Photographic News of the Conflict and Public Opinion. In *Media and Conflict: Framing Issues, Making Policy, Shaping Opinions,* ed. Eytan Gilboa, 313–32. Ardsley, N.Y.: Transnational Publishers.

Bohlen, Celestine. 2001. In New War on Terrorism, Words Are Weapons Too. *New York Times,* 29 September, A11.

Brace, Paul, and Barbara Hinckley. 1992. *Follow the Leader: Opinion Polls and the Modern Presidents.* New York: Basic Books.

Brody, Richard A. 1991. *Assessing the President: The Media, Elite Opinion, and Public Support.* Stanford: Stanford University Press.

———. 1994. Crisis, War and Public Opinion: The Media and Public Support for the President. In *Taken by Storm: The Media, Public Opinion, and U.S. Foreign Policy in the Gulf War,* ed. W. Lance Bennett and David L. Paletz, 210–30. Chicago: University of Chicago Press.

Brosius, Hans-Bernd. 1993. The Effects of Emotional Pictures in Television News. *Communication Research* 20: 105–24.

Brosius, Hans-Bernd, Wolfgang Donsbach, and M. Birk. 1996. How Do Text–Picture Relations Affect the Informational Effectiveness of Television Newscasts? *Journal of Broadcasting and Electronic Media* 40, no. 2: 180–95.

Budd, Mike, Robert M. Entman, and Clay Steinman. 1990. The Affirmative Character of U.S. Cultural Studies. *Critical Studies in Mass Communication* 7, no. 2: 169–84.

Burchell, Graham, Colin Gordon, and Peter Miller. 1991. *The Foucault Effect: Studies in Governmentality: With Two Lectures by and an Interview with Michel Foucault.* Chicago: University of Chicago Press.

Cacioppo, John T., and Wendi L. Gardner. 1999. Emotion. *Annual Review of Psychology* 50, no. 1: 191–215.

Cannon, Lou. 1988. Poll Finds Support for Ship's Action, U.S. Policy in Gulf. *Washington Post,* 21 July, A21.

Cappella, Joseph, and Kathleen H. Jamieson. 1997. *Spiral of Cynicism: The Press and the Public Good.* New York: Oxford University Press.

Carter, Bill, and Felicity Barringer. 2001. A Nation Challenged; Speech and Expression, in Patriotic Time, Dissent Is Muted. *New York Times,* 28 September, 1.

Chandler, David L. 1994. The Patriot; No Letup in War of Words; but Outside Studies Back Critics of Missile's Performance. *Boston Globe,* 4 April, 25.

Chang, Wen Chen, and Ya-Qin Zhang, eds. 1999. *Visual Information Representation, Communication, and Image Processing.* New York: Marcel Dekker.

Chestnut, Beatrice. 1995. *The Narrative Construction of Iran–Contra.* Ph.D. diss., Northwestern University.

Chicago Council on Foreign Affairs. 2002. A World Transformed: Foreign Policy Attitudes of the U.S. Public after September 11. Chicago: Chicago Council on Foreign Affairs. Available at http://www.worldviews.org/key_findings/us_911_report.htm#kf2.

Cohen, Bernard C. 1963. *The Press and Foreign Policy.* Princeton: Princeton University Press.

———. 1973. *The Public's Impact on Foreign Policy.* Boston: Little, Brown.

Coleman, William D. and Anthony Perl. 1999. Internationalized Policy Environments and Policy Network Analysis. *Political Studies* 47: 691–709.

Condit, Celeste M. 1989. The Rhetorical Limits of Polysemy. *Critical Studies in Mass Communication* 6, no. 2: 103–22.

Conley, Patricia H. 2001. *Presidential Mandates: How Elections Shape the National Agenda.* Chicago: University of Chicago Press.

Cook, Fay Lomax, Jason Barabus, and Benjamin I. Page. 2002. Policy Elites Invoke Public Opinion: Polls, Policy Debates, and the Future of Social Security. In *Navigating Public Opinion: Polls, Policy and The Future of American Democracy,* ed. Jeff Manza, Fay Lomax Cook, and Benjamin I. Page, 141–70. New York: Oxford University Press.

Cook, Timothy E. 1994. Domesticating a Crisis: Washington Newsbeats and Network News after the Iraq Invasion of Kuwait. In *Taken by Storm: The Media, Public Opinion, and U.S. Foreign Policy in the Gulf War,* ed. W. Lance Bennett and David L. Paletz, 105–30. Chicago: University of Chicago Press.

———. 1998. *Governing with the News.* Chicago: University of Chicago Press.

Corcoran, Ferrell. 1986. KAL-007 and the Evil Empire: Mediated Disaster and Forms of Rationalization. *Journal of Communication* 3, no. 3: 297–316.

Crigler, Ann, and Marion Just. 1994. Interpreting Visual versus Audio Messages in Television News. *Journal of Communication* 44, no. 4: 132–49.

Cumings, Bruce. 1992. *War and Television.* London: Verso Books.

Dahl, Robert A. 1989. *Democracy and Its Critics.* New Haven: Yale University Press.

Dallek, Robert. 1983. *The American Style of Foreign Policy: Cultural Politics and Foreign Affairs.* New York: Random House.

Dallin, Alexander. 1985. *Black Box: KAL007 and the Superpowers.* Berkeley: University of California Press.

Delli Carpini, Michael X., and Scott Keeter. 1996. *What Americans Know about Politics and Why It Matters.* New Haven: Yale University Press.

Destler, I. M. 2001. The Reasonable Public and the Polarized Policy Process. In *The Real and the Ideal: Essays on International Relations in Honor of Richard H. Ullman,* ed. Anthony Lake and David Ochmanek, 75–90. Lanham, Md.: Rowman and Littlefield .

Destler, I. M., Leslie H. Gelb, and Anthony Lake. 1984. *Our Own Worst Enemy: The Unmaking of American Foreign Policy.* New York: Simon and Schuster.

Dickson, S. H. 1994. Understanding Media Bias: The Press and the United-States Invasion of Panama. *Journalism Quarterly* 71, no. 4: 809–19.

Domke, David, Dhavan V. Shah, and Daniel B. Wackman. 1998. Media Priming Effects: Accessibility, Association, and Activation. *International Journal of Public Opinion Research* 10, no. 1: 51–74.

Dorman, William A., and Mansour Farhang. 1987. *The U.S. Press and Iran: Foreign Policy and the Journalism of Deference.* Berkeley: University of California Press.

Dorman, William A., and Steven Livingston. 1994. News and Historical Content:

The Establishing Phase of the Persian Gulf Policy Debate. In *Taken by Storm: The Media, Public Opinion, and U.S. Foreign Policy in the Gulf,* ed. W. Lance Bennett and David L. Paletz, 63–81. Chicago: University of Chicago Press.

Edelman, Murray. 1988. *Constructing the Political Spectacle.* Chicago: University of Chicago Press.

———. 1993. Contestable Categories and Public Opinion. *Political Communication* 10, no. 3: 231–42.

———. 2001. *The Politics of Misinformation.* New York: Cambridge University Press.

Edelman, S. 1998. Representation Is Representation of Similarities. *Behavioral and Brain Sciences* 21, no. 4: 449–66.

Edwards, George. 1990. *At the Margins: Presidential Leadership of Congress.* New Haven: Yale University Press.

Elliott, Michael, John Barry, and Karen Breslau. 1994. The Neurotic Lion. *Newsweek,* 26 September, 36.

Entman, Robert M. 1989. *Democracy without Citizens: Media and the Decay of American Politics.* New York: Oxford University Press.

———. 1991. Framing United-States Coverage of International News: Contrasts in Narratives of the KAL and Iran Air Incidents. *Journal of Communication* 41, no. 4: 6–27.

———. 1993. Framing: Toward Clarification of a Fractured Paradigm. *Journal of Communication* 43, no. 4: 51–58.

———. 1997. Mass Media and Policy Innovation: Opportunities and Constraints for Public Management. In *Innovation in American Government:Challenges, Opportunities, and Dilemmas,* ed. Alan Altshuler and Robert D. Behn, 202–18. Washington: Brookings Institution.

———. Forthcoming. *Private Lives in the Public Sphere: Scandals of Journalism.* Seattle: University of Washington Press.

Entman, Robert M., and Andrew Rojecki. 1993. Freezing out the Public: Elite and Media Framing of the U.S. Anti-Nuclear Movement. *Political Communication* 10, no. 2: 151–67.

———. 2000. *The Black Image in the White Mind: Media and Race in America.* Chicago: University of Chicago Press.

———. 2001. "Preface to the Paperback Edition." In *The Black Image in the White Mind: Media and Race in America,* rev. paperback ed. Chicago: University of Chicago Press.

Entman, Robert M., and Benjamin I. Page. 1994. The News before the Storm: The Iraq War Debate and the Limits to Media Independence. In *Taken by Storm: The Media, Public Opinion, and U.S. Foreign Policy in the Gulf War,* ed. W. Lance Bennett and David L. Paletz, 82–104. Chicago: University of Chicago Press.

Entman, Robert M., and David L. Paletz. 1980. Media and the Conservative Myth. *Journal of Communication* 30, no. 4: 154–65.

Entman, Robert M., and Susan Herbst. 2001. Reframing Public Opinion as We Have Known It. In *Mediated Politics: Communication in the Future of Democracy,* ed. W. Lance Bennett and Robert M. Entman, 203–25. New York: Cambridge University Press.

Erikson, Robert S, Michael B. MacKuen, and James A. Stimson. 2002. *The Macro Polity.* New York: Cambridge University Press.

Feldman, Stanley, and Lee Sigelman. 1985. The Political Impact of Prime Time Television: The Day After. *Journal of Politics* 47, no. 2: 556–78.

Fenno, Richard. 1978. *Homestyle: House Members in Their Districts.* Boston: Addison-Wesley.

Ferguson, Thomas, and Joel Rogers. 1986. *Right Turn: The Decline of the Democrats and the Future of American Politics.* New York: Hill and Wang.

Fishman, Mark. 1980. *Manufacturing the News.* Austin: University of Texas Press.

Fiske, Susan T., and Shelley E. Taylor. 1991. *Social Cognition.* New York: McGraw Hill.

Forbes, Grania. 1990. Thatcher and Bush Accused of a Cover-up on Lockerbie. *Sunday Times,* 28 January.

Forgas, Joseph, ed. 2001. *Handbook of Affect and Social Cognition.* Mahwah, N.J.: Erlbaum.

Fowler, Roger. 1991. *Language in the News: Discourse and Ideology in the Press.* New York: Routledge.

Foyle, Douglas. 1999. *Counting the Public In: Presidents, Public Opinion, and Foreign Policy.* New York: Columbia University Press.

Fraser, Nancy. 1990. Rethinking the Public Sphere: A Contribution to the Critique of Actually Existing Democracy. *Social Text* 25/26: 56–80.

Freedman, Lawrence, and Efraim Karsh. 1993. *The Gulf Conflict: 1990–91.* Princeton: Princeton University Press.

Fried, Amy. 1997. *Muffled Echoes: Oliver North and the Politics of Public Opinion.* New York: Columbia University Press.

Friedman, Thomas. 1993. Clinton Will End U.S. Opposition to Vietnam Loans, Officials Say. *New York Times,* 1 July, 1, 5.

———. 2002. *Longitudes and Attitudes.* New York: Farrar, Straus and Giroux.

Gabrieli, J. D. E. 1998. Cognitive Neuroscience of Human Memory. *Annual Review of Psychology* 49, no. 1: 87–116.

Galtung, Johan, and Marie Ruge. 1965. The Structue of Foreign News. *Journal of Peace Research* 2: 64–91.

Gamson, William A. 1988. The 1987 Distinguished Lecture: A Constructionist Approach to Mass Media and Public Opinion. *Symbolic Interaction* 11: 161–74.

———. 1989. News as Framing: Comments on Graber. *American Behavioral Scientist* 33, no. 2: 157–61.

———. 1992. *Talking Politics.* New York: Cambridge University Press.

Gamson, William A., and Andre Modigliani. 1987. The Changing Culture of Affirmative Action. In *Research in Political Sociology,* ed. Richard D. Braungart, 137–77. Greenwich, Conn.: JAI Press.

———. 1989. Media Discourse and Public Opinion on Nuclear Power: A Constructionist Approach. *American Journal of Sociology* 95, no. 1: 1–37.

Gamson, William A., David Croteau, William Hoynes, and T. Sasson. 1992. Media Images and the Social Construction of Reality. *Annual Review of Sociology* 18: 373–93.

Gans, Herbert J. 1979. *Deciding What's News.* New York: Pantheon.

———. 2002. *Democracy and the News.* New York: Oxford University Press.

Gaubatz, K. T. 1991. Election Cycles and War. *Journal of Conflict Resolution* 35, no. 2: 212–44.

———. 1995. Intervention and Intransitivity: Public Opinion, Social Choice, and the Use of Military Force Abroad. *World Politics* 47: 534–54.

Gelb, Leslie H. 1986. Speakes Defines His Role in Shaping Events. *New York Times,* 10 October, 1.

Gilboa, Eytan, ed. 2002. *Media and Conflict: Framing Issues, Making Policy, Shaping Opinions.* Ardsley, N.Y.: Transnational Publishers.

Gilliam, Franklin D., and Shanto Iyengar. 2000. Prime Suspects: The Influence of Local Television News on the Viewing Public. *American Journal of Political Science* 44, no. 3: 560–73.

Gitlin, Todd. 1980. *The Whole World Is Watching: News Media in the Making and Unmaking of the New Left.* Berkeley: University of California Press.

———. 1998. Public Sphere or Public Sphericles. In *Media, Ritual and Identity,* ed. James Curran and Tamar Liebes, 168–74. London: Routledge.

Gobet, F. 2000. Some Shortcomings of Long-Term Working Memory. *British Journal of Psychology* 91: 551–70.

Goffman, Erving. 1974. *Frame Analysis: An Essay on the Organization of Experience.* Cambridge: Harvard University Press.

Graber, Doris A. 1988. *Processing the News: How People Tame the Information Tide.* Washington, D.C.: CQ Press.

———. 2001. *Processing Politics: Learning from the Television in an Internet Age.* Chicago: University of Chicago Press.

———. 2002. *Mass Media and American Politics.* 6th ed. Washington, D.C.: CQ Press.

Greenberg, Maurice R., William F. Wechsler and Lee S. Wolosky. 2002. *Terrorist Financing.* New York: Council on Foreign Relations. Available at http://www.cfr.org/pdf/Terrorist_Financing_TF.pdf.

Groeling, Tim. Forthcoming. *Breaking the Eleventh Commandment: Divided Party Communication and Unified Government.*

Groeling, Tim J., and Samuel Kernell. 2000. Congress, the President, and Party Competition Via Network News. In *Polarized Politics: Congress and the President in a Partisan Era,* ed. Jon Bond and Richard Fleisher. Washington, D.C.: CQ Press.

Habermas, Jurgen. 1989. *The Structural Transformation of the Public Sphere.* Cambridge: MIT Press.

———. 1992. Further Reflections on the Public Sphere. In *Habermas and the Public Sphere,* ed. Craig Calhoun, 421–61. Cambridge: MIT Press.

Halberstam, David. 2001. *War in a Time of Peace.* New York: Scribner's.

Hall, Stuart. 1973. *Encoding and Decoding in the Television Discourse.* Birmingham, UK: University of Birmingham Centre for Contemporary Cultural Studies Stencilled Occasional Paper.

Hallin, Daniel C. 1986. *The "Uncensored" War.* New York: Oxford University Press.

———. 1992. The Passing of the High Modernism of American Journalism. *Journal of Communication* 42, no. 3: 14–25.

———. 1992. Sound Bite News: Television Coverage of Elections, 1968–1988. *Journal of Communication* 42, no. 2: 5–24.

———. 1993. *We Keep America on Top of the World.* New York: Routledge.

Hart, Peter, and Seth Ackerman. 2001. Patriotism and Censorship. *Extra!*, November/December. Available at http://www.fair.org/extra/0111/patriotism-and-censorship.html.

Hartley, Thomas, and Bruce Russett. 1992. Public Opinion and the Common Defense. *American Political Science Review* 86: 905–15.

Herbst, Susan. 1993. *Numbered Voices: How Opinion Polling Has Shaped American Politics.* Chicago: University of Chicago Press.

———. 1998. *Reading Public Opinion: How Political Actors View the Democratic Process.* Chicago: University of Chicago Press.

Herman, Edward S., and Noam Chomsky. 1988. *Manufacturing Consent: The Political Economy of the Mass Media.* New York: Pantheon.

Hermann, Richard K., and James F. Voss. 1997. Images in International Relations: An Experimental Test of Cognitive Schemata. *International Studies Quarterly* 41: 403–34.

Hersh, Seymour. 1986. *The Target Is Destroyed: What Really Happened to Flight 007 and What America Knew About It.* New York: Random House.

———. 2003. Selective Intelligence. *New Yorker*, 12 May, 44–51.

Hinckley, Ronald H. 1992. *People, Polls, and Policymakers: American Public Opinion and National Security.* New York: Lexington Books.

Hochschild, Jennifer L. 2001. Where You Stand Depends on What You See: Connections among Values, Perceptions of Fact, and Political Prescriptions. In *Citizens and Politics: Perspectives from Political Psychology,* ed. James H. Kuklinski, 313–40. New York: Cambridge University Press.

Holsti, Ole R. 1992. Public Opinion and Foreign Policy: Challenges to the Almond–Lippmann Consensus. *International Studies Quarterly* 36: 439–66.

———. 1996. *Public Opinion and American Foreign Policy.* Ann Arbor: University of Michigan Press.

Holsti, Ole R., and James N. Rosenau. 1984. *American Leadership in World Affairs: Vietnam and the Breakdown of Consensus.* Boston: Allen and Unwin.

Holzman, Franklyn D. 1989. Politics and Guesswork: CIA and DIA Estimates of Soviet Military Spending. *International Security* 14: 101–31.

Hunt, Michael H. 1987. *Ideology and American Foreign Policy.* New Haven: Yale University Press.

Huth, Paul K., and Todd L. Allee. 2002. Domestic Political Accountability and the Escalation and Settlement of International Disputes. *Journal of Conflict Resolution* 46: 754–90.

Independent Commission of Inquiry and Jane Franklin. 1991. *The U.S. Invasion of Panama : The Truth Behind Operation "Just Cause."* Boston: South End Press.

Ismael, Tareq Y., and Jacqueline S. Ismael, eds. 1994. *The Gulf War and the New*

World Order: International Relations of the Middle East. Gainesville: University Press of Florida.

Iyengar, Shanto. 1991. *Is Anyone Responsible? How Television Frames Political Issues.* Chicago: University of Chicago Press.

Iyengar, Shanto, and William McGuire, eds. 1993. *Explorations in Political Psychology.* Durham: Duke University Press.

Jacobs, Lawrence, and Robert Y. Shapiro. 2000. *Politicians Don't Pander: Political Manipulation and the Loss of Democratic Responsiveness.* Chicago: University of Chicago Press.

Jamieson, Kathleen H. 1992. *Dirty Politics: Deception, Distraction, and Democracy.* New York: Oxford University Press.

Jentleson, Bruce W. 1994. *With Friends Like These: Reagan, Bush, and Saddam, 1982–1990.* New York: Norton.

———. 1992. The Pretty Prudent Public: Post post-Vietnam American Opinion on the Use of Military Force. *International Studies Quarterly* 46: 49–74.

Jentleson, Bruce W., and Rebecca L. Britton.1998. Still Pretty Prudent: Post–Cold War American Public Opinion on the Use of Military Force. *Journal of Conflict Resolution* 42: 395–417.

Jervis, Robert. 1993. The Drunkard's Search. In *Explorations in Political Psychology,* ed. Shanto Iyengar and William McGuire, 338–60. Durham: Duke University Press.

Johnson, R. W. 1987. *Shootdown: Flight 007 and the American Connection.* New York: Penguin.

Jones, Bryan D. 1994. *Reconceiving Decision-Making in Democratic Politics.* Chicago: University of Chicago Press.

Kahneman, Daniel, and Amos Tversky. 1984. Choices, Values and Frames. *American Psychologist* 39: 341–50.

Keating, Susan Katz. 1994. *Prisoners of Hope: Exploring the POW/MIA Myth in America.* New York: Random House.

Kelley, Stanley Jr. 1983. *Interpreting Elections.* Princeton: Princeton University Press.

Kellner, Douglas. No date. Habermas, the Public Sphere, and Democracy: A Critical Intervention. Available at http://www.gseis.ucla.edu/faculty/kellner/papers/habermas.htm.

Kellner, Douglas. 1992. *The Persian Gulf TV War.* Boulder: Westview Press.

Keohane, Robert. 1986. *Neo-realism and Its Critics.* New York: Columbia University Press.

Kernell, Samuel. 1993. *Going Public: New Strategies of Presidential Leadership.* Washington, D.C.: CQ Press.

Kinder, Donald R., and Lynn M. Sanders. 1996. *Divided by Color: Racial Politics and Democratic Ideals.* Chicago: University of Chicago Press.

King, Elliot, and Michael Schudson. 1991. The Myth of the Great Communicator. *Columbia Journalism Review* 26 (November/December): 37–39.

Kintsch, Walter. 1998. The Representation of Knowledge in Minds and Machines. *International Journal of Psychology* 33, no. 6: 411–20.

Knightley, Phillip. 1975. *First Casualty: From the Crimea to Vietnam: The War*

Correspondent as Hero, Propagandist, and Myth Maker. New York: Harcourt Brace.

Knopf, Jeffrey W. 1998. How Rational Is "The Rational Public"? Evidence from U.S. Public Opinion on Military Spending. *Journal of Conflict Resolution* 42: 544–71.

Kotz, Nick. 1988. *Wild Blue Yonder: Money, Politics, and the B-1 Bomber.* New York: Pantheon Books.

Kuhn, Thomas. 1962. *The Structure of Scienctific Revolutions.* Chicago: University of Chicago Press.

Kuklinski, James H., ed. 2001. *Citizens and Politics: Perspectives from Political Psychology.* New York: Cambridge University Press.

Kuklinski, James H., and Paul J. Quirk. 2000. Reconsidering the Rational Public: Cognition, Heuristics, and Mass Opinion. In *Elements of Reason: Cognition, Choice and the Bounds of Rationality,* ed. Arthur Lupia, Matthew D. McCubbins, and Samuel L. Popkin, 153–82. New York: Cambridge University Press.

Kuklinski, James H., R. C. Luskin, and J. Bolland. 1991. Where Is the Schema: Going Beyond the S-Word in Political Psychology. *American Political Science Review* 85, no. 4: 1341–56.

Kull, Steven, and Clay Ramsay. 2000. Elite Misperceptions of U.S. Public Opinion and Foreign Policy. In *Decisionmaking in a Glass House: Mass Media, Public Opinion, and American and European Foreign Policy in the 21st Century,* ed. Brigitte Lebens Nacos, Robert Y. Shapiro, and Pierangelo Isernia, 95–110. Lanham, Md: Rowman and Littlefield.

———. 2002. How Policymakers Misperceive U.S. Public Opinion on Foreign Policy. In *Navigating Public Opinion: Polls, Policy and the Future of American Democracy,* ed. Jeff Manza, Fay Lomax Cook, and Benjamin I. Page, 201–20. New York: Oxford University Press.

Kull, Steven, and I. M. Destler. 1999. *Misreading the Public: The Myth of a New Isolationism.* Washington, D.C.: Brookings Institution.

Lakoff, George. 1987. *Women, Fire, and Dangerous Things: What Categories Reveal about the Mind.* Chicago: University of Chicago Press.

———. 2002. *Moral Politics: How Conservatives and Liberals Think.* 2nd ed. Chicago: University of Chicago Press.

LaMay, Craig. 1991. The Goals of War: Newspaper Editorial Coverage at Defining Moments of the Crisis. In *The Media at War: The Press and the Persian Gulf Conflict.* New York: Gannett Foundation.

LaMay, Craig, Martha FitzSimon, and Joan Sahadi, eds. 1991. *Media at War.* New York: Gannett Foundation.

Lane, Robert E. 1962. *Political Ideology: Why the American Common Man Believes What He Does.* New York: Free Press.

Lang, Annie, and Marian Friestad. 1993. Emotion, Hemispheric-Specialization, and Visual and Verbal Memory for Television Messages. *Communication Research* 20, no. 5: 647–70.

Lee, Martin A., and Norman Soloman. 1991. *Unreliable Sources: A Guide to Detecting Bias in News Media.* New York: Lyle Stuart.

Lee, Taeku. 2002. The Sovereign Status of Survey Data. In *Navigating Public*

Opinion: Polls, Policy and the Future of American Democracy, ed. Jeff Manza, Fay Lomax Cook, and Benjamin I. Page, 290–314. New York: Oxford University Press.

Lemann, Nicholas. 2002. The War on What? *New Yorker,* 16 September, 36–44.

Lewis, Justin. *Constructing Public Opinion.* New York: Columbia University Press.

Linsky, Martin, Jonathan Moore, Wendy O'Donnell, and David Whitman. 1986. *How the Press Affects Federal Policymaking: Six Case Studies.* New York: Norton.

Lippmann, Walter. 1922. *Public Opinion.* New York: Harcourt Brace.

———. 1925. *The Phantom Public.* New York: Harcourt Brace.

Lipsky, Michael. 1968. Protest as a Political Resource. *American Political Science Review* 62, no. 4: 1144–58.

Livingston, Steven. 1994. *The Terrorism Spectacle.* Boulder: Westview Press.

———. 1996. *Clarifying the CNN Effect: An Examination of Media Effects According to Type of Military Intervention.* Cambridge: Shorenstein Center, Harvard University.

Lodge, Milton, and Charles S. Taber. 2000. Three Steps toward a Theory of Motivated Political Reasoning. In *Elements of Reason: Cognition, Choice, and the Bounds of Rationality,* ed. James H. Kuklinski and Paul J. Quirk, 183–213. New York: Cambridge University Press.

Lodge, Milton, and Patrick Stroh. 1993. Inside the Mental Voting Booth: An Impression-Driven Process Model of Candidate Evaluation. In *Explorations in Political Psychology,* ed. Shanto Iyengar and William McGuire: 225–63. Durham: Duke University Press.

Lupia, Arthur, and Matthew McCubbins. 1998. *The Democratic Dilemma: Can Citizens Learn What They Need to Know?* New York: Cambridge University Press.

MacArthur, John R. 1992. *Second Front: Censorship and Propaganda in the Gulf War.* New York: Hill and Wang.

MacKuen, Michael. 1983. Political Drama, Economic Conditions, and the Dynamics of Presidential Popularity. *American Journal of Political Science* 27: 165–92.

Manheim, Jarol B. 1997. *Strategic Public Diplomacy and American Foreign Policy: The Evolution of Influence.* New York: Oxford University Press.

Manza, Jeff, and Fay Lomax Cook. 2002. The Impact of Public Opinion on Public Policy: The State of the Debate. In *Navigating Public Opinion: Polls, Policy and the Future of American Democracy,* ed. Jeff Manza, Fay Lomax Cook, and Benjamin I. Page, 17–32. New York: Oxford University Press.

Manza, Jeff, Fay Lomax Cook, and Benjamin I. Page, eds. 2002. *Navigating Public Opinion: Polls, Policy, and the Future of American Democracy.* New York: Oxford University Press.

Marcus, George E., W. Russell Neuman, and Michael MacKuen. 2000. *Affective Intelligence and Political Judgment.* New York: Cambridge University Press.

Margolis, Michael, and Gary A. Mauser. 1989. *Manipulating Public Opinion: Essays on Public Opinion as a Dependent Variable.* Pacific Grove, Calif.: Brooks/Cole.

Masters, Roger D. 2001. Cognitive Neuroscience, Emotion and Leadership. In *Citizens and Politics: Perspectives from Political Psychology,* ed. James H. Kuklinski, 68–102. New York: Cambridge University Press.

Masters, Roger D., and Denis G. Sullivan. 1993. Nonverbal Behavior and Leadership: Emotion and Cognition in Political Information Processing. In *Explorations in Political Psychology,* ed. Shanto Iyengar and William McGuire, 150–82. Durham: Duke University Press.

McCombs, Maxwell E., and Donald L. Shaw. 1993. The Evolution of Agenda-Setting Research: 25 Years in the Marketplace of Ideas. *Journal of Communication* 43, no. 2: 58–67.

McCombs, Maxwell, and Salma I. Ghanem. 2001. The Convergence of Agenda Setting and Framing. In *Framing Public Life: Perspectives on Media and Our Understanding of the Social World,* ed. Stephen D. Reese, Oscar Gandy, and August E. Grant, 67–83. Mahwah, N.J.: Erlbaum.

McLeod, Douglas M., and Benjamin H. Detenber. 1999. Framing Effects of Television News Coverage of Social Protest. *Journal of Communication* 49, no. 3: 3–23.

Mearsheimer, John J., and Stephen M. Walt. 2003. An Unnecessary War. *Foreign Policy* 134: 51–61.

Mendelberg, Tali. 2001. *The Race Card: Campaign Strategy, Implicit Messages, and the Norm of Equality.* Princeton: Princeton University Press.

Mermin, Jonathan. 1999. *Debating War and Peace: Media Coverage of U.S. Intervention in the Post-Vietnam Era.* Princeton: Princeton University Press.

Meyer, D. S. 1995. Framing National Security: Elite Public Discourse on Nuclear Weapons during the Cold War. *Political Communication* 12, no. 2: 173–92.

Meyrowitz, Joshua. 1986. *No Sense of Place: The Impact of Electronic Media on Social Behavior.* New York: Oxford University Press.

Miller, M. Mark, and Bonnie Parnell Riechert. 2001. The Spiral of Opportunity and Frame Resonance: Mapping the Issue Cycle in News and Public Discourse. In *Framing Public Life: Perspectives on Media and Our Understanding of Social Life,* ed. Stephen D. Reese, Oscar H. Gandy, and August E. Grant, 107–21. Mahwah, N.J.: Erlbaum.

Miller, Peter V. 2002. The Authority and Limitations of Polls. In *Navigating Public Opinion: Polls, Policy and the Future of American Democracy,* ed. Jeff Manza, Fay Lomax Cook, and Benjamin I. Page, 221–31. New York: Oxford University Press.

Mitchell, Timothy. 1991. The Limits of the State: Beyond Statist Approaches and Their Critics. *American Political Science Review* 85, no. 1: 77–96.

Morgan, T. C., and S. H. Campbell. 1991. Domestic Structure, Decisional Constraints, and War: So Why Kant Democracies Fight? *Journal of Conflict Resolution* 35, no. 2: 187–211.

Moriarty, Sandra E., and M. N. Popovich. 1991. Newsmagazine Visuals and the 1988 Presidential Election. *Journalism Quarterly* 68, no. 3: 371–80.

Mueller, John. 1994. *Policy and Opinion in the Gulf War.* Chicago: University of Chicago Press.

Murray, S. K., and J. A. Cowden. 1999. The Role of "Enemy Images" and Ideology in Elite Belief Systems. *International Studies Quarterly* 43: 455–81.

Mutz, Diana C. 1998. *Impersonal Influence: How Perceptions of Mass Collectives Affect Political Attitudes.* New York: Cambridge University Press.

Nacos, Brigitte Lebens. 1990. *The Press, Presidents, and Crises.* New York: Columbia University Press.

Nacos, Brigitte Lebens, Robert Y. Shapiro, and Pierangelo Isernia, eds. 2000. *Decision Making in a Glass House.* Lanham, Md.: Rowman and Littlefield.

Nelson, John S., and G. R. Boyton. 1997. *Video Rhetorics: Televised Advertisements in American Politics.* Urbana: University of Illinois Press.

Nelson, Thomas E., Rosalee A. Clawson, and Zoe M. Oxley. 1997. Media Framing of a Civil Liberties Conflict and Its Effect on Tolerance. *American Political Science Review* 91, no. 3: 567–83.

Neuman, W. Russell, Marion Just, and Ann Crigler. 1992. *Common Knowledge.* Chicago: University of Chicago Press.

Neustadt, Richard. 1991. *Presidential Power and the Modern Presidents.* New York: Free Press.

Newhagen, John E., and Byron Reeves. 1992. The Evening's Bad News: Effects of Compelling Negative Television News Images on Memory. *Journal of Communication* 42, no. 2: 25–41.

Noelle-Neumann, Elisabeth. 1993. *The Spiral of Silence: Public Opinion, Our Social Skin.* Chicago: University of Chicago Press.

Norris, Pippa. 2001. *Digital Divide: Civic Engagement, Information Poverty, and the Internet Worldwide.* New York: Cambridge University Press.

Nye, Joseph S. 2002. *The Paradox of American Power: Why the World's Only Superpower Can't Go It Alone.* New York: Oxford University Press.

Olson, Mancur. 1965. *The Logic of Collective Action: Public Goods and the Theory of Groups.* Cambridge: Harvard University Press.

Page, Benjamin I. 1996. *Who Deliberates? Mass Media and Modern Democracy.* Chicago: University of Chicago Press.

———. 2002. The Semisovereign Public. In *Navigating Public Opinion: Polls, Policy and the Future of American Democracy,* ed. Jeff Manza, Fay Lomax Cook, and Benjamin I. Page, 325–44. New York: Oxford University Press.

Page, Benjamin I., and Robert Y. Shapiro. 1992. *The Rational Public.* Chicago: University of Chicago Press.

Paletz, David L., and Robert M. Entman. 1981. *Media Power Politics.* New York: Free Press.

Pan, Zhondang, and Gerald M. Kosicki. 1993. Framing Analysis: An Approach to News Discourse. *Political Communication* 10, no. 1: 55–76.

———. 2001. Framing as a Strategic Action in Public Deliberation. In *Framing Public Life: Perspectives on Media and Our Understanding of Social Life,* ed. Stephen D. Reese, Oscar Gandy, and August E. Grant, 35–65. Mahway, N.J.: Erlbaum.

Parenti, Michael. 1993. *Land of Idols.* New York: St. Martin's Press.

Pasztor, Andy. 1995. *When the Pentagon Was For Sale.* New York: Simon and Schuster.

Patterson, Thomas E. 1993. *Out of Order.* New York: Knopf.

————. 1997. The News Media: An Effective Political Actor? *Political Communication* 14, no. 4: 445–55.

————. 2002. *The Vanishing Voter.* New York: Knopf.

Peffley, Mark, and Jon Hurwitz. 1992. International Events and Foreign Policy Beliefs: Public Response to Changing Soviet–U.S. Relations. *American Journal of Political Science* 36: 431–61.

Peffley, Mark, R. E. Langley, and Kirby Goidel. 1995. Public Responses to Presidential Usage of Military Force: A Panel Analysis. *Political Behavior* 17, no. 3: 307–37.

Petty, Richard E., and John T. Cacioppo. 1986. *Attitudes and Persuasion: Classic and Contemporary Approaches.* New York: Springer Verlag.

Pew Research Center. 1998. *Public Appetite for Government Misjudged: Washington Leaders Wary of Public Opinion.* Washington: Pew Research Center for the People and the Press. Available at http://people-press.org/reports/display.php3?ReportID=92.

————. 2003. *Public Wants Proof of Iraqi Weapons Programs.* Washington: Pew Center for the People and the Press. Available at http://people-press.org/reports/display.php3?ReportID=170.

Physicians for Human Rights. 1991. *Panama: "Operation Just Cause": The Human Cost of the U.S. Invasion.* Boston: Physicians for Human Rights.

Popkin, Samuel L. 1991. *The Reasoning Voter: Communication and Persuasion in Presidential Campaigns.* Chicago: University of Chicago Press.

Power, Samantha. 2001. Bystanders to Genocide: Why the United States Let the Rwanda Tragedy Happen. *Atlantic Monthly,* September, 84–108.

Powlick, Philip J. 1995. The Sources of Public Opinion for American Foreign Policy Officials. *International Studies Quarterly* 39: 427–51.

Powlick, Philip J., and Andrew Z. Katz. 1998. Defining the American Public Opinion/Foreign Policy Nexus. *International Studies Quarterly* 42, no. 1 (Supp. 1): 29–63.

Rachlin, Allan. 1988. *News as Hegemonic Reality: American Political Culture and the Framing of News Accounts.* New York: Praeger.

Reese, Stephen D. 2001. Prologue–Framing Life: A Bridging Model for Media Research. In *Framing Public Life: Perspectives on Media and Our Understanding of the Social World,* ed. Stephen D. Reese, Oscar Gandy, and August E. Grant, 7–31. Mahwah, N.J.: Erlbaum.

Reese, Stephen D., and B. Buckalew. 1995. The Militarism of Local Television: The Routine Framing of the Persian Gulf War. *Critical Studies in Mass Communication* 12, no. 1: 40–59.

Reese, Stephen D., Oscar Gandy, and August E. Grant, eds. 2001. *Framing Public Life: Perspectives on Media and Our Understanding of the Social World.* Mahwah, N.J.: Erlbaum.

Reilly, John E. 1991. *American Public Opinion and U.S. Foreign Policy 1991.* Chicago: Chicago Council on Foreign Relations.

Reta, Meseret Chekol. 2002. Effects of Ambiguous Policies on Media Coverage of Foreign Conflicts: The Cases of Eritrea and Southern Sudan. In *Media and Conflict: Framing Issues, Making Policy, Shaping Opinions,* ed. Eytan Gilboa, 239–64. Ardsley, N.Y.: Transnational Publishers.

Riker, William. 1986. *The Art of Political Manipulation.* New Haven: Yale University Press.

Robinson, Piers. 2002. *The CNN Effect: The Myth of News, Foreign Policy and Intervention.* London: Routledge.

Rojecki, Andrew. 1999. *Silencing the Opposition: Anti-Nuclear Movements and the Media in the Cold War.* Urbana: University of Illinois Press.

———. 2002. Media and the New Post–Cold War Movements. In *Media and Conflict: Framing Issues, Making Policy, Shaping Opinions,* ed. Eytan Gilboa, 3–24. Ardsley, N.Y.: Transnational Publishers.

Russett, Bruce. 1990. *Controlling the Sword: Democratic Governance of National Security.* Cambridge: Harvard University Press.

Schank, Roger C., and Robert P. Abelson. 1977. *Scripts, Plans, Goals, and Understanding: An Inquiry into Human Knowledge Structures.* Hillsdale, N.J.: Erlbaum.

Scheer, Robert. 1982. *With Enough Shovels: Reagan, Bush, and Nuclear War.* New York: Random House.

Schell, Jonathan. 2003. *The Unconquerable World.* New York: Metropolitan Books.

Scheufele, Dietram A. 1999. Framing as a Theory of Media Effects. *Journal of Communication* 49, no. 1: 103–22.

Schon, Donald A., and Martin Rein. 1995. *Frame Reflection.* New York: Basic Books.

Schudson, Michael. 1992. Was There a Public Sphere? If So, When? Reflections on the American Case. In *Habermas and the Public Sphere,* ed. Craig Calhoun, 143–63. Cambridge: MIT Press.

Schultz, Kenneth A. 1998. Domestic Opposition and Signaling in International Crises. *American Political Science Review* 92: 829–44.

Sears, David O. 1993. Symbolic Politics: A Socio-Psychological Theory. In *Explorations in Political Psychology,* ed. Shanto Iyengar and William McGuire, 113–49. Durham: Duke University Press.

———. 2001. The Role of Affect in Symbolic Politics. In *Citizens and Politics: Perspectives from Political Psychology,* ed. James H. Kuklinski, 14–40. New York: Cambridge University Press.

Semetko, Holli A., and Patti M. Valkenburg. 2000. Framing European Politics: A Content Analysis of Press and Television News. *Journal of Communication* 50, no. 2: 93–109.

Shapiro, Robert Y., and Lawrence Jacobs. 2002. Public Opinion, Foreign Policy, and Democracy: How Presidents Use Public Opinion. In *Navigating Public Opinion: Polls, Policy and the Future of American Democracy,* ed. Jeff Manza, Fay Lomax Cook, and Benjamin I. Page, 184–201. New York: Oxford University Press.

Sharkey, Jacquline. 1992. The Media's War. *Nation* 254: 617–18.

Sheehan, Neil. 1993. Prisoners of the Past. *New Yorker,* 24 May, 44–51.

Shrum, L. J. 1996. Psychological Processes underlying Cultivation Effects: Further Tests of Construct Accessibility. *Human Communication Research* 22: 482–509.

Sifry, Micah L., and Christopher Cerf. 1991. *The Gulf War Reader: History, Documents, Opinions.* New York: Random House.

Sigal, Leon. 1973. *Reporters and Officials.* Lexington, Mass.: D. C. Heath.

Simon, Adam, and Michael Xenos. 2000. Media Framing and Effective Public Deliberation. *Political Communication* 17, no. 4: 363–76.

Simon, Herbert. 1997. *Administrative Behavior.* New York: Free Press.

Smith, Donald C. 1985. KAL 007: Making Sense of the Senseless. Paper presented at the annual convention of the Speech Communication Association. Denver.

Smith, Hedrick. 1983. Capitol Hill Clamor Softens as Public Support Swells. *New York Times,* 4 November, 11.

Sniderman, Paul M. 2000. Taking Sides: A Fixed Choice Theory of Political Reasoning. In *Elements of Reason: Cognition, Choice and the Bounds of Rationality,* ed. Arthur Lupia, Matthew McCubbins, and Samuel L. Popkin, 67–84. New York: Cambridge University Press.

Sniderman, Paul M., Philip E. Tetlock, and Laurel Elms. 2001. Public Opinion and Democratic Politics: The Problem of Nonattitudes and Social Construction of Political Judgment. In *Citizens and Politics: Perspectives from Political Psychology,* ed. James H. Kuklinski, 254–88. New York: Cambridge University Press.

Sniderman, Paul M., Richard Brody, and Philip Tetlock. 1991. *Reasoning and Choice: Explorations in Political Psychology.* New York: Cambridge University Press.

Snow, David A., and Robert D. Benford. 1988. Ideology, Frame Resonance, and Participation Mobilization. *International Social Movement Research* 1: 197–216.

Sobel, Richard. 2001. *The Impact of Public Opinion on U.S. Foreign Policy since Vietnam: Constraining the Colossus.* New York: Oxford University Press.

Solomon, William. 1992. News Frames and Media Packages: Covering El Salvador. *Critical Studies in Mass Communication* 9, 56–74.

Stimson, James A. 1991. *Public Opinion in America: Moods, Cycles, and Swings.* Boulder: Westview Press.

Stubbing, Richard. 1986. *The Defense Game.* New York: Harper and Row.

Taber, Charles S., Milton Lodge, and Jill Glathar. 2001. The Motivated Construction of Political Judgments. In *Citizens and Politics: Perspectives from Political Psychology,* ed. J. H. Kuklinski, 198–226. New York: Cambridge University Press.

Talbott, Strobe. 1984. *Deadly Gambits.* New York: Knopf.

Taylor, Philip M. 1992. *War and the Media: Propaganda and Persuasion in the Gulf War.* Manchester, UK: Manchester University Press.

Tetlock, Phillip E. 2000. Coping with Trade-Offs: Psychological Constraints and Political Implications. In *Elements of Reason: Cognition, Choice, and the Bounds of Rationality,* ed. Arthur Lupia, Matthew McCubbins, and Samuel L. Popkin, 239–63. New York: Cambridge University Press.

Tuchman, Gaye. 1978. *Making News: A Study in the Construction of Reality.* New York: Free Press.

U.S. House of Representatives. 1988. *Declassified Intelligence Assessments of 1983 KAL Shootdown at Variance with Previous Administration Statements.* Washington, D.C.: U.S. House of Representatives.

Verba, Sidney, and Norman Nie. 1987. *Participation in America: Political Democracy and Social Equality.* Chicago: University of Chicago Press.

Vertzberger, Yaacov Y. I. 1990. *The World in Their Minds: Information Processing,*

Cognition, and Perception in Foreign Policy Decisionmaking. Stanford: Stanford University Press.

Walker, Stephen G., and Mark Schafer. 1999. Presidential Operational Codes and Foreign Policy Conflicts in the Post–Cold War World. *Journal of Conflict Resolution* 43, no. 5: 610–25.

Waltz, Kenneth N. 1991. America as a Model for the World: A Foreign Policy Perspective. *P.S. — Political Science,* December, 667–70.

Warner, Margaret G. 1987. Bush Battles the "Wimp Factor." *Newsweek,* 19 October, 28.

Warren, Kenneth F. 2001. *In Defense of Public Opinion Polling.* Boulder: Westview Press.

Warren, Mark. 1993. Can Participatory Democracy Produce Better Selves? Psychological Dimensions of Habermas's Discursive Model of Democracy. *Political Psychology* 14: 209–34.

White, Ralph. 1984. *Fearful Warriors.* New York: Free Press.

Wilson, George C., and Michael Weisskopf. 1986. Pentagon, Congress Seek Cure to Shortcomings Exposed in Grenada Invasion. *Washington Post,* 20 February, 24.

Wlezien, Christopher. 1996. Dynamics of representation: The Case of U.S. Spending on Defence. *British Journal of Political Science* 26, no. 1: 81–103.

Wittkopf, Eugene. 1990. *Faces of Internationalism.* Durham: Duke University Press.

Wolfinger, Raymond, and Steven Rosenstone. 1980. *Who Votes?* New Haven: Yale University Press.

Wolfsfeld, Gadi. 1997. *Media and Political Conflict: News from the Middle East.* New York: Cambridge University Press.

———. 2001. Political Waves and Democratic Discourse: Terrorism Waves during the Oslo Peace Process. In *Mediated Politics: Communication in the Future of Democracy,* ed. W. Lance Bennett and Robert M. Entman, 226–51. New York: Cambridge University Press.

———. 2003. *Media and the Path to Peace.* New York: Cambridge University Press.

Woodward, Bob. 1991. *The Commanders.* New York: Simon and Schuster.

———. 2002. *Bush at War.* New York: Simon and Schuster.

Wyer Jr., Robert S., and Sallie E. Gordon. 1984. The Cognitive Representation of Social Information. In *Handbook of Social Cognition,* ed. Robert S. Wyer Jr. and Thomas K. Srull. Hillsdale, N.J.: Erlbaum.

Yankelovich, Daniel, and John Immerwahr. 1994. The Rules of Public Engagement. In *Beyond the Beltway: Engaging the Public in U.S. Foreign Policy,* ed. Daniel Yankelovich and I. M. Destler. New York: Norton.

Young, Marilyn J., and Michael K. Launer. 1988. *Flights of Fancy, Flights of Doom: KAL 007 and Soviet–American Rhetoric.* Landham, Md: University Press of America.

Zaller, John. 1991. Information, Values and Opinion. *American Political Science Review* 85, no. 4: 1215–37.

———. 1992. *The Nature and Origins of Mass Opinion.* New York: Cambridge University Press.

———. 1994. Elite Leadership of Mass Opinion: New Evidence from the Gulf War. In *Taken by Storm: Media, Public Opinion, and U.S. Foreign Policy in the Gulf War,* ed. W. Lance Bennett and David L. Paletz, 186–209. Chicago: University of Chicago Press.

———. 2001. Monica Lewinsky and the Mainsprings of American Politics. In *Mediated Politics: Communication in the Future of Democracy,* ed. W. Lance Bennett and Robert M. Entman, 252–78. New York: Cambridge University Press.

Zaller, John, and Dennis Chiu. 2000. Government's Little Helper: U.S. Press Coverage of Foreign Policy Crises, 1946–1999. In *Decisionmaking in a Glass House: Mass Media, Public Opinion, and American and European Foreign Policy in the 21st Century,* ed. Brigitte Lebens Nacos, Robert Y. Shapiro, and Pierangelo Isernia, 385–405. Lanham, Md: Rowman and Littlefield.

INDEX